THE
THIRTIETH YEARBOOK

OF THE

NATIONAL SOCIETY FOR THE STUDY OF EDUCATION

PART I

The Status of Rural Education

FIRST REPORT OF THE SOCIETY'S COMMITTEE ON
RURAL EDUCATION

Prepared by the Society's Committee

J. E. BUTTERWORTH, KATHERINE COOK, FANNIE W. DUNN, NORMAN FROST,
GEORGE A. WORKS, and ORVILLE G. BRIM (*Chairman*)

Assisted by the Following Active Members of the Society

T. J. BAYNE, JR., W. H. BRISTOW, MABEL CARNEY, T. H. EATON,
E. N. FERRISS, W. H. GAUMNITZ, HELEN HEFFERNAN, HELEN
H. HEYL, R. E. JAGGERS, G. C. KYTE, H. C. MORRISON,
M. G. NELSON, M. S. PITTMAN, AND R. M. STEWART

Edited by

GUY MONTROSE WHIPPLE

THIS PART OF THE YEARBOOK WILL BE DISCUSSED AT THE DETROIT
MEETING OF THE NATIONAL SOCIETY, TUESDAY,
FEBRUARY 24, 1931, 8:00 P. M.

PUBLIC SCHOOL PUBLISHING COMPANY
BLOOMINGTON, ILLINOIS
1931

AGENTS

PUBLIC SCHOOL PUBLISHING COMPANY
BLOOMINGTON, ILLINOIS
PUBLISHERS OF ALL THE YEARBOOKS OF THE SOCIETY

———

Published February, 1931
First Printing, 6,000 copies

Printed by the
PUBLIC SCHOOL PUBLISHING COMPANY
Bloomington, Illinois

ii

OFFICERS OF THE SOCIETY
for 1930-31

Board of Directors
(Term of office expires March 1st of the year indicated)

W. C. BAGLEY (1934)*
Teachers College, Columbia University, New York City

WERRETT W. CHARTERS (1932)
University of Chicago, Chicago, Illinois

F. N. FREEMAN (1932)
University of Chicago, Chicago, Illinois

M. E. HAGGERTY (1934)†
University of Minnesota, Minneapolis, Minnesota

ERNEST HORN (1933)
State University of Iowa, Iowa City, Iowa

CHARLES H. JUDD (1931)
University of Chicago, Chicago, Illinois

LEONARD V. KOOS, *Chairman* (1933)
University of Chicago, Chicago, Illinois

GUY MONTROSE WHIPPLE (*Ex-officio*)
Danvers, Massachusetts

Secretary-Treasurer
GUY MONTROSE WHIPPLE (1932)
Danvers, Massachusetts

*Reëlected for three years beginning March, 1931.
†Elected for three years beginning March, 1931.

TABLE OF CONTENTS

For Minutes of the Annual Meeting, Proceedings of the Board of Directors, List of Members, and Other Information about the Society,
see Part II of this Yearbook.

MEMBERSHIP OF THE SOCIETY'S COMMITTEE ON RURAL EDUCATION

ORVILLE G. BRIM, (*Chairman*) Professor of Elementary Education, Ohio State University, Columbus, Ohio.

JULIAN E. BUTTERWORTH, Professor of Rural Education, Cornell University, Ithaca, New York.

KATHERINE M. COOK, Chief, Division of Special Problems, Office of Education, Department of Interior, Washington, D. C.

FANNIE W. DUNN, Associate Professor of Education, Teachers College, Columbia University, New York, N. Y.

NORMAN FROST, Professor of Rural Education, George Peabody College for Teachers, Nashville, Tennessee.

GEORGE A. WORKS, Professor of Education, University of Chicago, Chicago, Illinois.

ASSOCIATED CONTRIBUTORS ASSISTING THE COMMITTEE ON RURAL EDUCATION

THOMAS L. BAYNE, JR., Department of Rural Education, Cornell University, Ithaca, New York.

WILLIAM H. BRISTOW, Assistant Director of Secondary Education, Department of Public Instruction, Harrisburg, Pennsylvania.

T. H. EATON, Professor of Rural Education, Cornell University, Ithaca, New York.

EMERY N. FERRISS, Professor of Rural Education, Cornell University, Ithaca, New York.

W. H. GAUMNITZ, Specialist in Rural-School Problems, Office of Education, Washington, D. C.

HELEN HAY HEYL, Rural Education Bureau, State Education Department, Albany, New York.

R. E. JAGGERS, Supervisor of Rural Elementary Schools, Department of Education, Frankfort, Kentucky.

GEORGE C. KYTE, Professor of Elementary Education and Supervision, University of Michigan, Ann Arbor, Michigan.

HENRY C. MORRISON, Professor of Education, University of Chicago, Chicago, Illinois.

M. G. NELSON, Professor of Education, New York State College for Teachers, Albany, New York.

M. S. PITTMAN, Director of Training, Michigan State Normal College, Ypsilanti, Michigan.

R. M. STEWART, Professor of Rural Education, Cornell University, Ithaca, New York.

EDITOR'S PREFACE

It was in April, 1924, at the Dallas meeting of the Board of Directors that the idea of producing a yearbook dealing with rural
education was broached. At that time communications were read
from Professor Ernest Burnham and from Professor Norman Frost
and Mr. Harold Van Buren suggesting different approaches to the
topic. The Board deferred consideration of these several proposals
until a later meeting when more information could be at hand.

At the meeting in October, 1925, Professor Burnham submitted
a more detailed proposal, but the Board, though sympathetic, felt
disinclined to proceed until those actively interested had canvassed
the situation even more comprehensively, and had, in particular,
made it reasonably certain that a yearbook on rural education could
be produced that would be representative of all the important move-
ments and tendencies within the field.

At the Washington meeting, February, 1926, Professor Frost submitted in behalf of those interested in the rural education yearbook
a formal statement outlining some ten topics for discussion, suggesting contributors, and estimating the budget needed to carry on
the proposed program, but it was felt to be desirable, in view of the
Society's undertakings and certain difficulties of organization, to
defer the appointment of a yearbook committee for a year. However, when the year had elapsed, the Board, at its Dallas meeting,
February, 1927, still found difficulty in agreeing upon plans and
personnel, and it was not until the Boston meeting, February, 1928,
that, on the basis of extended correspondence between Professor
Koos, the Chairman of the Board, and Professor Frost, it was finally
decided to launch the enterprise. Professors Frost, Brim, and Works
were then asked to form the nucleus of a yearbook committee. Nine
months later the Board at its Rochester meeting approved the nomi-
nations recommended, whereby Professor Julian Butterworth, Mrs.
Katherine Cook, and Professor Fannie Dunn joined Professors Frost,
Brim, and Works to form a Committee on Rural Education, organized with Professor Brim as chairman and Professor Frost as
secretary.

Three hundred dollars was made available for the use of this
Committee in 1928; a like amount was added for use in 1929, and
four hundred dollars for use in 1930. The Society has to thank certain institutions and individuals, particularly the Chairman of the
Committee, for subsidiary contributions toward the expenses of
preparing this yearbook.

It was originally intended that the material published in 1931
by the Committee on Rural Education should comprise, within a

single volume, a first section descriptive of the present status of rural education and a second section setting forth fundamental principles and policies that should guide the development of rural education, together with a series of statements from various leaders in this field showing in what respects each of them agreed or disagreed with the several principles and policies thus set forth. Unfortunately, these intentions could not be realized, primarily because the amount of material submitted for the first section considerably exceeded the space available for the use of the Committee. The difficulty thus presented did not become fully clear until the MSS. for the present volume began to reach the editor's desk. Professor Brim was then just leaving this country for needed rest in Hawaii. Accordingly, the editor, after extended conference with Professor Butterworth, undertook to make the deletions of material necessary to bring it within the compass of the space assigned.

Of the first of the original two sections, some portions have been omitted and other portions rearranged and condensed. The editor accepts the responsibility for these omissions and rearrangements. He desires to thank various contributors for their acquiescence to these dispositions of their material and their willingness to coöperate in carrying out this never-pleasant task of discarding what has been laboriously created for publication; one contributor, for example, not only withdrew a carefully prepared and scholarly chapter, but also, at the editor's eleventh-hour request, wrote a substitute chapter to fit the limited space available.

Of the second of the original two sections, only the first of the chapters submitted could be retained—the one by Professor Brim which appears as Chapter XI. This chapter is included in the present report because members of the Committee were agreed (in Professor Brim's absence) that the formulation of the general principles he presented ought to be made public now, despite the fact that the other chapters discussing these principles had to be deferred until some later report can be made. On this account the present volume is published as the ''First Report of the Committee.'' The editor is certain that it contributes a valuable account of the present status of rural education and that those who read it will look forward toward a second report, with its discussion of principles and policies, at an early date.

G. M. W.

FOREWORD

The function of this study is twofold: to make a summary and an appraisal of the status of rural education in the United States, and to set forth the conclusions of its leaders concerning guiding values and principles of procedure.

Because of the scope of the field to be covered, the absence of reliable data, the limited number of trained leaders and dependable field workers, scientific studies of rural education have been and are extremely difficult. However, in spite of the obstacles and handicaps that might have overwhelmed less adventurous and courageous spirits, those engaged in the field have made significant progress in the study of the various problems, in planning forward-looking programs, and in actual achievements in the schools.

For evident reasons, such studies have not always attracted wide attention. Rural educators have lacked a medium of communication, save for a brief period, and even then but a small number was reached. Consequently, the reports of investigations have not become widely known among rural superintendents, principals, supervisors, and teachers. Because other duties called or other problems challenged, those not engaged specifically with the rural problem are only partially informed as to its status and achievements.

Moreover, as in the field of general education, not all these studies and the deductions drawn from them have been without fault. A critical evaluation is needed in order that later studies may be more carefully guarded and that a more critical attitude may be fostered among those who use them.

A summary of the existing studies, then, it was felt might bring the status of rural education before educators generally and rural educators particularly, in a concise yet comprehensive way. The critical evaluation of existing studies would help to reveal any tendencies to superficial study and unwarranted applications. It would challenge workers to more rigorous research, more critical interpretation, and the rank and file to a better evaluation of the findings. As a source book for those who are training workers in this field, it was thought such a book would furnish a much needed body of materials. Furthermore, it was expected that such a study, by presenting the limitations and errors in existing studies, would reveal problems for further study. It was decided, therefore, to devote the major portion of this Yearbook to a critical summary of the existing literature of rural education[1] and to add such supplementary studies as proved essential for purposes of connection or organization.

It early became evident that for interpretation of available information as to status, as well as for guidance in further study, some consideration would have to be given to the philosophy or philosophies underlying the rural educator's work. Science represents an attitude toward problems and a method of answering questions. It contributes somewhat in determining what goals are possible and what values are tenable. In the main, however, the values man holds high and the goals he seeks are determined by his own philosophy of life. While a scientific study of education or a review of the findings of preceding studies serves to reveal further questions, science does not determine which of these shall be investigated. The determination must be made on the basis of one's system of values or one's purposes. The Yearbook was accordingly to be divided into two parts; Section I, devoted to a critical summary of status; and Section II, devoted to a statement of principles and criteria.

Each contributor to the first section, now represented by Chapters I to X, was urged to deal with his field in an impersonal manner. The purpose was not to 'set rural education right' or to give personally approved answers to the questions that arose, but rather to set forth the facts impartially.

Chapter I, "The Social and Economic Status of Rural Life," presents the background against which all questions of rural education must be considered. Chapters II to IX consider the major phases of public education. Chapter X presents the status of the coöperative extension work in agriculture and home economics. Our original plan was to include a section on "The Visiting Teacher in Rural Schools," and another on other aspects of "Adult Education" not included under Chapter XI. Limited space, however, has prevented this.

In Section II we intended to present the judgments of leaders in the several fields of rural education as to what should be our guiding values and principles. To accomplish this end we planned to bring

---

[1] In certain fields space permitted the inclusion or review of only a part of the many studies available.

into the open the points upon which the many leaders agree and upon which they differ in their philosophies of rural education, to set forth the nature of these differences and the reasons for them in the hope that each reader might thus be led to think more critically about his own point of view and more effectively about the entire question of principles of rural education.

These plans, unfortunately, have turned out to consume more space than had been anticipated. A compromise has been effected, as explained elsewhere by the editor. As a result of the necessary reduction the contributions found in Chapters I to X may seem inadequate. It was impossible in the limited space to get a picture of the whole field before the profession and yet treat each topic elaborately. Many important studies have been entirely eliminated and merely brief mention made of others. Moreover, all criticisms of the chairman's formulation of principles had to be omitted and this formulation incorporated as Chapter XI, leaving the discussion of the principles to a subsequent volume.

ORVILLE G. BRIM, Chairman.

CHAPTER I

ECONOMIC AND SOCIAL FACTORS OF RURAL LIFE[1]

GEORGE A. WORKS
Professor of Education
The University of Chicago, Chicago, Illinois

I. INTRODUCTION

During the first quarter of the twentieth century, much was written and said in favor of using the rural schools as a means of stemming the movement of population from the farm to urban centers. It was assumed that the decline in percentage of the population that was rural as a result of this migration was unfortunate for the country as a whole and that the program of instruction in the rural school should be so organized as to reduce, if not to stop, the movement of population cityward. More recently this view has been rejected for one that is more consistent with the purposes of publicly supported education in a democratic society. There is now general acceptance of the idea that the aims and objectives of our public schools are the same for the rural as for the urban elements in our population.

The acceptance of this view, which from the writer's angle is the only sound one, may result in the disregard of important factors in the situation unless a more careful analysis is made than is frequently done. Common statements are to the effect that "there is no such thing as rural education" or that "there is no difference between rural and urban education." These statements are in danger of being accepted as an excuse for failing to make the critical analyses that are necessary to determine the extent to which there are differences between the difficulties involved in developing programs of education for the open country and the city that are consistent with our ideals of the place of education in a democratic society.

It is the purpose of this chapter to point out some of the problems on the economic and social side that have a significant bearing on the

---

[1] In the preparation of this chapter the writer is indebted to Dr. M. Slade Kendrick, Cornell University, for various helpful suggestions. R. M. Tisinger, a graduate student at Cornell University, prepared the material presented in the section dealing with social factors.

1

possibilities of the development of a program of education conceived in terms of the welfare of the entire people. The reader is certain to be impressed with the inadequacy of the data that are presented, but the chapter will serve its purpose if it does no more than make clear the importance of having in our possession more information than we now have before the decision is made that there need be no difference between rural and urban education. It seems clear that in their objectives there should be no difference, but the economic and social conditions under which the realization of the objectives is undertaken may be so different that their attainment is impossible unless cognizance is taken of the differences between the two situations, the rural and urban.

On the economic side the data presented relate to three questions: (1) the ability of the open country to support schools as compared with that of centers of population; (2) the burden of education in the open country; and (3) taxation in relation to the support of schools.

The ability of a population group to support education may be measured in terms of its income or of the wealth per person for which schooling is to be provided. It is only in recent years that significant studies have been undertaken in this field. The magnitude of the problem and the complexity of the situation mean that the data obtained, while significant, are too incomplete to justify final conclusions.

II. FARM INCOME

Table I is based on a report of the National Bureau of Economic Research (12:61, 91)[2]. The authors of this report comment on the data incorporated in Table I in the following words (11:61):

> The figures show that the gross value of the output per person engaged in agriculture is about the same as the average annual earnings of factory or railway employees. From this gross output the agriculturist must subtract payments for interest, insurance, fertilizers, machinery, etc., before arriving at his net income and this net income includes not only payment for his services but also for the use of any property which he may possess and for any farm labor performed by his wife or children. It seems clear, then, that when farm laborers and farmers are considered as a joint group, their economic condition,

---

[2] Citations in parentheses refer by number and page to the numbered references at the end of this chapter.

if measured in monetary terms, compares unfavorably with that of employees of railways or of manufacturing concerns.

Again, in considering the income of farmers as contrasted with other groups, the statement is made (12:64) that:

> The indications are that farmers, even though they are entrepreneurs, and belong to the class usually considered to consist of men of higher talent than mere employees, nevertheless obtain on the average less money value in return for their efforts than do the average employees in most lines of industry. Only in the years 1918 and 1919 did they receive more than the average earnings for all employees in the United States, while in 1920 their reward fell to a mere fraction of the average wage in other lines. Even though money will buy considerably more of certain commodities in the county than in the city, it nevertheless appears that the average farmer can scarcely with justice be considered a pampered child of fortune.

TABLE I.—OUTPUT PER PERSON ENGAGED IN AGRICULTURE, COMPARED WITH THE AVERAGE ANNUAL EARNINGS OF FACTORY AND RAILWAY EMPLOYEES (After King)

Year	Value of output per person engaged in agriculture at prices of 1918	Purchasing power of average annual compensation of factory employees in terms of 1913 retail prices	Purchasing power of average annual compensation of railway employees in terms of 1913 retail prices
1909........	$617	$597	$571
1910........	727	634	620
1911........	694	619	609
1912........	683	659	655
1913........	678	705	705
1914........	736	610	616
1915........	766	634	653
1916........	635	794	873
1917........	647	792	1,022
1918........	786	726	1,148
1919........	821	....	.....
1920........	977	....	.....

In another report (14) the Bureau of Economic Research presents data on the proportion of the total current income that went to the population living on farms for the years 1919, 1920, and 1921. For these years the percentages of the current income received by the farm population were 17.7, 13.4, and 9.9, respectively. According to the Census of Agriculture for 1920, 29.9 percent of the population of continental United States lived on farms. In interpreting these figures, it should be borne in mind that according to Table I the years 1918 and 1919 were ones of relatively large returns for farmers.

When the comparison is made between the monetary return of the farming and the non-farming population, the contrast is striking. The data for the years 1919, 1920, and 1921 are here assembled in Table II.

TABLE II.—PER CAPITA TOTAL INDIVIDUAL CURRENT INCOME FROM ALL SOURCES, 1919, 1920, 1921*

	1919	1920	1921
Farm population......................	$362	$298	$186
Non-farm population..................	723	816	701

*After Levin, Tables XLVI, XLVII, and XLVIII.

These percentages are for the country as a whole and might, therefore, be misleading for any given state. The detailed data show that in a few states the proportion of the current income going to the farming population is approximately equivalent to the percentage the farm population is of the total population.

King's latest study (11) gives more complete data on the agricultural income on a somewhat different basis than was used in some of the figures quoted above. Table III, based on this report (11:58, 98), shows the percentage of those gainfully employed who are engaged in agriculture. The percentage drawn by individuals from agriculture is somewhat larger than the return received by farmers, but in spite of this fact it is evident that for most of the period from 1909 to 1927, inclusive, there existed a marked disparity between the percentage of those gainfully employed in agriculture and the percentage of total income drawn from agriculture. The difference has been very pronounced since 1920, and at no time has it shown any material improvement.

These figures should be interpreted with care or erroneous ideas of conditions will be obtained. A warning on this phase has been sounded by Dr. Black, one of the leading agricultural economists of this country, who says (2:30f.):

> If one were satisfied with a comparison of farming and non-farming incomes in terms of all adult workers in city and country and for the

TABLE III.—ESTIMATED PERCENTAGE OF THE GAINFULLY OCCUPIED POPULATION ENGAGED IN AGRICULTURE, AND PERCENTAGE OF INCOME DRAWN BY INDIVIDUALS FROM AGRICULTURE (After King)

Year	(1) Percentage of Gainfully Employed	(2) Percentage of Total Income	(3) Ratio of (1) to (2)
1909	25.49	16.85	.66
1910	25.11	16.60	.66
1911	24.77	15.11	.61
1912	24.28	15.58	.64
1913	23.79	14.37	.60
1914	23.27	14.25	.61
1915	23.27	14.75	.63
1916	22.78	15.32	.67
1917	22.44	17.90	.79
1918	21.95	18.85	.86
1919	22.21	18.47	.83
1920	22.17	14.94	.67
1921	21.71	10.99	.50
1922	20.91	11.07	.53
1923	20.46	10.80	.52
1924	20.11	10.79	.53
1925	19.72	11.09	.56
1926	19.14	9.60	.50
1927	18.58	9.49	.57
1928	.....	9.27	.....

same geographic units, agriculture would not appear at much disadvantage in the years 1918 to 1920 if the two incomes were reduced to terms of what they were able to buy in the goods and services that constitute living. Those who try to prove the contrary are insulting the agricultural population of the United States. If our population of farm people continued on farms with average real incomes as low as they are made to appear by the data published by the National Bureau of Economic Research, the Industrial Conference Board, and others, most of them would properly be called 'boobs' and 'ignoramuses.' And they are not that. Most of them, instead, are small business men working to make a good return on their investments and to improve their financial status.

However, Dr. Black believes the economic situation to be far from satisfactory with the farmer, as is shown by the following quotations:

It is customary to compare incomes of farmers with those of city workmen. As already indicated, these are scarcely comparable social groups. The farmer is to be compared with the small business man of the city—the retail merchant; or with the city man with a trade—the carpenter or plumber; or with the city man with a profession—the small city lawyer, doctor, or teacher. Nevertheless it is of some consequence that weekly earnings of New York factory workers are now 135 percent above their prewar level, whereas gross incomes of farmers are only 70 percent above prewar; that these same weekly earnings are now appreciably higher than in 1919 to 1920, whereas net cash incomes of farmers are now at only 60 percent of their 1919 to 1920 level. (2:27 f.).

We must all admit that the nation has done many things for its agriculture. But the point is that it has done much more for the city, and farming is of such a nature that it needs to have vastly more done for it than the city if it is to maintain equality with the city. The saying that there is no greater inequality than the equal treatment of unequals is all to the point here; and yet we have not even treated agriculture as well as we have the city (2:54).

The strongest case in favor of raising the incomes and scale of living of farm people is the simple and obvious one that if the objective of national policy is to improve human welfare, then it ought to begin with those groups of the population whose welfare is distinctly below the general level, which surely would include much of agriculture at present. The mere numbers in the agricultural groups make it highly important that their welfare be promoted. The farm population of the United States is at present suffering from important deficiencies in the matter of health, housing, and education that the nation cannot afford to tolerate. The foregoing statement is made in full consciousness of the fact that the farm population of many areas is living on a distinctly higher plane than are the inhabitants of many quarters of our large cities. But there are slums in the country too. Obviously, it is important that the poorest sections both in the city and the country be helped most (2:59 f.).

III. Farm Wealth

The farmer's income is undoubtedly a better measure of his ability to provide education for his children than is wealth alone. However, some data will be submitted on this phase of the problem. Significant figures on the wealth per teacher for different types of districts in New York State are reported by Updegraff. He found (27:85) the median equalized valuation per teacher for the common school districts (country) to be $108,157 and for cities and villages to be $182,857. In a similar study Updegraff and King (28) showed a median true valuation for the different types of districts in Pennsylvania to be: fourth class, $100,000; third class, $129,375; and first and second class cities combined, $250,000. As far as wealth per teacher is a true index to the ability to support schools, it is evident from these figures that the larger centers of population in those two states were in a much better position than the small villages and the open country. We do not know the extent to which these two states are representative of conditions throughout the country without further investigation. That the condition does not obtain in all states is shown by the following statement by Sears and Cubberley (25 :322) :

> It is clear that, aside from less than a dozen large cities in the state, the economic strength of the rural districts of California is relatively greater than is that of city districts.

Black presents data that apply to the country as a whole. He compares the farmer with non-farmers in the following words (2 :23f.) :

> It is fully as important to understand the state of mind of the farm population at present as it is their economic condition. In order to understand this state of mind, one must do more than make comparison with prewar or 1921-1922 agriculture. Of more importance is comparison with the changes in the prosperity of other economic classes. The outstanding feature of this comparison is the changes in valuation. While the capitalization of the farms of the United States has been declining from $79,000,000,000 to $58,000,000,000, that of urban industry has greatly increased. The Dow-Jones index for 20 leading industrial stocks has risen from a low of 64 in 1921 to 322 at present writing; for 20 railroad stocks, from a low of 66 to 161 at present writing. No doubt the ordinary sorts of industrial and commercial enterprises do not show the phenomenal gains of these leaders; but that they have made large gains in capitalization, no one will doubt. The census no longer gives a figure for valuation of industrial plants comparable to that for farms. The one it gave until 1919 is apparently valueless. The total capital of corporations, as nearly as it can be figured from the corporation income-tax returns, increased from $123,000,000,000 in 1921 to $151,000,000,000 in 1926. Neither of these figures is at all dependable, and some of the increases represent new corporations and growth of old corporations. The Census of Manufactures' figures for value of product of manufacturing plants are $61,737,000,000 for 1919, and $62,713,000,000 for 1925, nearly the same in dollars. If cost of materials and wages and salaries are subtracted from these two figures, the difference is $10,968,000,000 in 1919, and $12,300,000,000 in 1925, the 1919 figure being equal to $8,461,000,000 in 1925 dollars. These figures represent profits, taxes, and insurance mostly. There is surely basis here for an increase in capitalization beyond that representing additional equipment. The vast difference in the valuation of agriculture and urban industry represented by these figures—a phenomenal

decline in one set against a phenomenal rise in the other—is the principal basis for the continuing agricultural discontent.

IV. BURDEN OF EDUCATION IN THE OPEN COUNTRY

Adequate data are lacking on the relative cost of furnishing schooling in the open country and of comparable schooling in centers of population. The fact that the population of the open country is relatively scattered means that ordinarily the financial burden involved in providing schools will be greater in the country than in the city. Some indirect evidence on this phase is to be found in practically every comparative study that has been made of the per capita costs of schooling. Two illustrations will be given: Updegraff (27:63) reports the median per capita expenditure for common school districts in New York State as $64.82. In the same state the corresponding figure for cities and larger villages (places over 4500) was $61.66. In the interpretation of these costs it should be borne in mind that in spite of the fact the higher per capita cost is found in the common school districts, on the whole the schooling in these districts was very much more limited than was true in the urban centers. Had it been comparable for the two situations, the per capita cost for the country would have been much greater than reported.

A study made in Iowa showed (21:47) the average (arithmetic mean) current expense per pupil in 1922 to be as follows: city schools, $66; consolidated schools, $84; rural schools, $71. A further analysis shows that in the case of the consolidated schools other items than salary constitute a relatively large proportion of the expenditures. A large share of this extra cost is due to the expense of transportation. In the rural district schools of the one-teacher type the per pupil costs are likely to run high owing to the small number of pupils per teacher. Question may fairly be raised regarding the extent to which the farmer should be subjected to a heavy school cost as a result of the conditions under which the business must be conducted.

The school burden of the open country is increased by the relatively large proportion of persons of school age in rural communities. The census for 1920 is the source of the figures in Table IV, whence it is evident that in the rural districts the numbers of children for which schooling must be provided are appreciably greater in proportion to the adult population than is the case in the urban districts.

TABLE IV.—PERCENTAGES OF PERSONS OF DIFFERENT AGES CLASSIFIED AS RURAL AND URBAN IN THE FEDERAL CENSUS FOR 1920

Ages	Rural	Urban
5– 9	12.1	9.9
10–14	10.4	8.7
15–19	8.8	8.0

V. FARM TAXES

An interesting comparison of the relation between taxes and income for three population groups has been made in Dane County, Wisconsin. Table V has been taken from this study (9:18).

TABLE V.—PERCENTAGES OF PRE-WAR, WAR PERIOD, AND PRESENT NET INCOMES ABSORBED BY TAXES (From Hibbard and Allin)

Class	Percentage of Net Income Absorbed by Taxes						Number of Reports
	Pre-War Period		War Period		Present Period		
	1913	1914	1918	1919	1923	1924	
Farm	12.3	13.9	6.7	9.0	19.1	22.5	214
City	4.8	4.9	7.2	7.8	9.5	8.9	1,353
Village	4.9	5.0	4.6	4.8	8.0	8.2	133

In commenting on their data the authors of the report attribute the heavy farm tax burden to two factors: (1) "failure of farm incomes to increase in proportion to tax increases;" and (2) "peculiarities of the general property system of taxation."

It would be unwise to assume that the conditions found in Dane County are representative of the situation in the entire country. However, the study represents the type of information that should be more generally available in considering the support of rural schools. Most of the taxes paid by farmers are local, and the school tax usually constitutes between a third and a half of the local taxes.

M. Slade Kendrick (10:8) summarizes the results of the comparative studies that had previously been made in the following words:

> A summing up of the evidence presented by these comparisons of taxes with income indicates that, in five of the eight states, taxes on rural real estate comprised the larger percentage of net income, and that in the three instances where the difference was significant rural

taxes absorbed a larger percentage of income than did urban taxes. Admittedly, eight states may not be sufficiently representative of the whole forty-eight. But, in so far as this particular group is representative, the evidence indicates that a larger, though not a greatly larger, percentage of the income from rural property is paid in taxes than is paid from the income of urban property. Additional evidence in support of this conclusion is afforded by the fact that during the last few years the agricultural industry has been relatively depressed in relation to the average city industry. It is to be expected that real estate taxes would take a larger percent of the income of a relatively depressed industry than of a relatively prosperous one.

The question may well be raised whether this conclusion means precisely what it says, or more. Let it be supposed, for example, that thirty percent of the income of rural real estate is paid in taxes and that twenty-five percent of the income of urban real estate is so paid. Does the difference between thirty percent and twenty-five percent express the full difference in the burdens on the two classes of property? Probably it does not if there be included a consideration of relative dollars' worth of benefits, added to the incomes of urban and rural real properties from the expenditure of taxes collected on these properties. How much do efficient fire and police departments, a good school, and a convenient park add to the incomes of urban real estate? How much does a paved road or a muddy one affect the income from rural real estate? Considerations such as these must be included in any true comparison between tax burdens on urban and on rural properties. Failure to include them is an error precisely analogous to that committed by a comparison of two corporations in terms of their expense outlays with no reference to their income statements. It is indeed unfortunate that at present, on account of lack of data, this error is inevitable in any comparison of the relative tax burdens on urban and rural real estate.

The most comprehensive consideration of farm taxes that has appeared comes from the United States Department of Agriculture. The following statement is made by Dr. Combs as a result of consideration of the data available (4: 33):

> The comparison which has been made of the taxes and yields of urban and rural properties does not give a satisfactory indication of the relative burdens of taxation on these types of property. From the point of view of current income to the owner of rented land, the comparison is exceedingly important. Examination indicates that both types of property pay high proportions of their net yields in taxes and that on the basis of the few states for which figures are available, farm property seems to pay a slightly greater proportion.

Too much importance should not be attached to the meager conclusions that may be drawn from the comparative data that have been presented. Urban and rural taxes are, in part, different things. That is, the taxpayer in the city is purchasing, through his tax payments, types of services that are different from those paid for in rural tax payments. The city government provides fire and police protection. It maintains a school system which may be no better in its individual units than are the rural schools, but which enables pupils to carry their education further and provides a greater variety of training and more elaborate equipment. The streets maintained by city taxes are of a higher grade and are usually kept in better condition than are roads in rural sections. Street cleaning and lighting are city services that rarely have rural counterparts. Thus, it is apparent that the things for which city taxes are paid are much more extensive than the things which the rural property owner purchases through his tax payments.

In a letter to the writer, Dr. M. Slade Kendrick, of Cornell University, makes this statement:

As local expenditures increase, the burden is inevitably placed upon real property. Other taxes are levied at percentage rates and are subject to change only by legal action; therefore, since a change means a legislative battle, such changes are rather infrequent. But the property rate is not fixed by law but by necessity; as the demands for revenue increase, the burden is automatically placed upon property. This situation, it seems to me, emphasizes the need, from a rural point of view, of the greater sharing of revenues collected by the state government. The economic evolution of the last century has been responsible for the possibility of income taxes, corporation taxes, stamp taxes, and various other taxes. These cannot be administered successfully by small local units; they can be administered only by a large unit such as the state or nation.

VI. Social Factors

"Society," says Kolb (13), "is never a fixed or static thing and rural society is no exception." Similarly, Morgan and Howells (20) say: "Improved means of communication and transportation, are rapidly breaking down the isolation of country life. There is, as a result, a dissolution of the old groupings and a constant rearrangement of the new."

1. Various Communities in Rural Society

Galpin (5), in 1918, presented a "method of analysis and inquiry into the structure of rural society" which led the way in a number of researches in this field in later years. His method of analysis consisted of mapping the county in such a way as to show the "trade communities," "banking communities," "local paper communities," "village or city-milk communities," "village or city church communities," "high-school communities" and "public-library communities." Three years later Kolb presented his study just cited of rural primary groups which he defined as "that first grouping beyond the family which has significance and which is conscious of some local unit." By means of a map system he presented a further refined technique for discovering these primary groups.

Sanderson and Thompson (23) carried the process of analyzing still further and classified the neighborhoods in Otsego County, New York, according to type as follows: (1) the hamlet; (2) the institutional neighborhood; (3) the business neighborhood; (4) the ethnic neighborhood; (5) the kinship neighborhood; (6) the topographical neighborhood; (7) the village neighborhood. In brief, these writers found that "the hamlet type is persisting because of the investment in its homes and central location," and that "the business neighborhood is practically gone and there seems little probability of recovery." "The kinship neighborhood, although still evident, is passing." "The topographic neighborhood has little more significance than giving a name to a locality." "Institutional neighborhoods maintain themselves in localities somewhat isolated from village centers."

Their next step was the definition and location of the 'community.' "The rural community consists of the people in a local area tributary to the center of their economic interests. The community is the smallest geographical unit of organized association of the chief human activities."

Similar means were used for locating communities as were used for locating the neighborhoods, and in general the community areas were found to coincide closely with the trade areas of the village centers. This type of community, in which the high-school patronage area is perhaps the most important measure used, became the basis for the formation of the new "central rural-school district," as it is now being organized in New York State.

Two years after the New York study was published, Morgan and Howells (20) published the results of a similar study in Boone County, Missouri. In part, these authors conclude:

> The school was found to be the strongest factor in maintaining primary group consciousness. Intergroup consciousness was developed

best through the consolidated high school, followed by the church, the lodge, and the store. Neighborhood boundaries were cut across in the effort of the people to reach preferred points for such services as church, trade, school, lodge, and blacksmith shop. Thus a farm family has at a given time a number of separate and conflicting group loyalties. In the midst of this the neighborhood is losing much of the force it once had. 'This is being transferred to the larger community, which usually includes a town or village. This larger rural grouping is new and now has less vitality and intensity of group consciousness than the neighborhood, although it appears to be on the gain. It is this larger group, which is the combination of country and town, that will be of increasing importance in the development of rural affairs. The status of the community depends upon physical, economic, and social factors which in a few cases are entirely beyond the power of the community to modify. The future of most community centers depends upon the ability to render superior services to the adjacent farm group.

2. Urbanization of Rural Communities

Improvements in transportation and communication have made possible a change which might be termed the 'urbanization' of certain rural communities. This trend is most evident in the Northeastern states and in certain selected areas in the remaining states where cities and towns have grown rapidly during the last two decades. This does not refer to such items as the installation of modern improvements upon the farm, but rather to the tendency for people employed in the city, with city social contacts, to live in the country and to commute.

New York is one of the states which has been greatly influenced by this movement. The population of this state has increased steadily since 1855. In 1928 Melvin (17) investigated the rural population trends of this state. Table VI, assembled from his study, shows the nature of the change which is taking place.

The total rural population, according to Melvin, steadily declined in numbers from 1880 up to 1920. From 1920 to 1925 the trend changed and the rural population showed a sudden large increase. Thereafter the farm population continued to decline at about the same rate as during the period from 1880 to 1920. Likewise, the village population was approximately stationary from 1880 to 1920, with a very slight rise during the period from 1920 to 1925. The explanation for the sudden increase in rural population from 1920 to 1925

TABLE VI.—TOTAL RURAL POPULATION AND ITS CLASSES IN NEW YORK, 1855-1925
(After Melvin)

Year	Total Rural Population	Population in Incorporated Villages	Farm Population	Unincorporated Villages and Non-farming, Non-Village Population
1855	2,081,183	182,109	1,153,286	745,788
1870	2,092,291	200,733	1,041,771	849,787
1880	2,125,722	268,358	1,076,705	780,659
1890	1,998,885	308,355	986,072	704,458
1900	1,964,165	345,716	969,064	649,385
1910	1,925,287	348,510	916,009	660,768
1920	1,795,383	346,877	796,516	651,990
1925	2,003,265	353,256	762,509	887,500

lies in the group listed as "unincorporated village, and non-farming, non-village population," which grew at a high rate in the state as a whole (41 percent). The greatest growth was in the urban counties (52 percent) and the least was in the mountain counties (11.9 percent).

This phenomenal growth of a non-rural group within the bounds of rural areas presents many perplexing problems in the field of rural education—occupational and cultural differences tend to complicate curricular offerings and new standards of activity are thrust upon the more or less conservative rural population.

Another population study by the same author (18) brings out a tendency for the female group to predominate in the incorporated and unincorporated agricultural villages and for the males to predominate in the open country. The ratios found were 93.6 females to 100 males in rural population as a whole, 108.5 females to 100 males in incorporated villages, and 89.5 females to 100 males in the open country. It was found that the older people live in the incorporated villages—29.5 percent of the rural population are 50 years of age and above, while for the total rural population 26.9 percent fall within this age group. Both of these groups, however, showed a much higher percentage than in the United States as a whole (14.7 percent).

3. Social Contacts

There is a widespread belief that rural areas are lacking in social contacts. In a recent study by Burt (3) in a trade-area rural community in Missouri, the author sought "to discover in one rural community, for a period of three months, the nature, frequency, distribution, and costs of contacts.'' He found that

of the total contacts within the community, 92,148, or 58.3 percent, were educational contacts of school children; 46,047, or 29.1 percent, were social contacts due to visiting; and 19,923, or 12.6 percent, were of all other types. [The 18,889 trade contacts were not included here.] A large number of persons had no contacts at all *within* the community during the three months' period of study. About one-fourth had no social contacts. More than one-half had no religious contacts. Nearly two-thirds had no educational contacts. Exactly five-sixths had no recreational contacts.

With the exception of one type of contact (the recreational) a still greater number of persons had no contacts at all *outside* the community during the three months' period of study. Almost exactly one-half had no recreational contacts. A few more than half had no social contacts. Somewhat under three-fifths had no religious contacts. Exactly three-fourths had no educational contacts.

[There was] no correlation between road passability and number of contacts. The people of this community had about as many contacts in a period of poor roads as in a period of excellent roads. A reasonable interpretation seems to be that in fair weather the press of farm work tends to keep the farmer at home, and in wet weather poor roads tend to keep him at home. Unless farm work can be so organized as to leave the farm family freer to go during favorable weather, the most likely way to increase contacts is to provide hard-surfaced roads so that farm people can go more easily during periods of wet weather.

This was a quantitative type of study, presenting a cross-section of social contacts over a comparatively brief period of time. Two obvious questions point towards the need for similar studies in other situations: First, what kind of a qualitative analysis could be made of these contacts? Second, what changes are taking place both as to the quality and quantity of contacts in this community? In other words, what change or changes are taking place in our rural areas in the way of opportunities for ''socialization'' as Hawthorne (8) uses this term? Have modern means of communication, such as the radio, telephone, rural delivery, automobile, improved highways, etc., in reality improved the social conditions of these rural areas, or is this just a potentiality?

According to Hawthorne (8):

1. The school with its teaching staff works not with old age, which is 'set' in its ideas, but with youth which is open-minded and plastic to the thought of evolving society.

2. The school is a mobilization or concentration point for the devices of social heredity, which are to be brought into play upon the plasticity of childhood.

3. The school can compel the attention of adaptable minds to the subject matter, experimental projects, and the socializing events selected by experts.

4. The human material with which the school works is not under the strain of the economic effort to obtain a livelihood.

5. Through the invention of cheap printing and rapid communication, the school can extend its range of influence, so that it is no longer limited to its own little miniature society.

6. The school can adapt and grade the subject matter of education and socialization to the intelligence and maturity of the group.

7. The school has a commanding prestige as a community institution.

4. Health Conditions

Turning now from social contacts to health conditions, we find that "the efforts of medical science have been concentrated in the cities, leaving for the open country only those health values of a quiet life close to nature upon which the early concept of the country as a healthy place in which to live was based." "Health standards today include not only a general environment but ready access to a variety of health agencies which society has developed and come to look upon as indispensable.... Trained nursing and hospital service are only meagerly used by country people; public-health organization, though established in many rural districts, is only beginning to be effective."

To substantiate these statements, Lively and Beck (16) surveyed all the health agencies in Ross County, Ohio. The mere presence of agencies tells little about the service rendered. An ignorant and superstitious patient may die in the shadow of a hospital without knowing the possibilities for medical aid. These investigations went a step further and included a systematic study of the use which was being made of the existing institutions, checking such items as extent of illness, expenditures for health, composition of the population, expenditures for physicians' services, expenditure for dental service, expenditures for hospital and nursing service, and expenditures for optical services. The use of these facilities appears to be conditioned by a number of factors, such as extent of illness, distance, ability to pay, sex, age, size of family, and education of family.

In this county, which is "about as well supplied with medical and health agencies as any semi-rural county in Ohio," it was found that (16):

> Physicians were becoming urban in their location, standards of practice, and fees. This greatly increased the cost of medical services to country people that live some distance from the city and sometimes increased the difficulty of obtaining a physician because of poor communicative facilities, bad roads, and the reluctance of urban physicians to make calls by means other than motor transportation. . . The country doctor of the older type complained that his clientele deserted him in serious cases. These were taken to the urban physician, leaving for the rural physician the less profitable and emergency cases. . . Country people used the hospital only in extreme cases. Nursing service, when obtained, was done by the practical nurse rather than by the graduate nurse. . . Due to the educational work of the county public-health organization, dental work was increasing, but rural dentists reported that rural work is "eleventh-hour work." . . There was much variation in the economic conditions in various sections of the country and also much variation in the prevailing standards of health. In general, the standards and costs of medical and health agencies have risen more rapidly than the health standards of the people and their ability to pay. . . The results were infrequent use of medical agencies, misunderstanding of the nature and value of service rendered by the physician, the use of patent medicines and office calls when the patient should be in bed. . .
>
> It is evident that limited ability to pay, low health standards, and relative inaccessibility to modern medical and health agencies were serious handicaps in the hilly sections of the county. With no clinics or free service available, many persons either obtained no medical service or they called a physician and paid him nothing, or in part. . . The people in these areas are, in both health practices and ability to pay, so far below current medical standards and costs that satisfactory readjustment may be expected following only extended and sympathetic aid on a low cost level.

Dr. Wm. C. Savage in an article issued under the auspices of the central council for health education (24), advocates the adoption of "Compulsory Health." By that he means the duty of all individuals in the community to maintain themselves in health, or, if they are in charge of children, to see that they are maintained in health, all of course as far as practicable—a duty, if necessary, to be enforced by compulsion. In the old days such an idea would have seemed absurd; but many persons are advancing toward an acceptance of it. If it is right for the community to expend large sums of money on maintaining and assisting its members to maintain or regain health, it is but a logical sequence that its members must themselves play their part in maintaining their own health. Before, however, any such demand can be made on members of the community they should have the opportunity of knowing much more about how health can be maintained. There is urgent need for an extensive system of general instruction on health matters; Savage believes that in a few years this will be recognized as an essential part of the work of every health department.

In his effort to secure a further measure of health conditions, Sanderson (22) well illustrates the difficulty in securing comparable data on sickness in rural areas by seeking answers to such questions as "What is the effect of sickness on the life of the farm family"; "Is medical service adequate for farm families?" "Is there more sickness on the farm or in the village?"

From a house to house canvass made in three townships in Cortland County, N. Y., he found that

> In recent years there has been a dcrease in the number of county doctors and a marked tendency for physicians to settle in larger towns and cities. The increasing difficulty of securing prompt medical service has become a real problem in many rural communities. [The data] seem to show that the village cases are more frequently visited by physicians than are those on the farms, and that the farm people make more calls at the physician's office. This is doubtless due to the expense of bringing a physician to the farm as well as to the larger proportion of aged persons in the village and a consequent larger number of serious illnesses in the village.

Sanderson found that the physician's charges are "fairly reasonable," considering the distance travelled. However, the cost for these farms more than five miles distant from a physician is so great as to deter the employment of one except when absolutely necessary. Irrespective of costs, there is a question whether physicians are available when needed. There seemed to be general agreement that only two or three of the city's (Cortland) physicians could be depended upon for country calls.

5. The Social Status of Rural Young People

A general social problem evolves from the economic side of rural life. Child labor laws in general do not function on the farm. The child has been considered an economic asset, and much of his labor has been uncompensated for. He has had little time for individual recreation and play and limited opportunities for group recreation or social life. This situation is reflected in the "attitudes, interests, activities, and activity-wishes and migration" of young people living in these areas. Morgan and Burt (19) studied four trade-area communities in Missouri, having as their purpose

> to ascertain for certain limited areas something of what rural young people are thinking, what attitudes they have developed toward rural life and its institutions and toward such general interests as education, religion, play, science, and urban life . . . to discover what these young people are now doing, what they would do if they had a chance, and what they would like to learn how to do, together with what the community provides for the satisfaction of these activity-wishes, and what appear to be unsatisfied needs.

Their findings involve much of interest to the rural school and are therefore given here in full:

> 1. Young people express a greater number of recreational activity-wishes (56 percent) than any other kind, while the communities are providing a smaller number of recreational organizations (7 percent) than any other type.
>
> 2. Young people express a smaller number of religious activity-wishes (3 percent) than any other type, while the communities are providing a greater number of religious organizations (66 percent) than any other type.
>
> 3. The conflict of the Old and the New is evident in this study. The most numerous class of old people (the farmer group) expresses the most friendly attitude toward the church and the least friendly attitude toward play and recreation for young people. On the other hand, the young people express the least appreciation for the church and the greatest appreciation for play and recreation for young people.
>
> 4. The type of organization toward which young people express the fewest activity-wishes (religious) is increasing in membership, while the type toward which they express the greatest number of activity-wishes (recreational) is decreasing in membership.
>
> 5. Experience of village young people and country young people with environment other than their own tends to break down the preference for their own environment, but the tendency for country young people with village experience to prefer the village is stronger than the tendency of village young people with country experience to prefer the country.
>
> 6. The most frequent reasons [for which] young people leave the rural communities are economic.
>
> 7. Assuming these findings to be fairly typical for the state, it would appear that the rural communities of Missouri must provide in-

creased economic opportunities if they wish to check the migration of
their young people, and must provide, above all, more numerous opportunities for recreational activities in order to satisfy the most generally expressed needs of the young people who remain.

A different type of approach to the problem of rural recreation
has been made by Lively (15) in two agricultural counties in Ohio.
A survey was made of the recreational agencies in each of these two
counties and the results anlyzed from the standpoint of the communities. Lively also analyzed the same activities of the family and the
individual. We quote from his conclusions:

> Paulding County is the newer and wealthier, and possesses a more
> youthful population. The social organization of Gallia County is
> simpler than that of Paulding County, and is organized much more on
> the neighborhood basis, with the one-room school and country store still
> the type institutions. The people of Paulding County have gone fur-
> ther toward abandoning these outworn neighborhood agencies, replac-
> ing them with modern institutions and organizations, and making the
> necessary adjustments to them. Neighborhood agencies have largely
> disappeared in this county. Organization life is chiefly centered in
> the village. The open country is in a state of disorganization, having
> not yet been welded into the larger community whole which in this
> locality has such a splendid opportunity to emerge.

In either of these Ohio counties, where the one-room school is
found, it has practically no recreational functions as a neighborhood
institution; where the schools are consolidated, organized recreation
for school pupils begins to appear, and in some cases the school begins
to develop some social center functions.

6. Movement To and From Rural Areas

The urban world has been expanding; the rural world has been
decreasing and the proportion of population engaged in agriculture
has been decreasing while that engaged in urban occupations has been
growing, according to Sorokin and Zimmerman (26). There is always an exchange of population between urban and rural areas. The
following figures from Galpin (5) show the net movement from farm
to cities in the United States from 1922 to 1928.

The general causes of this cityward trend have been given by
Sorokin and Zimmerman (26) as:

1. The demographic factor of a higher fertility of the rural population.
2. A series of economic factors, such as:

TABLE VII.—MOVEMENT TO AND FROM FARMS OF THE UNITED STATES, 1922-1928
(From Galpin)

Year	Persons Leaving Farms for Cities	Persons Arriving at Farms from Cities	Net Movement from Farms to Cities
1922	2,000,000	880,000	1,120,000
1924	2,075,000	1,396,000	769,000
1925	1,900,000	1,066,000	834,000
1926	2,155,000	1,135,000	1,020,000
1927	1,978,000	1,374,000	604,000
1928	1,960,000	1,362,000	598,000

    a. Certain land laws or customary methods of inheritance such that the estate goes to the elder or younger son.

    b. City populations manufacture products of elastic demand, whereas, relatively, the products of the farm are inelastic.

    c. There is a tendency for population to migrate from lower-income communities to the cities.

    d. Increased efficiency of agricultural production coupled with inelastic demand pushes more workers to the city.

    e. The moving of many industries to the cities.

3. The progress of science and invention.

It has been found by various researches that this movement is rather highly selective in several respects. According to Hart (7) more than half of the native white and Negro migrants from the rural areas go between the ages of 20-29, and an additional fourth between the ages of 10-19.

Again quoting Sorokin and Zimmerman (26) :

The chief causes of age selectivity in migration are that such a movement requires great energy, great adaptability, and adult judgment. A child or an old man cannot take care of himself and therefore cannot afford to leave either the parental home or the local community where he is guided, supported, and advised.

A second selective factor is sex. The city appears to draw more women than men and at a slightly younger age than men.

This congregation of young adults and more females than males in cities has much to do with the peculiar characteristics of city populations. It increases the per capita incomes, decreases the proportion of dependent persons per 100 wage-earners, adds to the mobility and life of the cities, reduces marriage, adds to the amount of vice and prostitution, and gives cities the appearance of greater vitality than they really possess.

If this conclusion be true, it becomes readily apparent that the absence in the country of the group mentioned also determines characteristic population tendencies in these areas and involves many problems of an educational nature, such as the kind of vocational training to be given, the fundamental philosophy which is to underlie rural education, school financial problems, etc.

A slightly different approach to the problem was made by Anderson and Loomis (1) in Wake County, North Carolina. Their approach was from the rural angle, in that from a given group of owner and tenant farmers there was secured specific data on the migration of their sons and daughters. An attempt was made to answer such questions as: (1) What proportion of the sons and daughters of farm operators leave the parental home to establish homes of their own? (2) At what period of life do they leave the parental home? (3) Where do they go? (4) What occupations do they enter? (5) What preparation do they have for entering the occupational world, and do those who are best prepared leave farming and rural areas for the town and city? (6) How far, on the average, do they go from the parental home?

In the analysis of the data secured, farm owners and farm tenants were grouped separately.

Of the 1703 sons and daughters 14 years of age or over, 823, 48 percent, have left the parental home. Relatively more daughters leave the parental home than sons among Wake County farmers. By the age of 30, 70 to 80 percent of the owner and tenant sons and daughters have left the parental home. The movement begins at about 18 years, both for boys and girls, and is practically completed at 30 years.

The greatest single factor influencing the mobility of sons and daughters of farmers from the parental home is the establishment of homes of their own.

Taking the group as a whole, 80 percent of all the sons and daughters settled within a radius of 50 miles from the parental home. Sixty-five percent settled within a radius of 25 miles, while 30 percent located within 10 miles of the parental home. Of the total group migrating, 37 percent live in cities of 10,000 population or above. As farmers' sons and daughters move greater distances from the parental home, they locate in larger places of residence.

The significant conclusions to be drawn from the occupational activities is that there is a high degree of transmission of farming as a life work from parents to sons and daughters.

7. Other Social Problems

Many aspects of the social status of rural life have been omitted because of lack of space, and not for lack of importance. For example, sectarian and denominational strife of rural churches and their struggle for existence creates a problem in character building which may conceivably concern the school. Several studies, *e.g.*, those by Hamilton and Garnet (6), by White (29), and by Williams (30), are available on this question. Again, the father apparently continues to dominate the home in many rural areas, with the result of lack of understanding and sympathy with the younger generation. Williams discusses this question.

No attempt has been made to evaluate the material herein presented. Students of rural problems will find that the authors quoted have recognized the limitations of their studies and have given suggestions for more extensive research. The presentation of their material in this chapter will, it is hoped, lead to further study of these social problems of the rural community. The rural social status must be looked upon as a changing status, not as something fixed. Adequate understanding of the changes in rural social life is essential to effective rural education.

References

1. ANDERSON, W. A. and LOOMIS, C. P. *Migration among Sons and Daughters of White Farmers in Wake County, N. C.* (North Carolina Agricultural Experiment Station, Bulletin 275) 1929.
2. BLACK, J. D. *Agricultural Reform in the United States.* New York, 1929.
3. BURT, H. J. *Contacts in a Rural Community.* (Missouri Agricultural Experiment Station, Bulletin 125) 1929.
4. COMBS, WHITNEY. *Taxation of Farm Property.* (U. S. Dept. of Agriculture), Washington.
5. GALPIN, C. J. *Rural Life.* New York, 1918.
6. HAMILTON and GARNET. *Rôle of Church in Rural Community Life in Virginia.* (Virginia Agricultural Experiment Station, Bulletin 267.)
7. HART, HORNELL. *Selective Migration.* (University of Iowa Studies) 1921.
8. HAWTHORNE, B. H. *The Sociology of Rural Life.* New York.
9. HIBBARD, B. H. and ALLIN, B. W. *Tax Burdens Compared.* (Univ. of Wisconsin) Madison, 1927.
10. KENDRICK, M. S. "A comparison between urban and rural taxation on real estate values." Offprint from *Annals Amer. Acad. Pol. and Social Sci.*, March, 1930.

11. KING, W. I. *The National Income and Its Purchasing Power.* New York, 1930.

12. KING, W. I. *et al.* *Income in the United States.* (Vol. II) New York, 1922.

13. KOLB, J. H. *Rural Primary Groups.* (Univ. of Wisconsin Agri. Expt. Station, Research Bull. 51) 1921.

14. LEVIN, MAURICE. *Income in the Various States.* New York, 1925. 306 pp.

15. LIVELY, C. E. *Rural Recreation in Two Ohio Counties.* (Ohio State Univ. Studies) 1923.

16. LIVELY, C. E. and BECK, P. G. *The Rural Health Facilities of Ross County, Ohio.* (Ohio Agri. Exp. Station Bull. 412) 1927.

17. MELVIN, BRUCE L. *Rural Population of New York 1855 to 1925.* (Cornell Univ. Agri. Expt. Station, Memoir 116) 1928.

18. MELVIN, BRUCE L. *Rural Population, Tompkins and Schuyler Counties, New York.* (Cornell Univ. Agri. Expt. Station Bull. 487) 1925.

19. MORGAN, E. L. and BURT, HENRY J. *Community Relations of Rural Young People.* (Univ. of Missouri Agri. Expt. Station Bull. 110) 1927.

20. MORGAN, E. L. and HOWELLS, OWEN. *Rural Population Groups.* (Univ. of Missouri Agr. Expt. Station Bull. 74) 1925.

21. RUSSELL, W. F. *et al.* *The Financing of Education in Iowa.* New York.

22. SANDERSON, DWIGHT. *A Survey of Sickness in Rural Areas in Courtland County, N. Y.* (Cornell Univ. Agri. Expt. Station, Memoir 112) March, 1928.

23. SANDERSON, DWIGHT and THOMPSON, WARREN S. *The Social Areas of Otsego County.* (Cornell Univ. Agri. Expt. Station Bull. 422) 1923.

24. SAVAGE, WM. C. "Compulsory health," *Jour. Amer. Med. Assoc.* July 6, 1929.

25. SEARS, J. B. and CUBBERLEY, E. P. *The Cost of Education in California.* New York, 1924.

26. SOROKIN and ZIMMERMAN. *Principles of Rural-Urban Sociology.* New York.

27. UPDEGRAFF, HARLAN. "Financial Support." In *Rural School Survey of New York State.* Ithaca, New York, 1922.

28. UPDEGRAFF, HARLAN and KING, LEROY A. *A Survey of the Fiscal Policies of the State of Pennsylvania in the Field of Education.*

29. WHITE, R. CLYDE. *Denominationalism in Certain Rural Communities in Texas.* (Indiana University).

30. WILLIAMS, J. W. *Our Rural Heritage.*

CHAPTER II

PUPIL STATUS IN THE RURAL ELEMENTARY SCHOOL

GEORGE C. KYTE
Professor of Elementary Education and Supervision
University of Michigan, Ann Arbor, Michigan

The data treated in this chapter were gathered by the writer from published and unpublished materials, integrated, and organized to present various aspects of the status of children enrolled in rural elementary schools. In order to give added significance to the information collected regarding the rural-school children, the writer has included frequently the analogous data obtained about the city-school children. The limited space available for presenting an adequate and representative picture of these pupils precludes any possibility of including a similar account regarding the rural high-school pupils.

An effort has been made to depict briefly various phases of the status of the rural-school pupils, as disclosed by a study of the considerable amount of data found in state and county surveys published since 1920, in recent state and county reports containing usable statistical information, in published and unpublished research studies, and in mimeographed materials generously furnished the writer by many rural-school officers throughout the country. In the following pages of this chapter, the data are presented to show representative conditions as found in the state-wide studies made in representative states together with supporting information regarding similar aspects in smaller areas. The reader will find much valuable information contained in the tables which are not discussed in the chapter because of the lack of space.

AGE-GRADE STATUS OF PUPILS

Age-grade status and progress records of children are general measures of how schools are operating in accordance with: (1) the legal requirements regarding age of admission to school, compulsory attendance, continuation in school, and the like, (2) general attitudes

25

of the people toward the legal requirements and the extent to which the laws are enforced, and (3) the promotion standards maintained by teachers in dealing with pupils.

The central tendencies in age-grade status of children in various types of schools located in representative states are shown in Table I.[1]

TABLE I.—CENTRAL TENDENCIES IN AGE-GRADE STATUS OF PUPILS IN VARIOUS
TYPES OF ELEMENTARY SCHOOLS
(Median Chronological Age in Months)

	Grade I	Grade II	Grade III	Grade IV	Grade V	Grade VI	Grade VII	Grade VIII
In Twenty States:[1]								
One-teacher schools........	—	—	113	128	139	151	163	174
Consolidated schools.......	—	—	115	127	140	152	163	174
In Mississippi:[2]								
Fewer than 2,500..........	77	97	111	124	139	155	168	178
2,500 to 9,999.............	85	95	106	123	133	148	161	173
10,000 and over............	80	95	110	124	133	149	161	170
In New York:[3]								
One-teacher schools........	—	—	115	126	143	154	161	172
Four-teacher schools........	—	—	110	126	139	150	162	·173
In Texas:[4]								
Fewer than five teachers....	—	—	125	137	152	164	176	—
Five teachers and more.....	—	—	119	134	143	158	169	—
City schools...............	—	—	—	—	141	—	164	—
In Utah:[5]								
Rural schools..............	—	—	106	122	136	150	164	174
Urban schools.............	—	—	108	122	—	—	162	—

[1] Data from 374 one-teacher schools and 135 consolidated schools in 1922.
[2] Data from three types of population groups in 1925—white children only. O'Shea, M. V. *A State Educational System at Work.* (1927 Mississippi Survey).
[3] Haggerty, M. E. *Educational Achievement.* (Rural School Survey of New York State). 1922. Pp. 176-180.
[4] White children only. Kruse, P. J. *Educational Achievement.* (Texas Educational Survey Report, Volume IV.) Austin, 1925. Pp. 114-127.
[5] Data from 1926 survey.

---

[1] The data regarding conditions in individual states compiled in Table I and in many of the following tables have been taken from or computed from the materials in the following publications:

Bachman, F. P. *Public Education in Indiana.* New York, 1923.
Bachman, F. P. *Public Education in Kentucky.* New York, 1921.
Haggerty, M. E. *Educational Achievement.* (Rural School Survey of New York State) 1922.
Kruse, P. J. *Educational Achievement.* (Texas Educational Survey Report, Vol. IV) 1925.
O'Shea, M. V. *A State Educational System at Work.* (Mississippi Survey) 1927. *State School Facts.* Published semi-monthly by the State Superintendent of Public Instruction of North Carolina.

From the data included, at least three significant conclusions can be drawn. (1) The size of the school and the nature of the population center in which it is located affect only slightly the age-grade status of the pupils enrolled in any one grade. (2) The greatest differences between the ages of city-school pupils and those of rural-school pupils in corresponding grades occur in the middle grades. (3) The median age of children enrolled in the highest grade of common types of rural elementary schools varies slightly throughout the nation and is only slightly more than that of children enrolled in the corresponding grade of city schools.

The larger the school and the larger the population in a community are, the younger are the children enrolled in corresponding grades. A marked difference does not begin to occur until after the first grade; it becomes significantly large in the fourth to sixth grades; and then it diminishes considerably in the seventh and eighth grades. A statistically checked sampling in California disclosed that the mean age of pupils, 14.57 years, enrolled in the eighth grade of rural schools differed by a small margin from that of pupils, 14.33 years, in the corresponding grade of city schools (6:307).[2] The difference is in agreement with the data in Table I and is typical of the conditions found in numerous unpublished reports obtained by the writer from county superintendents of schools and city-school superintendents in various parts of the country.

There is a surprising agreement in the central tendencies of age-grade status throughout the nation. A study of state reports and of mimeographed materials from smaller educational units indicated that the distributions included in Table I are typical. As far as the age-grade status of children who continue in school is concerned, it seems to make little difference, therefore, in what type of school they are enrolled, in what part of the country it is located, and into how many grades the elementary school is divided. Data in state reports indicated that pupils, finishing the last, or seventh, grade of a seven-year elementary school in Maryland, for example, were about the same age as pupils in the corresponding type of school in Texas or in North Carolina, and about the same age as the pupils finishing the last, or eighth, grade of an eight-year elementary school in California, Utah, Michigan, Mississippi, or New York.

---

[2] References in parentheses refer by number and page to the list at the end of this chapter.

This condition has its beginning in the universal tendency to fix the age for admission to the first grade of elementary schools at six years in eight-grade and seven years in seven-grade elementary schools. These practices establish about fourteen years as the age at which children making normal progress will finish the highest grade of the traditional elementary school, whether the system provides for an eight-year elementary school or for a seven-year elementary school. It is facilitated by the trends in promoting elementary-school pupils by grades and according to such standards as each teacher considers sound.

TABLE II.—AGE-GRADE STATUS OF ELEMENTARY-SCHOOL CHILDREN IN VARIOUS TYPES OF SCHOOLS IN SEVEN STATES

	Under Age (Percent)	Normal Age (Percent)	Over Age (Percent)
Alabama (Elmore County, 1927):			
One-teacher schools	4.9	36.9	58.2
Two-teacher schools	3.0	45.4	51.6
Three-teacher schools and larger	4.7	47.0	48.3
Illinois (Schools having annual promotions, 1923):			
Rural communities	29.0	42.0	29.0
In other communities under 2,500	21.0	46.0	33.0
In communities of 2,500 to 9,999	21.0	43.0	36.0
In communities of 10,000 to 25,000	19.0	40.0	41.0
Indiana (1923):			
Rural	9.2	54.6	36.1
City	7.2	60.7	32.6
Kentucky (1921):			
Sub-district	7.8	33.3	58.9
District	6.3	40.3	53.4
City	4.2	49.1	46.7
Maryland (White children, 1927):			
One-teacher schools	——	69.9 [1]	30.1
Two-teacher schools	——	73.0 [1]	27.0
Graded schools	——	78.1 [1]	21.9
New York (1922):			
One-teacher schools	8.0	55.2	36.8
Four-teacher schools	5.6	61.4	33.0
North Carolina (White children, 1927):			
Rural schools	——	55.0 [1]	45.0
City schools	——	72.7 [1]	27.3

[1] Under age and normal age combined.

The age-grade data included in Table II disclose why the median and the mean ages of pupils in corresponding grades may not be expected to differ much in the various types of schools. The deviations from regular status tend to balance each other. The percentage of under-age children in rural schools is higher than that found in city schools and higher in small rural schools than in larger ones. On the other hand, the percentage of over-age pupils is even higher in the rural communities than in the urban communities, and in the smaller rurals schools than in the larger ones.

PROGRESS OF PUPILS ACCORDING TO PROMOTION

Practices in promoting pupils in the various grades, which tend to produce the conditions just noted, are illustrated by the data found in the promotional record of the white children enrolled in the North Carolina elementary schools during the year 1927-1928. The general conditions are typical of those found in the records of other states. In Table III, they are shown to be as follows: (1) The smallest percentage of promotions occurs in the lowest grade. (2) The percentages of promotions tend to increase quite rapidly after the first grade and until the last grade or two, where there is a slight decrease. (3) The percentage of promotions is less in rural schools than in city schools. (4) The difference in percentages in the two types of schools is large in the first grade, smallest in the second, increasing in successive upper grades, and largest of all in the highest grade.

TABLE III.—PERCENTAGES OF WHITE PUPILS PROMOTED IN EACH GRADE OF THE ELEMENTARY SCHOOLS IN RURAL AND IN URBAN COMMUNITIES OF NORTH CAROLINA DURING THE YEAR 1927-1928

Type of School	Grade I	Grade II	Grade III	Grade IV	Grade V	Grade VI	Grade VII	Total
Rural schools	52.1	67.4	67.2	64.9	64.3	64.2	60.6	61.7
City schools	69.1	77.9	78.5	77.7	78.8	76.9	78.8	75.9

The results of differences in ages at which children enter a school system and of the trends in promotion practices are clearly typified in the enrollment data accumulated in North Carolina during a five-year period beginning with 1924 (21). Assuming the enrollment in the first grade in that year to be 100 percent, the enrollment in the second grade in 1925 becomes 63 percent of it; in the third grade in 1926, 61 percent; in the fourth grade in 1927, 57 percent; and in the fifth grade in 1928, 52 percent. There is little difference between the series of percentages computed from these consecutive records of enrollment and the percentages similarly computed regarding the enrollments in the various grades in any one school year. In 1927-1928, for instance, the North Carolina enrollment, when thus computed in percents, shows 100 percent in Grade I; 61 percent in Grade II, 57 percent in Grade III, 55 percent in Grade IV, and 50 percent in Grade V.

TABLE IV.—PERCENTAGE DISTRIBUTION OF PUPILS ACCORDING TO GRADES IN TYPES OF ELEMENTARY SCHOOLS IN FIVE STATES

	Grade I	Grade II	Grade III	Grade IV	Grade V	Grade VI	Grade VII	Grade VIII	Total
California:[1]									
Urban schools..............	19.1	13.2	12.0	12.1	11.2	10.7	11.1	10.6	100
Rural schools..............	20.1	12.9	12.1	11.8	11.5	11.0	10.7	9.9	100
Maryland:[2]									
Urban schools..............	17.5	15.5	14.1	14.3	14.1	13.0	11.6	____	100.1
Rural schools..............	18.1	15.0	14.0	14.3	13.8	13.0	11.8	____	100
Minnesota:[3]									
Rural schools..............	18.7	12.6	12.7	12.6	11.4	10.5	9.9	11.6	100
New York:[4]									
Four-teacher schools.........	13.6	11.5	13.0	13.6	11.7	13.3	10.9	12.4	100
One-teacher schools.........	17.3	15.2	13.5	13.8	11.9	12.4	8.5	7.4	100
North Carolina:[5]									
Urban schools..............	21.3	16.0	14.5	13.8	12.8	11.4	10.2	____	100
Rural schools..............	25.9	15.0	14.2	13.6	12.0	10.3	9.1	____	100.1

[1] In 1927-1928; four markedly urban counties (Alameda, Los Angeles, Orange, and San Francisco) contrasted with the other fifty-four counties, by the writer.
[2] In 1927-1928; Baltimore City for urban distribution; remainder of the state for rural distribution.
[3] In 1922-1923; rural schools in thirty counties.
[4] From the data in the rural school survey of 1922.
[5] In 1927-1928.

The data in Table IV regarding percentage of elementary-school children enrolled in each grade of various types of schools in five representative states are characteristic of percentage distributions of school children in the grades in a school year. In rural schools as well as city schools, the largest enrollment occurs in the first grade. The difference between the number of pupils in Grade I and the number in Grade II is large. The percentages show that this marked difference is not typical of the differences between the enrollments of succeeding pairs of grades. In fact, the decreases in successive grades from the second to sixth are comparatively small in the five states, with the exception of North Carolina. In that state, significantly larger decreases occur after Grade IV which correspond to those occcurring after Grade VI in Maryland, Minnesota, and New York. These decreases in the upper grades are due in part to eliminations from school.

In the rural schools, larger percentages of enrollment occur in the first grade than in the same grade in urban schools. On the other hand, smaller percentages of enrollment in the upper grades are to be noted in the rural schools than in the city schools. The percentages in corresponding middle grades are approximately the same in rural schools as in urban schools.

The data regarding the one-teacher schools and the four-teacher schools in New York disclose that the same contrasts and similarities are to be noted in the two sizes of rural schools as occur in the two sizes of population groups. The relative conditions are to be seen also in the percentage distributions in schools of various sizes in Elmore County, Alabama. These data are presented in Table V (2).

TABLE V.—PERCENTAGE OF CHILDREN IN EACH GRADE BY TYPES OF ELEMENTARY SCHOOLS IN ELMORE COUNTY, ALABAMA, DURING THE SCHOOL YEAR 1927-1928[1]

Grade	One Teacher	Two Teacher	Three Teacher	Four Teacher	Five or More
I.	37.6	23.6	22.0	20.7	18.9
II.	9.8	15.1	16.0	13.8	13.1
III.	18.8	14.6	14.7	11.7	15.2
IV.	15.0	11.9	12.2	12.4	13.5
V.	2.3	13.6	11.1	17.9	12.5
VI.	9.0	14.2	12.6	17.3	14.0
VII.	7.5	7.0	11.4	6.2	12.8
Total.	100	100	100	100	100

[1] Adapted from Alabama, *The Report of the Survey of Elmore County Schools.* 1929. p. 50.

Odell's intensive study of the effects of the promotion programs on the average rates of progress of elementary-school pupils presents types of distributions of progress status according to types of schools. From this investigation have been taken the data organized in Table VI (22:20). In the Illinois school systems providing for annual promotions, the percentage of children making rapid progress in rural schools is twice that of the same type of pupils in urban schools, and

TABLE VI.—RATE OF PROGRESS OF PUPILS IN THE ELEMENTARY SCHOOLS OF ILLINOIS
ACCORDING TO SIZE OF COMMUNITY, 1923
(After Odell)

CLASSIFICATION OF SCHOOLS ACCORDING TO COMMUNITY	SCHOOLS HAVING SEMESTER PROMOTIONS			SCHOOLS HAVING ANNUAL PROMOTIONS		
	Rapid	Regular	Slow	Rapid	Regular	Slow
30,000 population and more.............	13	63	24	—	—	—
10,000-29,999 population................	7	54	39	2	66	32
2,500- 9,999 population................	7	58	35	2	71	27
Less than 2,500 population..............	10	67	23	2	71	27
Rural-school population.................	—	—	—	4	72	24

the percentage of pupils making slow progress in the rural schools is less than the percentage of pupils making slow progress in the city schools. The percentage of rural-school children making regular progress is greater than the corresponding percentage attending the other types of schools. The study shows also that city school systems and village school systems providing for semi-annual promotions have much larger percentages of pupils making rapid progress than have the other school systems. On the other hand, cities between twenty-five hundred and thirty thousand population providing for half-year promotions have large percentages of pupils making slow progress.

An intensive treatment of the data to obtain average rates of progress per year produced numerical values from which two conclusions can be drawn: (1) The average child in any one type of school progresses through the grades at about the same rate as the average child in every other type of school. (2) The progress of rural-school children who have moved from school to school is retarded slightly more than that of the same type of city-school children (22).

In the Illinois study, it was found that pupils spending their whole career in one school system progressed at the rate of .98 school years per annum in city schools with semiannual promotions; .94 school years in city and village schools with annual promotions; and .96

school years in rural schools. Of the pupils moving from system to system while in the elementary schools, the average city-school child progressed .93 school years per year; the village-school child, .92 school years; and the rural-school child, .89 school years (22:57). The data accumulated in the California study indicate that similar conditions existed in that state in 1925 (6: 295ff.). Foote's report (9) shows that consolidation of rural schools does not contribute to producing a marked change; in the one-teacher schools, the annual progress was .67 school years and in the consolidated schools, .69 years.

One of the series of investigations reported regarding the pupils in California (6) indicates clearly that pupils of superior ability progressed less rapidly in the rural schools than similar pupils in city schools. The study also shows that the superior pupils 'skipped' most frequently one of the grades from the second to the sixth, and especially Grade II. Such of these pupils as were not promoted sometime during their elementary-school careers found Grades I, III, IV, and V to be the most difficult ones (6: 323ff.).

Causes of Non-Promotion in the Rural Schools

Percival's thorough study (26) of why the teachers in one state failed pupils in each of the elementary grades indicates the specified causes and the subjects reported markedly difficult in each case. A close correlation between factors and conditions in city schools and those in rural schools was found. Such marked agreements included in the study make it possible to discuss here, briefly, the failures of pupils in the rural schools.

Of the pupils failed in the county schools in California in June, 1925, 35.7 percent were not promoted because of one reported cause; 36.3 percent, because of two causes; 19.3 percent, because of three causes; and the remainder, because of four to six causes. Table VII contains the distribution of all the causes reported (26:333). Learning very slowly, lack of application and the like, weak schooling foundation, low mentality, and changing schools during the year were the outstanding causes contributing to failure of pupils reported by the rural school teachers. One of the two significant differences between causes of failure in city schools and those in rural schools occurred in cases of absence due to illness. The percentage of cases was considerably less in rural than in urban schools (26).

TABLE VII.—DISTRIBUTION OF REPORTED FAILURES IN CALIFORNIA ELEMENTARY
SCHOOLS IN 1925 ACCORDING TO CONTRIBUTING CAUSES LISTED BY THE TEACHERS
(From Bagley and Kyle, after Percival)

CAUSE CONTRIBUTING TO NON-PROMOTION	NUMBER OF CASES		PERCENTAGE OF CASES	
	Cities	Counties	Cities	Counties
Learns very slowly	2,760	667	36.7	36.9
Lack of application, etc	2,677	603	35.5	33.3
Entered with weak foundation	1,697	403	22.5	22.3
Change of schools during year	1,341	343	17.8	19.0
Absent due to illness	1,260	196	16.7	10.9
Foreign language handicap	977	264	13.0	14.6
Pupil subnormal (tested)	974	371	12.9	20.5
Immaturity	957	198	12.7	11.0
Poor home conditions	755	247	10.0	13.7
Absence (other than illness)	640	149	8.5	8.2
Poor health (pupil not absent)	394	71	5.2	3.9
Defective vision	172	55	2.3	3.0
Other physical defects	161	51	2.1	2.8
Defective speech	137	28	1.8	1.6
Defective hearing	74	20	1.0	1.1
Total number of pupils failed	7,531	1,811	100	100

Pearson $r = .985$ PE$r = .005$

When single causes and combinations of causes of reported non-promotions were tabulated, it was found that 12.4 percent of the failures in the rural schools were attributed to a combination of learning slowly and lack of application, attention, and the like; 10 percent to lack of application, and entering the grade with a weak foundation; 8.6 percent to weak foundation and learning very slowly; and 8 percent to low mentality as indicated by test data.

Outstanding causes of failure were noted in various grades. Immaturity, for instance, was a significant factor in Grade I only. The first combination mentioned above accounted for approximately 18 percent of the failures in the fourth grade and in the seventh; the second combination accounted for 15.4 percent in Grade VI and 23 percent in Grade VIII (26:343).

Table VIII taken from Percival's study (26:349) indicates the extent to which teachers believed that weaknesses in the various subjects were sufficient to cause non-promotion of their pupils. The subjects of arithmetic and reading occurred with extreme frequency, while language, spelling, geography, and history occurred with marked frequency. Over 99 percent of those failing were weak in reading in Grade I; 90 percent, in Grade II; 67 percent, in Grade III; 56 percent, in Grade IV; 40 percent, in Grade V; and so on with decreasing percents to 24 percent in Grade VIII. Arithmetic was a reported subject weakness in 49 percent of Grade II and more than 72 percent in each of the grades above that. Language weaknesses were reported in 49 percent to 56 percent of the cases of failure in Grades III to VIII. Spelling weaknesses occur in 51 percent of the non-promotions in Grade III; 48 percent in Grade IV; and over 31 percent of the cases in each of the Grades II, V, and VI. Large percentages of subject weaknesses were listed in geography and in history in grades above the third. The percentages in these subjects increased grade by grade, those in history outstripping the corresponding ones in geography. Seventy-four percent of eighth-grade failures were reported in the former subject and 59 percent in the latter.

Among the 1,414 rural-school pupils reported as failing because of specified subject weaknesses, 418 were listed as not promoted because

TABLE VIII.—DISTRIBUTION OF PUPILS FAILING IN CALIFORNIA ELEMENTARY SCHOOLS ACCORDING TO SPECIFIED SUBJECTS IN WHICH WEAKNESS LED TO THE NON-PROMOTION
(From Bagley and Kyte, after Percival)

SUBJECTS IN WHICH WEAKNESSES WERE REPORTED	Number of Cases		Percentage of Cases	
	Cities	Counties	Cities	Counties
Reading......................................	3,879	820	67.3	58.0
Arithmetic.................................	3,118	871	54.1	61.6
Language....................................	2,173	306	37.7	21.6
Spelling......................................	1,555	360	27.0	25.5
Geography...................................	1,072	350	18.6	24.8
History......................................	1,048	317	18.2	22.4
Writing......................................	401	70	7.0	4.9
Grammar....................................	324	121	5.6	8.6
Science......................................	90	——	1.6	——
Art...	74	15	1.3	1.1
Civics..	65	16	1.1	1.1
Music..	39	37	.8	2.6
Hygiene......................................	20	45	.4	3.2
Industrial arts.............................	14	1	.3	.1
Home economics............................	11	——	.2	——
Foreign language...........................	10	——	.2	——
Typewriting.................................	4	——	.1	——
Miscellaneous...............................	4	——	.1	——
Total number of pupils failed..............	5,758	1,414	100	100

of weakness in only one subject. Of this number, 95 cases were in arithmetic and 307 in reading. The latter subject accounted for 205 out of 216 single-subject failures in Grade I and 68 out of 73 in Grade II. The cases listed with a single weakness in arithmetic were scattered over the grades, from the first to the sixth especially, with the largest numbers and percentages recorded in Grades III, IV, and VI. Combinations of two or more subject weaknesses causing non-promotions also presented groupings by grades which included subjects in marked agreement with the grade-placement of subject weaknesses just discussed.

HEALTH OF PUPILS

Another factor affecting the progress of pupils in school and in their lives out of school is health. Table IX contains data recently compiled with respect to the public-school children in Virginia showing the extent and nature of reported defects and the results of efforts to eliminate the conditions. The distributions of cases reported are similar in the city schools and in the rural schools, but

TABLE IX. HEALTH DATA REPORTED REGARDING THE SCHOOL CHILDREN IN THE
CITIES AND COUNTIES OF VIRGINIA FOR THE YEAR ENDING JUNE 1, 1929
(From mimeographed reports)

	PERCENTAGE OF CHILDREN	
	City	County
Enrollment inspected...	77.5	94.6
Found with defects...	67.6	75.6
Defective vision..	10.5	14.8
Defective hearing...	2.2	4.3
Defective teeth...	46.9	57.0
Defective throats...	22.5	19.2
Ten percent or more underweight..............................	18.5	23.0
Not Vaccinated...	3.3	29.4
Defective vision reported corrected............................	25.5	15.8
Defective hearing reported corrected...........................	17.7	13.8
Defective teeth reported corrected.............................	46.5	23.9
Defective throats reported corrected...........................	17.4*	8.7
Underweight improving to normal weight.......................	*	32.7
Given toxin-antitoxin†...	16.9	37.2
Vaccinated†..	87.5	53.1

*Not obtainable from the data.
†During 1928-1929.

the percentages are larger in the latter group. The conditions are typical of the ones found in other states where inspections have been made and reported. The various localities discussed in the report of the Joint Committee on Health Problems in Education exhibit similar conditions in the rural schools (33).

The survey of the rural schools of Buffalo County, Nebraska (23), presented similar conditions with respect to the various items included in the physical examination. Over 41 percent of the pupils had defective teeth; 26 percent, defective nose or throat; 20 percent, defective eyes; 11 percent, defective eyes and teeth; 10 percent, defective nose or throat and teeth; 8 percent, defective ears; 2 percent, all the defects mentioned; and 36 percent with combinations of two or more defects other than the combinations already listed.

How effectively the conditions are being met in some places is to be seen in Table IX. Although the rural schools in Virginia are making progress in overcoming health handicaps of school children, the extent of improvement lags behind that achieved in the city schools. The greater difficulty of obtaining medical attention in the rural districts, the marked concentration of health specialists in cities, and the slower introduction of intensive health-education programs in rural school systems are some of the causes of the disparities existing.

In a communication to the writer, Superintendent Calvin S. Smith, of the Granite School District, Utah, reported how one phase of the health program dealing with physical defects was met.

> In 1927, an examination of the teeth of the children revealed that 4,153 cases out of 5,402 examined needed dental care. The establishment of a dental clinic by the school board and county officers acting jointly was responsible for 1,118 extractions, 923 fillings, 395 treatments, and 581 cases of cleaning of the teeth by the school dentist.

Reports from various county school officers in different parts of the country show the effectiveness of health-education programs where school nurses are employed. The use of the health club by a nurse in Smythe County, Virginia, as a mean of creating pupils' interest in the forming of good health habits is included in the Joint Committee's report. The data in Table X, from Wood (33), indicate the extent to which children reported that they had formed certain health habits. The number of habits to be reported was increased annually as the health-education program was expanded, thus providing for a growing number of different health habits. The information throws some light on the varying degrees of difficulty encountered in coping with the habits listed. Getting children to use individual towels, for example, was a much harder educational habit to secure than influencing pupils to use individual drinking cups. Sleeping with open windows was readily accepted and practiced by almost all the pupils, but many of them continued to drink tea or coffee. Other significant points can be seen in the table, which limited space precludes treating in detail.

TABLE X.—REPORTS OF SCHOOL CHILDREN IN SMYTHE COUNTY, VIRGINIA, REGARDING HEALTH HABITS BEING FORMED—EXPRESSED IN PERCENTAGES
(From Wood)

ITEMS REPORTED BY THE CHILDREN	Before Health Club	SINCE HEALTH CLUB BEGAN			
		1917–1918	1918–1919	1919–1920	1920–1921
Sleeping with open windows	55	90	93	96	97
Brushing teeth twice a day	25	75	73	68	72
Washing face, hands, neck and ears	67	94	98	97	95
Cleaning finger nails	34	75	74	75	72
Brushing and combing hair	75	96	——		98
Doing without tea and coffee	33	76	76	78	75
Practicing physical training each day	——	97	99	97	100
Playing a game each day	——	——	99	97	100
Improving in posture	——	84	85	67	84
Using individual towels	——	44	65	59	53
Using individual drinking cup	40	85	87	82	85
Keeping desk and surroundings in good order	——	——	93	93	87
Doing at least one daily helpful deed	——	——	96	——	99
Carrying clean handkerchief each day	——	——	——	80	71
Drinking at least two glasses of milk per day	——	——	——	70	70
Chewing food properly	——	——	——	86	96
Attending to needs of body at the proper time	——	——	——	97	97
Drinking six glasses of water per day	——	——	——	——	91
Eating fruit and vegetables each day	——	——	——	——	99
Number having dental work done	——	——	——	——	30
Number reporting	——	1,750	3,000	3,500	6,000

Godfrey's investigation of the distribution of communicable diseases according to size of community in New York shows positively that the environment of the open country compensates to some extent for the lack of available medical attention. In Table XI, adapted from the data, it can be seen that in the three diseases listed—typhoid fever, diphtheria, and measles—the rate of occurrence is lower in the unincorporated districts than in the cities (12: 620, 622, 626). The low percentages of fatality in the rural communities in the case of typhoid fever and measles more than offset the slightly higher percentage of fatality in cases of diphtheria (12).

TABLE XI.—DISTRIBUTION OF TYPHOID FEVER, DIPHTHERIA, AND MEASLES IN NEW YORK ACCORDING TO SIZE OF COMMUNITY
(After Godfrey)

Type of Community	TYPHOID FEVER			DIPHTHERIA			MEASLES		
	Rate[1]	Deaths[2]	Percent Fatality	Rate[1]	Deaths[2]	Percent Fatality	Rate[1]	Deaths[2]	Percent Fatality
New York City.......	22.0	3.5	15.9	220	18.0	8.2	470	9.5	2.0
200,000-1,000,000......	25.5	4.2	16.5	270	22.0	8.1	550	7.0	1.3
50,000-200,000........	35.0	5.0	14.3	230	17.0	7.4	710	8.0	1.1
20,000-50,000.........	46.0	5.6	12.2	155	12.5	8.1	870	6.0	.7
10,000-20,000.........	69.5	8.8	12.7	180	13.0	7.2	810	7.6	.9
5,000-10,000..........	63.0	7.9	12.5	165	11.5	7.0	760	5.8	.8
2,500-5,000...........	50.0	6.8	14.0	137	9.5	6.9	870	4.5	.5
Under 2,500..........	47.0	6.7	14.3	95	6.0	6.3	870	3.6	.4
Unincorporated.......	42.0	5.2	12.4	70	7.5	10.7	610	4.2	.7

[1] Cases per 100,000.
[2] Deaths per 100,000.

If the information regarding the geographical variations in the incidence of poliomyelitis occurring in Vermont from 1912 to 1925, reported in Aycock's article (3), is typical, this serious disease occurs during the school ages of children in villages and rural districts, but at a much younger age in cities. The percentage distributions by age groups and types of population communities, in Table XII, indicates how clearly this specific health problem is one which seemingly challenges rural-school officers rather than city-school officers.

Table XIII indicates the prevalence of tuberculous infection in children under sixteen years of age in a Minnesota rural community. If this information, taken from the recent report by Vories (32: 1007), is typical of conditions elsewhere, it indicates another health problem to be dealt with in the rural schools. The lack of additional data in reports makes it impossible to assert that the situation is typical. The dearth of statistical information about many health items in rural

TABLE XII.—DISTRIBUTION OF CASES OF POLIOMYELITIS IN VERMONT, 1912 TO 1925,
ACCORDING TO AGE GROUPS AND TO TYPES OF COMMUNITY
(After Aycock)

PATIENTS' AGES IN YEARS	CITIES		VILLAGES		COUNTRY	
	Number	Percent	Number	Percent	Number	Percent
Under 5 years.............	122	62.2	104	38.1	99	26.1
5 to 14.9 years............	56	28.6	116	42.5	175	46.2
15 years and over.........	18	9.2	53	19.4	105	27.7
Total.................	196	100	273	100	379	100

TABLE XIII.—INCIDENCE OF TUBERCULOUS INFECTION IN CHILDREN OF A
MINNESOTA RURAL SCHOOL COMMUNITY IN 1924
(After Vories)

CHILDREN'S AGES IN YEARS	BOYS			GIRLS		
	Number Examined	Number of Cases	Percent	Number Examined	Number of Cases	Percent
0.5 to 2 years............	21	——	——	13	3	23.0
2 to 5 years.............	110	11	10.0	99	13	13.1
5 to 10 years............	220	36	16.3	186	32	17.2
10 to 15 years............	181	33	18.2	170	41	24.1
Total.................	532	80	15	468	89	19

communities, in fact, precludes as accurate an account of the health
status of the pupils as it is desirable to obtain.

MENTALITY OF PUPILS

Although the data in Table VII indicate that rural-school teachers
reported a larger percentage of children not promoted because of low
mentality than city-school teachers reported, mental ages of rural-
school children in a grade average lower than those of city-school
children in the same grade. This condition is especially true after
the first grade. Table XIV illustrates the differences in the grades
above the second. The findings in less extensive surveys in various
states (1, 7, 14, 18, 20) are in marked agreement with the data presented in the table and supplement them with respect to the mentality
of children in the lower grades.

TABLE XIV.—COMPARISON OF MENTAL AGE OF CHILDREN IN RURAL AND IN
CITY SCHOOLS IN THREE STATES
(Indicated by Median Ages Expressed in Months)

	Grade III	Grade IV	Grade V	Grade VI	Grade VII	Grade VIII
Mississippi (white children, 1925):						
Fewer than 2,500............................	87	113	131	138	147	157
2,500-9,999.................................	103	128	140	147	159	175
Over 10,000.................................	109	126	140	150	161	177
New York (1922):*						
One teacher................................	100	109	126	143	155	163
Four teachers..............................	106	119	136	152	168	178
Texas (1925):						
One and two teachers......................	94	109	122	133	146	——
Three and four teachers...................	94	111	126	136	146	——
Five and more teachers....................	100	118	136	147	160	——
City†......................................	——	——	140	——	168	——

*"Rural schools" defined as those in districts with less than 4,500 population.
†"City" defined arbitrarily as a place having more than 10 teachers in the high school.

The mean or the median scores of mentality by grades in most states
from which information was obtained disclose that the differences between first-grade city-school scores and first-grade rural-school scores
are comparatively slight, the advantage being held by the city schools.
Grade by grade, the differences increase, however, to such an extent
that the intelligence score of the fifth-grade city-school child is generally the same as, or slightly higher than, that of the sixth-grade
rural-school child. In each of the upper grades, the average mental
age of rural-school pupils is less than the mean chronological age. A
study of the data in Kraybill's investigation (15) indicated, for example, that the mean chronological age of rural-school graduates applying for admission to Pennsylvania high schools is thirteen years
eleven months, but the mean mental age is only thirteen years.

The data in the studies show that the mean or the median mental
age of pupils in a grade of a small school is lower than in the corresponding grade of a larger school. Table XIV illustrates this point
with respect to the rural schools in three of the states. In discussing a similar condition found in a California county, Adams
(1:4 ff.) showed the difference to be such that the children in a grade
in a one-teacher school are mentally "53.51 percent of a grade below" children in the same grade in rural schools with more than one

teacher. In the small rural schools, children are promoted from grade to grade with lower mental ages than are children in larger rural schools. Children in rural schools, irrespective of size, are promoted from grade to grade with lower mental ages than are children in city schools.

That the differences just noted are not merely differences in mental ages, but also differences in intelligence quotients is to be seen in Table XV. The median of intelligence quotients in a rural-school grade is lower than that in the corresponding grade of city schools. While the medians in the successive grades of city elementary schools continue to be those of children of normal mentality, those of children in the rural elementary schools point to low normal intelligence scores and even to types of pupils classified as "dull" (29 : 78-104). Whether the conditions are due to nature or nurture or both, the data do not disclose.

TABLE XV.—MEDIAN INTELLIGENCE QUOTIENTS OF PUPILS IN VARIOUS TYPES OF ELEMENTARY SCHOOLS IN FOUR STATES

	Grade I	Grade II	Grade III	Grade IV	Grade V	Grade VI	Grade VII	Grade VIII
Sonoma County (California, 1924):								
Rural schools.............	90	92	90	—	—	—	—	—
Mississippi (Representative white, 1925):								
Fewer than 2,500...........	103	103	87	89	88	93	93	80
2,500-9,999...............	98	103	99	96	103	116	99	100
More than 10,000..........	100	101	100	100	108	99	107	116
Texas (1925):								
Fewer than 5 teachers......	—	—	75	80	82	82	83	—
Five and more teachers.....	—	—	84	88	95	93	95	—
City teachers..............	—	—	—	—	99	—	102	—
Utah (1926):								
Rural schools.............	—	—	94	98	97	95	91	95
City schools...............	—	—	107	109	—	—	107	—

ACHIEVEMENT OF PUPILS

Since the promotion records of children in various types of schools and the intelligence scores of these pupils are not in agreement, what does the measured achievement of the pupils show? Table XVI contains a partial answer which coincides with that which should be expected. Of the records from five states, only one presents a situation in which the poorest reading achievement score of fifth-grade pupils was not found in the smallest schools. The fifth grade was selected as the point where the accumulated effects of a type of school would be seen before many children had dropped out of school. Table XVI presents clearly the fact that the larger the school, the better is the achievement in reading. The reading achievements of the city-school pupils are superior to those of the rural-school pupils in corresponding grades.

TABLE XVI.—FIFTH-GRADE READING ACHIEVEMENT IN VARIOUS TYPES OF ELEMENTARY SCHOOLS IN FIVE STATES

Type of School	Indiana (1923)	Kentucky (1921)	Maryland (1928)*	New York (1922)	Texas (1925)†
One teacher	4.4	37.0	36.1	31.5	40.5
Two teachers	4.6	38.1	51.8	28.9	40.5
Three teachers	4.9	38.3	50.5	40.4	40.8
Four teachers	4.8	38.9	47.8	41.6	41.4
Five teachers	4.8	38.6	55.6	——	——
Six teachers	——	41.4	44.3	——	——
Five or more teachers (rural)	——	——	——	——	45.3
Six or more teachers (rural)	4.9	——	——	——	——
Seven or more teachers (rural and city)	——	——	59.2	——	——
Town	5.0	——	——	——	——
City	5.3	43.0	——	——	46.8
Standards	5.5	46.5	——	——	44.9

*Percentage of pupils at or above standard.
†White children only.

Van Wagenen's intensive study of the achievement of Minnesota children shows the same conditions with respect to arithmetic, language, and spelling, as well as reading. Table XVII, constructed from his findings (31:15), presents representative data. Achievement scores in the rural schools are significantly lower than in the city schools in all three subjects. Comprehension in reading, the fundamental operations in arithmetic, and mastery of words in spelling especially have been developed in the large city schools to the point that in the eighth grade the achievement of the pupils exceeds that of the rural-school pupils by almost a year.

The data show also the disadvantages of the eight-month school
as compared with the nine-month school. The pupils who are given
an additional month of schooling per year are achieving better results
in the 'three R's' than their less fortunate fellows in the eight-month
schools. Frost's study (11) of types of schools in Kentucky indicates
markedly also the handicaps which children suffer in achievement
because of the short school terms.

TABLE XVII.—MID-DIFFERENCES IN READING, ARITHMETIC, AND SPELLING BETWEEN
VARIOUS TYPES OF MINNESOTA ELEMENTARY SCHOOLS AS INDICATED
BY THE ACHIEVEMENTS OF EIGHTH-GRADE BOYS
(After Van Wagenen)

PAIRS OF TYPE SCHOOLS FOR WHICH DIFFERENCES ARE COMPUTED	READING		ARITHMETIC		Spelling
	Compre-hension	Inter-pretation	Funda-mentals	Prob-lems	
Nine-month rural minus eight-month rural....	2	0.0	3.5	0.0	2.5
Very small village minus nine-month rural....	2	1.0	2.0	3.0	1.0
Small village minus nine-month rural........	2	1.0	1.0	3.0	2.5
Small city minus nine-month rural..........	2	0.5	2.0	0.75	1.0
Large city minus nine-month rural..........	2	−0.25	1.5	1.0	3.0
Large city minus eight-month rural.........	6	1.0	5.0	1.0	6.0
Grade VIII minus Grade VII..............	4	4	6	6	4

Orleans and Baer (24) found that third-grade children in the
rural schools of New York wrote with a less satisfactory quality of
handwriting than did village-school pupils in the same grade. By the
time the fifth grade was reached, however, the differences were practically eliminated. Table XVIII, adapted from the study, shows that
in the matter of speed the children in the smaller schools did less well
(24:9, 14). The larger the school, the greater the speed achieved by
the children without sacrificing quality. Children in the third grade
of one-teacher schools, for example, write nine words per minute less
than third-grade children in village schools, and eighth-grade children
in the former write eleven words per minute slower than eighth-grade
children in the latter. How significant this difference is can be seen
from the additional fact that village-school children in the grades
above the fourth write as fast or faster than children in the next
higher grade in one-teacher schools.

TABLE XVIII.—RATE AND QUALITY OF HANDWRITING IN THE UPPER GRADES OF
VARIOUS TYPES OF NEW YORK ELEMENTARY SCHOOLS IN 1927
(After Orleans and Baer)

Type of School	Rate						Quality					
	III	IV	V	VI	VII	VIII	III	IV	V	VI	VII	VIII
One teacher*.............	40.6	51.2	64.1	71.6	76.5	82.9	35.9	41.2	46.6	53.4	60.1	66.8
Two and three teachers...	45.9	58.9	69.7	76.3	80.4	83.1	38.3	44.2	46.9	53.8	61.2	68.2
Four to ten teachers......	48.2	61.7	67.8	77.1	82.0	87.3	39.2	42.0	46.6	52.6	56.4	61.8
Ten or more teachers.....	46.9	56.5	68.0	76.3	85.1	89.0	40.1	43.6	48.8	54.3	60.9	65.9
Village†.................	49.3	61.6	70.4	78.7	87.2	94.1	40.4	42.6	48.7	53.2	57.2	65.5
Grade standards.......	49	59	67	74	78	82	43.6	47.6	51.6	55.6	59.6	63.6

*All types listed except village schools are rural.
†Village schools with annual promotions.

Achievements of pupils in the social studies in rural schools as
compared with results in city schools present even more serious contrasts. In the New York survey, Haggerty found eighth-grade children in one-teacher schools achieving lower scores in history than
the seventh-grade children in New York City. The pupils in four-
teacher rural schools were achieving less satisfactory results in the
eighth grade than were the city-school children in the same grade.
These data, derived from Haggerty (13 : 177, 178), are shown in
Table XIX.

O'Shea's findings in the Mississippi survey (25 : 243) present a
greater difference. The median scores in the history-literature test
(25 : 312), listed in Table XX, disclosed that the children in Grade IV

TABLE XIX.—HISTORY ACHIEVEMENT IN THREE TYPES OF NEW YORK
ELEMENTARY SCHOOLS
(After Haggerty)

TYPE OF SCHOOL	GRADE	ACHIEVEMENT SCORES	
		Information	Thought
One teacher...	VIII	31	29
Four teachers.......................................	VIII	39	37
New York City.......................................	VII	32	32
New York City.........................	VIII	42	42

TABLE XX.—MEDIAN SCORES IN AGES BY MONTHS ACHIEVED IN HISTORY-LITERA-
TURE BY MISSISSIPPI WHITE CHILDREN ATTENDING SCHOOLS IN
THREE TYPES OF COMMUNITY

(After O'Shea)

Population Groups	Grade Medians of Pupils*				
	IV	V	VI	VII	VIII
Cities over 10,000..........................	128	139	145	158	171
Cities 2,500 to 9,999.......................	122	139	143	157	171
Population below 2,500.....................	117	127	131	140	147
Standard age............................	126	137	149	161	172

*Medians computed by the writer.

of large city schools were doing better than children in Grade V of
the rural schools, and that children in Grade V of the former were
doing as well as children in Grade VII of the latter.

In Minnesota, Van Wagenen (31) found the rural-school pupils
achieving less satisfactory results in geography than were the city-
school pupils. He found the length of the school year in rural schools
affected the results sufficiently to give the child in the nine-month

TABLE XXI.—MID-DIFFERENCES* IN PHASES OF GEOGRAPHY BETWEEN TYPES OF
SCHOOLS IN MINNESOTA AS COMPUTED FROM THE ACHIEVEMENTS OF
PUPILS IN GRADES VII AND VIII

(After Van Wagenen)

PAIRS OF TYPE SCHOOLS FOR WHICH DIFFERENCES ARE COMPUTED	INFORMATION PHASE				THOUGHT PHASE			
	Grade VII		Grade VIII†		Grade VII		Grade VIII†	
	Boys	Girls	Boys	Girls	Boys	Girls	Boys	Girls
Nine-month rural minus eight-month rural............................	2.00	1.00	2.50	2.00	1.00	1.00	1.00	.25
Very small village minus nine-month rural............................	0.00	0.00	—1.00	—3.50	2.00	2.50	2.00	1.00
Small village minus nine-month rural..	1.00	1.50	—1.00	—3.25	1.00	1.00	1.00	1.00
Small city minus nine-month rural....	1.25	2.00	—0.50	—3.25	2.75	2.75	1.75	1.00
Large city minus nine-month rural....	1.75	1.50	—1.50	—3.00	2.25	2.50	1.00	0.50
Large city minus eight-month rural....	4.50	2.00	1.00	—1.50	3.00	3.00	2.00	2.00

*A mid-difference of 6 is approximately equivalent to one year of progress.
†Geography not studied in the first half of the eighth grade.

school an advantage over one in the eight-month school. Table XXI illustrates these and other differences (31:41, 47).

In the Mississippi survey, achievements of children in nature study are also included. Table XXII, constructed from the data in the report (25:311), indicates that the achievements of rural-school children, as compared to those of city-school children, are not quite so poor in this subject, as they were in history. The results in the rural schools, however, are still far from satisfactory in the subject dealing with environmental factors which should prove more advantageous to rural than to city children. By the time the latter are in the seventh grade, they are able to achieve a slightly higher score than their country cousins in the next higher grade.

TABLE XXII.—MEDIAN AGE SCORES OF WHITE PUPILS IN MONTHS IN NATURE STUDY IN VARIOUS TYPES OF MISSISSIPPI COMMUNITIES*

(After O'Shea)

Types of Community	Age Scores by Grades				
	IV	V	VI	VII	VIII
Cities over 10,000	129	140	151	157	172
Cities 2,500 to 9,999	125	137	148	157	172
Population below 2,500	123	134	142	148	155
Standard age	126	137	149	161	172

*Medians computed by the writer.

Rainey's extensive study of the achievements of Oregon school children (27) shows the marked superiority of city-school children in a grade over rural-school children in the same grade in the social studies, literature, and science. His findings regarding achievements in the "three R's" are similar to those indicated in the data included earlier in this chapter. If all the data found in such state surveys as have been made and in other published and unpublished reports could be included here, they would point to the same facts as have been illustrated in the materials included.

Data from two representative studies need to be included, however, in order to indicate the results of endeavors to determine relative differences in achievement obtained in schools of different sizes. In the one-teacher schools and in the consolidated schools located in the open country, Morrison (19) administered tests to discover what differences in achievement were occurring in the two types of rural schools. Data from his study (19: 355-359) are presented in Table XXIII to illustrate the differences found by grades and by types of schools. On the whole, the results in the larger school are better than those in the smaller; the greatest difference and the only marked one occurs in spelling.

TABLE XXIII.—COMPARISON OF ACHIEVEMENTS IN THE 'THREE R'S' OF PUPILS IN CONSOLIDATED AND IN ONE-ROOM RURAL SCHOOLS IN NEW YORK
(After Morrison)

	Grade III	Grade IV	Grade V	Grade VI	Grade VII	Grade VIII	Super-iority
Reading (Rate):							
Consolidated..............	62.4	71.8	91.6	105.7	100.1	112.5	4.2
One-room.................	47.6	68.7	75.1	103.6	106.5	117.2	
Reading (Comprehension):							
Consolidated..............	8.2	10.9	16.5	17.7	22.2	25.6	1.6
One-room.................	6.1	11.2	13.1	17.5	19.6	24.2	
Arithmetic:							
Consolidated..............	13.8	17.7	22.2	26.0	29.6	29.7	0.6
One-room.................	13.1	17.0	21.9	25.4	27.6	30.5	
Language:							
Consolidated..............	8.4	10.6	12.7	12.5	13.8	14.8	0.6
One-room.................	7.8	10.4	12.0	12.2	12.8	14.2	
Spelling:							
Consolidated..............	86.7	82.0	75.4	73.1	75.0	80.6	8.1
One-room.................	82.5	80.9	72.2	69.3	58.5	60.9	
Writing (Speed):							
Consolidated..............	38.9	52.1	64.8	73.5	77.4	83.6	4.1
One-room.................	39.4	46.4	58.9	66.8	71.3	83.1	
Writing (Quality):							
Consolidated..............	28.1	31.1	33.1	39.5	42.6	50.6	1.1
One-room.................	26.3	30.1	34.8	40.0	40.3	47.1	

Stone and Curtis (28) endeavored to obtain more refined measures of the differences in achievements of pupils in one-teacher schools and those of pupils in graded rural schools by carefully matching pupils. Pairings were made by matching a pupil from one type of school with one from the other type of school. The bases of matching included the same chronological age, the same intelligence-test score, and the same grade in school. The data regarding the differences in achievement were assembled from the report (28:261) to present in Table XXIV a composite picture of the achievement differences found. These differences are in favor of the children in the graded schools, showing them to be approximately a half-year advanced over the children in the one-teacher schools.

TABLE XXIV.—DIFFERENCES IN ACHIEVEMENT OF PUPILS IN ONE-ROOM SCHOOLS AND IN GRADED SCHOOLS WHEN MATCHED ACCORDING TO CHRONOLOGICAL AGE, GRADE, AND INTELLIGENCE TEST SCORES
(After Stone and Curtis)

Achievement Test Used	SUPERIORITY OF GRADED SCHOOL PUPILS	
	Percent	Months
Courtis Arithmetic, Series B	10.4	5.0
Stone Arithmetic	6.5	3.0
Whipple Reading	10.9	4.6
Thorndike Word Knowledge	2.7	2.7
Briggs English Form	4.9	4.9
Stanford Achievement (Grade VII)	——	5.6
Stanford Achievement (Grade VIII)	——	4.5
Stanford Achievement (Grade IX)	——	3.8

Other studies, such as those made by Covert (8) and McCracken (17), indicate that the conclusions drawn from the two studies above are typical of those to be made from the data found in practically all the studies.

ACHIEVEMENT IN TERMS OF POTENTIAL ABILITY

In conclusion, one other type of data needs to be included—a type which will aid in clarifying the seemingly confused findings presented up to this point. When the several general conclusions thus far arrived at in this chapter are brought together, they indicate that the size of the school (or of the community in which it is located) has (1) affected slightly the age-grade status of pupils; (2) retarded slightly the promotional progress of pupils; (3) proved handicapping to children in the smaller units in matters of elimination of health defects; (4) proved advantageous to these children in case of some common communicable diseases; (5) led to their promotion when they possessed lower mental ages and less potential ability; and (6) resulted in their promotions when their actual achievement has been lower than that of children in larger schools. What, then has been the achievement of the pupils in terms of their potential ability?

Several investigations have been made to find the answer to the question. Studies made in California, Minnesota, Texas, and Utah contain approximately the same results with respect to the "three R's". Table XXV was constructed from the data included in Kruse's investigation (16) to illustrate typical findings. When achievement scores are equated with mental scores which have been expressed in comparable terms, the resulting accomplishment quotients show clearly that rural-school children are accomplishing results which are as good as those accomplished by city-school children. In fact, the accomplishment quotients in reading, arithmetic, and spelling of the rural-school children tested indicate that they are working up to their capacity in the three subjects. The same facts were ascertained in the other three investigations published (10, 30, 31).

TABLE XXV.—RATIOS OF ACHIEVEMENT AGE TO MENTAL AGE OF TEXAS WHITE CHILDREN IN VARIOUS TYPES OF ELEMENTARY SCHOOLS ACCORDING TO MEDIAN SCORES IN THREE SUBJECTS IN GRADES V AND VII
(After Kruse)

| TYPE OF SCHOOL | ACHIEVEMENT QUOTIENTS IN THREE SUBJECTS IN GRADES V AND VII | | | | | |
| | Reading | | Arithmetic | | Spelling | |
	V	VII	V	VII	V	VII
One-teacher rural...........................	103	102	—	—	108	110
Two-teacher rural...........................	100	101	—	—	105	106
Three-teacher rural.........................	98	101	—	—	104	109
Four-teacher rural..........................	98	98	—	—	103	105
One-to-four-teacher rural...................	99	101	95	93	105	107
Five-and-more-teacher rural.................	100	98	93	91	105	104
City.......................................	100	101	94	89	104	104

Since the achievement scores of rural-school children in social studies, literature, and science were lower than their scores in the 'three R's' and much lower than the scores of city-school children in the social studies, literature, and science, the accomplishment quotients of the rural-school children in these enriching subjects will be less satisfactory. The data found in various state surveys especially support this final conclusion.

Conclusions

The reader will readily appreciate the difficulties which confront the writer in his endeavor to generalize from the large amount of data of different kinds treated in this chapter. If central tendencies regarding each phase of the status of rural-school pupils are assumed to be typical, the significance of deviations from such tendencies will be omitted. A summation of the most commonly occurring facts and factors, however, serves to indicate disagreements existing between general conditions as depicted by one type of data and those shown by another type. It aids, therefore, in pointing to further research needed to arrive at the details involved in the differences and in indicating fields for experimentation designed to improve the status of the rural-school child.

In general, the *age-grade status* of the rural-school child who continues in school is relatively the same as that of the child in the city schools. In the middle elementary grades, there are larger percentages of over-age children in rural schools than in city schools. The rural-school teachers tend to promote a smaller percentage of their pupils than do the city-school teachers, the greatest differences occurring in the first, seventh, and eighth grades. The number of non-promotions together with the number of eliminations produce in both types of schools much larger enrollments in the lower elementary grades than in the upper ones. The smaller the school, however, the greater is the percentage of enrollment in the lower grades. The causes of non-promotion and the subjects causing the greatest difficulty in these cases are quite similarly distributed in the rural schools and the urban schools.

The limited data regarding *health conditions* indicate the existence of conflicting influences operating in different types of communities. While rural-school pupils are working under a greater handicap than urban-school children, owing to the greater number of physical defects found in the former, the rates of occurrence of cases and of deaths due to typhoid fever, diphtheria, and measles indicate that the country child is more fortunately situated than is his city cousin.

On the other hand, poliomyelitis seems to be primarily an infant's disease in the city and a disease of children of school age in the country.

The *mental ages* of rural first-grade children are only slightly lower than those of urban first-grade children in the various states from which data could be obtained. In succeeding higher grades the differences increase until by the time children reach the sixth grade the average rural-school child in a grade is mentally a year or more younger than the average city-school child in the corresponding grade.

The corresponding data regarding *intelligence quotients* yield central tendencies similar to those found regarding the mental ages. In the first two grades, the intelligence quotient of the average child in the rural school is slightly lower than that of the average child in the corresponding grade in the city school. The differences between mean and median intelligence quotients become significant in the third grade and even more marked in the upper grades; the higher quotients occur among the average children in urban schools as contrasted with those of the average rural-school children in the same grade.

School achievement of pupils in rural schools, as measured by standardized educational tests, is less satisfactory than that of city-school pupils. Size of school and length of school term seem to be factors operating to cause some of the differences existing. The poorest results in rural schools, as contrasted with those in city schools, occur in subjects other than the "three R's." The achievements in the conventional subjects, however, are less satisfactory in each grade of the rural school than in the corresponding grade of the city school.

With respect to the *achievement quotient,* when intelligence and achievement scores are considered together, with intelligence rendered constant between children in rural schools compared with children in city schools, the former are found to be achieving as satisfactory results as the latter in the "three R's," which are in keeping with their general readiness. In such studies as history, geography, and nature study, however, the relative accomplishments of the rural-school pupils are meager as compared with those of their city cousins.

The *general status* of the rural elementary-school pupil is, therefore, a clearly less satisfactory one than that of the city elementary-school pupil. In order to ascertain with a high degree of accuracy, the specific causes of the difference and the interrelation of each factor operating with every other one, numerous intensive studies involving a series of controlled factors need to be made. When such new and refined data are obtained as these investigations will yield, experimentation can be carried on for the purpose of eradicating the apparent handicaps under which the rural-school child must now compete with the city-school child. As has been already pointed out, many beginnings have been made in these types of research. In spite of these initial efforts and of all the research carried on to date, it is possible to undertake a study in almost every phase of research regarding the rural-school pupil and make a much needed contribution in his behalf.

BIBLIOGRAPHY

1. ADAMS, F. J. *Modoc County Mental Survey.* Berkeley, 1922. 7 pp. (Univ. of Calif. Bur. of Research in Educ. Study, No. 4.)
2. Alabama. *The Report of the Survey of Elmore County Schools.* Montgomery, 1929.
3. AYCOCK, W. L. "A study of the significance of geographical and seasonal variations in the incedence of poliomyelitis." *Jour. of Preventive Medicine,* 3: 1929, 245-278.
4. BACHMAN, F. P. *Public Education in Indiana.* New York, 1923.
5. BACHMAN, F. P. *Public Education in Kentucky.* New York, 1921.
6. BAGLEY, W. C. and KYTE, G. C. *The California Curriculum Study.* Berkeley, 1926. Pp. 295-317; 323-330; 331-381.
7. COOK, J. H. *A Study of the Mill Schools of North Carolina.* New York, 1925. 55 pp. (Teachers College, Columbia University, Contributions to Education, No. 178.)
8. COVERT, T. *Educational Achievements of One-Teacher and of Larger Rural Schools.* Washington, 1928. 24 pp. (U. S. Bureau of Education Bulletin, No. 15.)
9. FOOTE, J. M. *et al.* "A comparative study of instruction in consolidated and one-teacher schools." *Nat. Educ. Assoc. Proc.* Washington, 1923. Pp. 812-826.
10. FRANZEN, R. H. and HANLON, W. H. *The Program of Measurement in Contra Costa County.* Martinez, California, 1923. 94 pp.
11. FROST, N. *A Comparative Study of Achievement in Country and Town Schools.* New York, 1921. 70 pp. (Teachers College, Columbia University, Contributions to Education, No. 111.)
12. GODFREY, E. S. "The age distribution of communicable disease according to size of community." *Amer. Jour. of Public Health,* 18: 1928, 616-631.
13. HAGGERTY, M. E. *Rural School Survey of New York State; Educational Achievement.* Albany, 1922. Pp. 176-180.

14. IRION, T. W. H. and FISCHER, F. C. "Testing the intelligence of rural-school children." *Amer. School Master*, 4: 1921, 221-223.
15. KRAYBILL, D. B. *The Problem of Admitting Rural Pupils to High School.* State College, 1927. 66 pp. (Pennsylvania State College Bulletin, Vol. XXI, No. 30.)
16. KRUSE, P. J. *Texas Educational Survey Report; Educational Achievement.* Austin, 1925. Vol. IV, pp. 114-127.
17. McCRACKEN, C. C. *Logan County and Bellefontaine, Ohio, School Survey.* Columbus, 1923. 66 pp.
18. MOORE, R. C. "Survey report." *Illinois Teacher*, 14: 1928, 75-78.
19. MORRISON, J. C. "A comparative study of instruction in consolidated and one-room rural schools in New York State." *Jour. of Rural Educ.* 1: 1922, 355-359.
20. NEWBERRY, M. C. "Intelligence and reading tests in a rural county." *Jour. of Rural Educ.* 1: 1921, 174-176 .
21. North Carolina. *State School Facts*, June 1, 1929.
22. ODELL, C. W. *The Progress and Elimination of School Children in Illinois.* Urbana, 1924. 76 pp. (University of Illinois Bulletin, Vol. XXI, No. 38.)
23. OLSEN, H. C. "Some shortcomings revealed by a school survey of a typical rural county." *Jour. of Rural Educ.* 1: 1922, 456-463.
24. ORLEANS, J. S. and BAER, J. A. *Handwriting in the Rural and Village Schools of New York State.* Albany, 1929. 52 pp. (University of the State of New York Bulletin, No. 922.)
25. O'SHEA, M. V. *A State Educational System at Work.* Hattiesburg, 1927. Pp. 243-250 (Mississippi Survey.)
26. PERCIVAL, W. P. "A study of the causes and subjects of school failure." *The California Curriculum Study*, Berkeley, 1926. Pp. 331-381.
27. RAINEY, H. P. *A Survey of Achievement of Oregon School Pupils in the Fundamental School Subjects.* Eugene, 1927. 168 pp. (University of Oregon Publications, No. 3.)
28. STONE, C. W. and CURTIS, J. W. "Progress of equivalent one-room and graded-school pupils." *Jour. of Educ. Research*, 16:1927, 260-264.
29. TERMAN, L. M. *The Measurement of Intelligence.* Boston, 1916. Pp. 78-104.
30. TIGERT, J. J., et al. *Survey of Education in Utah.* Washington, 1926. Chap. IV. (U. S. Bureau of Education Bulletin, 1926, No. 18.)
31. VAN WAGENEN, M. J. *Comparative Pupil Achievement in Rural, Town, and City Schools.* Minneapolis, 1929. Chaps. II, IV, V, and VI.
32. VORIES, R. E. "Incidence of tuberculosis infection in children from rural-school districts." *Amer. Jour. of Public Health*, 18: 1928, 1006-1009.
33. WOOD, T. D. et al. *Health Improvement in Rural Schools*, Chicago, 1922. 52 pp.

CHAPTER III
AVAILABILITY OF SCHOOLS IN RURAL COMMUNITIES

KATHERINE M. COOK
Chief, Division of Special Problems
and
W. H. GAUMNITZ
Specialist in Rural School Problems
Office of Education, Washington, D. C.

I. INTRODUCTION

This section aims to show, so far as the facts are available, to what extent educational facilities, elementary and secondary, supported at public expense, are available to children in rural communities. 'Rural communities,' as the term is used herein, are roughly defined as 'population centers of twenty-five hundred or less.' However, the territory and population compassed in the study were selected to include chiefly children from farm homes or from communities in which agriculture or closely allied industries are dominant. 'School age' means 'five to twenty years old.'

The two large factors considered are 'accessibility' as hereinafter defined, referring chiefly to the distance rural children travel between home and school, with certain closely related information and results; and 'types of schools' available to children in rural communities. 'Types of schools' as used in this section refers chiefly to size measured by number of teachers employed, but also to quality, insofar as that factor is measurable by the criteria presented.

The facts presented are gleaned from a thorough canvass of available studies, laws, and other materials bearing directly and indirectly on accessibility and types of schools in rural communities, supplemented by special sampling studies from five states and by less complete information from one county in each of two additional states, North Carolina and South Carolina. Complete information concerning these studies, the manner of collecting data, questionnaire forms, and additional information collected are given in Bulletin, 1930, No. 34, United States Office of Education. The data collected were detailed in character, involving information from individual children as to age, educational status, and distance between home and school, as indicated later in this chapter. Approximately sixty thousand children are involved.[1]

II. ACCESSIBILITY AND THE RURAL SCHOOLS

1. Problems of School Accessibility

Accessibility has been defined as the presence or absence of distance or other physical obstacles affecting regular school attendance of normal children of legal school age (2:1).[2] This definition is accepted for purposes of this study. However, since objective data obtainable are confined to the distance factor, discussion will center around it chiefly. Accessibility of schools in rural situations offers difficult and important problems; farm families, for the most part, live on their own land rather than in communities and villages. There are vast areas of low population density, and even when the farming population is relatively dense and evenly distributed, many homes are isolated. The task of selecting central and suitable sites for schools on or adjacent to improved highways is no simple matter.

The most common means of reaching schoolhouses are: through transportation at public expense, a means usually confined to large consolidated districts; at private or individual expense, one dependent in part on the economic status of the family; and by walking. A large majority of the three and one-half million children enrolled in one-teacher schools walk the distance between home and school at least

---

[1] The coöperating educators are Delia Kibbe, Supervisor of Elementary Schools, State Department of Education, Wisconsin; Frederick L. Whitney, Director of Research, Colorado State Teachers College, Greeley, Colo.; R. E. Jaggers, Supervisor of Rural Schools, State Department of Education, Kentucky; Helen Heffernan, Chief, Division of Rural Education, State Department of Education, California; and Agnes Samuelson, State Superintendent of Public Instruction, Iowa. These studies are referred to hereinafter as 'special studies in five states.' Supplementary data from one county in North Carolina and from one county in South Carolina were collected by Hattie Parrott, Supervisor of Elementary Instruction, State Department of Public Instruction, North Carolina; and Kate Wofford, County Superintendent, Laurens County, South Carolina, respectively. Certain compilations, supplementations, and coördinations were made in the United States Office of Education by W. H. Gaumnitz, Specialist in Rural School Problems. O. L. Troxel, Colorado State Teachers College, Greeley, Colorado, canvassed available literature for evidence of the effects of transportation on availability of schools.

[2] Citations in parenthesis refer by number and page to the references listed at the end of this chapter.

twice a day. With the beginning of free public education in rural communities the aim was to solve the accessibility problem by placing schools within easy walking distance of the children's homes. The resulting multiplicity of small schools and small administrative units, with its attendant evils of inadequate support and instructional inefficiency, is well known. Problems of school accessibility increase in importance and difficulty, as the policy of public universal education gains ground, and as laws of compulsory school attendance gain in public favor and effectiveness. The conflict between efficiency on the one hand and accessibility on the other looms larger than ever, as the demands of modern education increase.

Certain Legal Considerations. With the adoption of free public education as a state policy and responsibility, school accessibility seemed adequately provided for through the delegation of authority for local school systems to local officials. It became necessary to consider and to fix definite limitations of distance and therefore, indirectly at least, to set up legal accessibility standards as later developments when compulsory-attendance laws and the policy of expending public funds for transportation were inaugurated.

Distance as a factor in compulsory attendance is recognized in 22 states in which exemptions on this basis are set up in the statutes. Distance limitations are stated in terms of a given number of miles between home and school or left to the judgment of school officials. In 17 of the 22 states exemption is dependent on number of miles from school when transportation is not furnished at public expense. It varies from one and a half miles to three miles (9:5). In the other states acceptable reasons for non-attendance are set up, such as unreasonable distance, weather, travel conditions, undue hardships. Age is recognized as a factor in exemption from law enforcement in Michigan and Oregon.

With a few exceptions, two or two and a half miles is accepted in statutory provisions as a reasonable distance within which non-transported children can be compelled to attend school. Two miles is the maximal walking distance in 7 states (9:5). Blankenship (2:30) found "that in at least 28 states it is entirely possible that children may be expected to walk to school or transport themselves two miles or more.

In general, laws regulating distance children must be transported apply only where consolidation has been effected. Drewes (9:6f.)

discerns a tendency to require transportation at public expense for all pupils living more than three miles from school. That requirement is effective in two states, Texas and Kansas.

A careful canvass of the literature of the subject fails to reveal any basis in research or scientific study for an acceptable definition of accessibility as a guide in furnishing transportation or for the enforcement of compulsory-attendance laws. This situation is more difficult to reconcile with modern policies in universal education in view of the following facts: (1) The administrative machinery for enforcement of compulsory-education laws is not so well organized in rural as in urban territory. (2) Child-labor laws apply specifically to children in farm work in a *few* states only (21:47). Cooper (8:294) states that the largest factor in absence from rural schools in Delaware is farm work. Failure to fix by statute a reasonable definition of accessibility applicable in the enforcement of compulsory-education laws operates to deprive a large number of rural children of an education. State-wide surveys testify to this. The following is an example: "In case of the sparsely settled areas of Southwest Texas, more than 50 percent of the area is geographically exempt from the operation of the compulsory attendance law.... The aggregate [of children concerned] is undoubtedly considerable" (33:224).

Opinion and Tradition Influence Practice. The location of rural schoolhouses, the extent of public transportation, and legal distance regulations are influenced by an apparently widely accepted tendency to consider one and a half miles a reasonable walking distance to school for children in rural communities. Blankenship (2:39ff.) points out a tendency, especially when population density is from 18 to 45 per square mile, to form districts containing four to five square miles, thereby insuring that the majority of homes are within one and a half miles from a selected center. After an extensive study of rural-school attendance, he suggests that administration proceed on the policy that normal children seven to twelve years old should not walk more than one and a half miles to school. Reavis (26:15) found that attendance dropped off rapidly when children lived more than one and a half miles from school, and Cooper's Delaware studies (7:276) show that attendance drops off extensively after a mile and considerably after the first half-mile.

The criterion, one and a half miles distance, apparently influences transportation provisions. Decisions as to which children need to be transported, the distance children may be expected to walk to meet vehicles, and the reasonable time on the road when transported are apparently influenced frequently by this measure. "Transportation should be provided for all children living beyond the accessibility distance of one and a half miles of a school" (12:40). Economy in the costs of transportation suggests that "the walking accessibility distance of one and a half miles should be strictly enforced" (12:54). These are typical of expressions found in surveys of consolidated school districts.

Accessibility and the Locating of Schoolhouses. Locating schoolhouses, especially in non-consolidated districts, is generally a function of local boards of education of three to five laymen with very little professional guidance. In some states the county superintendent's approval is required or sought. When state aid is granted, building sites must be approved by state or county officials. Regulations concerning state grants for building purposes usually concern hygienic conditions rather than accessibility. In a few states provisions are made for surveys by the staff of the state department of education preliminary to redistricting counties when consolidation is contemplated.

While the multiplicity of small schoolhouses is probably due to efforts to achieve accessibility, these efforts are not always sufficiently intelligent to accomplish the purpose. It is certain that there are still large areas in which many children live, yet in which schools are inaccessible. The existence of these areas is due to a number of causes, among which are the following: sparsity and inequitable distribution of population and wealth; poor distribution of schools; inadequate transportation, especially in consolidation in villages (49 percent of children outside the villages in one county in Texas live more than one and a half miles from school); unfortunate methods of forming districts; ineffective and inadequate compulsory-attendance laws; separate schools for colored and white children; common practice of measuring distances from school by radii of a circle without due relation to roads; policies for promoting consolidation, such as inadequate study of territory consolidated, too small or too large units, state subsidies based on factors other than accessibility, as average daily attendance, certificate held by teacher, equipment—the cost of which may be beyond the possibilities of small, poor districts (2:24ff.).

Blankenship found not a few overlapping accessibility areas in Texas, as well as large and numerous inaccessibility areas. He suggests two remedies, the formation of districts on the basis of the number of homes rather than the size of the pupil group, and the consideration of the bias square with diagonals parallel to the prevailing direction of roads as nearer than the circle to the true locus of all points at a given distance from the schoolhouse (2:5).

A canvass of recent state school surveys indicates that, while the policy of locating consolidated schools on or near main and improved highways is fairly well established, it has not been so extensively practiced in locating small schools. Paved highways are establishing new lines of communication. Small schoolhouses antedate these roads. Thus, a recent survey of education in West Virginia (5:169f.) shows that the median distance one-teacher schools are from hard roads is nearly five miles. More than half the one-teacher schools are located on unimproved roads. Thirty-seven percent are on roads impassable by auto in winter. Of 1,820 rural teachers replying to a questionnaire on this subject, 25 percent were teaching more than ten miles from hard roads. In La Salle Parish, Louisiana, "Nearly all the school buildings are either off the main highways or are reached with difficulty" (11:31). Undoubtedly similar conditions exist in many localities in other states.

Standards scientifically worked out as to what constitutes school accessibility in rural communities are lacking. Eells (10:42) has pointed out that city surveys show that one-half mile is accepted as the maximal walking distance from home to school for elementary-school children in cities. In view of the less favorable walking conditions in the country, the many schoolhouses on unimproved roads, weather hazards, and the like, the disparity between one and one-half miles (as acceptable for rural children) and one-half mile (as acceptable for urban children) is difficult to account for. The extension of the good-roads movement may not have improved conditions for children who walk.

2. The Status of School Accessibility in Rural Communities

Although distance children live from school is recognized as of fundamental importance in surveys of school systems, both urban and rural, few studies are available which show the actual distance rural children walk to school, walk to meet buses when transportation is furnished, or are transported at public expense. General statements rather than specific data are commonly used to indicate conditions. The following are examples:

> A number of children live outside the compulsory attendance limit. . . . Information obtained in Rusk County. . . showed over two -fifths of the white children and half the negro children living 2½ miles or more from a school. In Hill County the situation was similar. Under these circumstances children reached the end of the compulsory school period without ever having gone to school (30:8).

> Five hundred children in Tangipahoa Parish, or 7 per cent of the registration of the Parish, live so far from any educational facilities that they are unable to attend school (12:23).

Two studies of the distance farm families live from school are available: In four counties in Ohio and Michigan 23 percent, 70 percent, 18 percent, and 54 percent, respectively, live one and one-half miles or more from the schoolhouse (4:23). The educational survey of Texas (33:397) shows that 40 to 100 percent of farm families live more than one and one-half miles from the schoolhouse in 38 percent of the one-teacher school districts studied.

Cooper shows that more than half the rural white children studied in Delaware live within the first mile of school. They are about equally distributed as between the first and second half-mile residence areas. Twenty-two percent live from one to one and one-half miles; 15 percent, one and one-half to two miles; and approximately 10 percent over two miles from school. If one and one-half miles or more from school is an unreasonable walking distance, it appears that approximately 25 percent of the children in Delaware live that distance or beyond it (8:127).

Throughout this chapter reference is made to special studies[3] of specific phases of school availability made in 22 representative counties in five states. The first of the tables resulting from the studies presented is Table I, a percentage distribution of non-transported children according to stated distances between their homes and schools. It may be read as follows: In the counties studied in Colorado there are 4,622 non-transported children, representing 75 percent of all

---

[3] Special studies in five states by Whitney, Heffernan, Kibbe, Jaggers, and Samuelson (see footnote, page 56).

TABLE I.—PERCENTAGE DISTRIBUTION OF CHILDREN CLASSIFIED IN TWO GROUPS—THOSE IN SCHOOL NOT TRANSPORTED, AND THOSE NOT IN SCHOOL—ACCORDING TO GIVEN DISTANCES BETWEEN HOME AND SCHOOL

PERCENTAGE DISTRIBUTION BY STATES

DISTANCE	Colorado In School (4,622 Children)	Colorado Not in School (1,205 Children)	California In School (7,027 Children)	California Not in School (848 Children)	Wisconsin In School (4,264 Children)	Wisconsin Not in School (1,367 Children)	Kentucky In School (6,632 Children)	Kentucky Not in School (1,348 Children)	Iowa In School (18,655 Children)	Iowa Not in School (5,023 Children)
Less than 1 mile	45	28	65	35	46	40	51	30	58	45
1–1.5 miles	20	23	15	16	28	24	23	22	22	24
1.5–2 miles	14	13	7	11	17	15	12	16	12	16
2–3 miles	14	17	8	16	8	12	10	15	4	8
3–4 miles	4	8	3	8	.4	6	2	7	1	3
4–5 miles	2	4	1	5	.2	1	1	4	1	2
5 miles or more	1	7	1	9	.04	2	1	6	2	2
Children living										
1.5 miles or more from school	35	49	20	49	26	36	26	48	20	31
2 miles or more	21	36	13	38	9	21	14	32	8	15
3 miles or more	6	19	5	22	1	9	4	17	4	9
Percent of enrollment transported	75		68		91		78		83	
Percent of children not in school		16		8		23		14		18

those in attendance at school; 45 percent live less than one mile from school; 20 percent, one to one and one-half miles; 14 percent, one and one-half to two miles, and so on.

Considering first the children who live within a mile of the schoolhouse, the percentages vary from 45 in Colorado to 65 in California. Similar data for one county each in South Carolina and North Carolina show that approximately 48 and 83 percent, respectively, of nontransported children live within the one-mile area. As shown in the table, percentages differ among states in each distance area; for example, from 15 percent of the children in California to 28 percent in Wisconsin live from one to one and one-half miles from school; from 7 to 17 percent live one and one-half to two miles in the same states, and 8 to 21 percent live more than two miles away.

The table also shows the distance areas in which rural children in the same counties and school districts live who are not enrolled in any school. These out-of-school children constitute the following percentages (by states) of the whole group five to twenty years old: Colorado 16 percent, California 8 percent, Wisconsin 23 percent, Kentucky 14 percent, and Iowa 18 percent. Comparing percentages of enrolled and non-enrolled children living within the given distance areas, the table shows larger proportions of the latter living at excessive distances, and it suggests that the distance from school is a probable cause of non-enrollment.

Many Children Live beyond 'a Reasonable Walking Distance.' The percentage of non-transported children enrolled in school living one and one-half miles or more from schoolhouses will be seen from the table to be as follows: Colorado, 35 percent; California, 20 percent; Wisconsin, 26 percent; Iowa, 20 percent; Kentucky, 26 percent. The percentage in Delaware, as previously shown, is 25. This distance is considered by students of the subject as unreasonable unless public transportation is furnished, especially for children of elementary-school age. It is of interest also that, except in Wisconsin, from 4 to 7 percent of non-transported enrolled children live three miles or more from school; and from 2 to 3 percent, four miles or more—the latter is characterized by Cooper as 'prohibitive' for non-transported children. Another important question for further study raised by the table arises from the high percentages of children two or more miles from school now out of school who might be in school

TABLE II.—PERCENTAGES OF NON-TRANSPORTED CHILDREN ENROLLED IN RURAL SCHOOLS WHO LIVE AT VARIOUS DISTANCES FROM SCHOOL: DATA FROM STUDIES IN EIGHT STATES

Distance	Colorado	California	Wisconsin	Kentucky	Iowa	North Carolina	South Carolina	Delaware	Total Number of Children	Percent
Less than 1 mile	45	65	46	51	58	56	83	48	29,305	55
1 to 1.5 miles	20	15	28	24	22	16	12	33	11,005	21
1.5 to 2 miles	14	7	17	12	12	12	4	12	6,232	12
2 to 3 miles	14	8	8	10	4	12	1	6	4,249	8
3 to 4 miles	4	3	.4	2	1	3		.3	1,149	2
4 to 5 miles	2	1	.2	.8	1	1		.2	587	1
5 miles or more	1	1	.04	.9	2			.1	457	1
Total	100	100	99.64	100.7	100	100	100	99.6	52,984	100

if effective laws were enacted. Table V indicates that about 25 percent of the out-of-school children are six to fourteen years old.

Distance Exempts Rural Children from Compulsory Attendance.
Reference has been made elsewhere to certain evidences that many
rural children are exempt from provisions of compulsory-education
laws because of distance from school. The need of research to show
the number of such children is evident and imminent. Exact data
are not available. In three of the states included in the studies just
referred to, Iowa, California, and Wisconsin, as in several others, non-
transported children who live more than two miles from school by
the nearest traveled road are exempt from the provisions of the compulsory-attendance laws. While age limitations differ among states,
efforts to extend compulsory-attendance laws to all children of school
age are not uncommon. Table I gives an indication of the number
of rural children who would not be reached by laws of the type suggested, namely, those living two miles or more from school. For the
five states the average is 13 percent of the children, enrolled but non-
transported, whose ages range from five to twenty years. In 1920
(U. S. Census Report) there were nearly 18,500,000 children five to
twenty years old in rural communities; 13 percent of this group
means about 2,400,000.

Summary of Data Concerning Distance. In Table II are combined
data from all available sources collected on a comparable basis, showing the percentages of enrolled, non-transported children who live the
indicated distances from school. Over fifty thousand rural children
living in eight different states are represented. Living in the territory
studied in the "special studies in five states" are over ten thousand
other children not enrolled in school; higher percentages of these children than of enrolled children live excessive distances from school.

In so far as one can judge the situation in the United States as a
whole from the data in this table, approximately half (55 percent)
of non-transported children in rural districts live within a mile of
the school which they attend. If conditions in Delaware (8:127)
are typical of those in other states, approximately half of 55 percent
within the first mile actually live within the first half-mile. One-half
mile is the distance considered as the maximal reasonable walking distance for city children to cover between home and school. If the areas
from which data in Table II were collected were urban areas, approxi-

mately 73 percent of the children would be considered as living an unreasonable distance from the schoolhouse.

If one and one-half miles is the limit of a reasonable walking distance, approximately 24 percent of non-transported rural children enrolled live that far or farther from school. About 12 percent attend school who live two miles or more, and about 4 percent who live three miles or more from school. These children walk, unless they can afford transportation at their own expense, over highways prepared for vehicles rather than for pedestrians.

3. Probable Effects of Distance on School Attendance

Distance from school was found the most significant cause of absence among rural children in Maryland and to have a "negative relationship to attendance for all types of schools, for all sections of the State and all subdivisions of pupils" in Delaware. Reavis (26:15) found distinct zones within which attendance was somewhat similar, as follows: (1) Within one-fourth mile from school; (2) one-fourth to one and one-half miles; (3) more than one and one-half miles. Children living more than one-fourth of a mile from school do not, by virtue of that fact alone, have equal educational opportunities with those living nearer school. Cooper found that children living nearer the school attend better, irrespective of age, grade, parentage, section of the state, or type of school. After the first half-mile, decreases in attendance are constant and fairly regular.

> The attendance average of pupils within the first half-mile is 134.4 days. This is the only distance group in a total of 10 distance groups in which 50 percent of the pupils attend as much as 150 days. About one-third of all pupils living from one to four miles attend from 50 to 99 days; one-third attend school from 100 to 149 days; the other third is divided between those who attend 150 days and over and those who attend not less than 50 days (8:203 f.).

> The median attendance of colored pupils aged 8 to 10 living on farms is from 20 to 46 days better if they live near school than if they live more than 1½ miles from school. Pupils living over 4 miles from school are apparently at a prohibitive distance unless special conveyance is provided. This is true irrespective of age (8:254).

Tables III and IV show median days attended by non-transported and transported children respectively living at designated distances, and percentages with high and low attendance records as found in several states. The data may be interpreted as follows: in Iowa, to

TABLE III.—ATTENDANCE OF NON-TRANSPORTED CHILDREN LIVING AT STATED
DISTANCES FROM SCHOOL

DISTANCE	MEDIAN DAYS ATTENDED	PERCENT ATTENDING	
		70 days or fewer	151 days or more
California:			
Less than 1 mile	158	12	65
1–2 miles	163	9	77
2–3 miles	161	7	73
3–4 miles	159	4	75
4 miles or more	163	12	68
Colorado:			
Less than 1 mile	146	18	47
1–2 miles	138	21	42
2–3 miles	139	18	40
3–4 miles	139	17	37
4 miles or more	132	27	11
Iowa:			
Less than 1 mile	162	8	69
1–2 miles	150	11	50
2–3 miles	153	12	54
3–4 miles	169	3	81
4 miles or more	170	4	83
Kentucky:			
Less than 1 mile	109	32	18
1–2 miles	72	49	3
2–3 miles	68	51	6
3–4 miles	98	29	10
4 miles or more	140	11	40
Wisconsin:			
Less than 1 mile	156	7	61
1–2 miles	151	7	51
2–3 miles	144	11	42
3–4 miles	135	14	38
4 miles or more	—	—	—
Five States:			
Less than 1 mile	157	12	61
1–2 miles	145	17	46
2–3 miles	143	19	45
3–4 miles	155	13	57
4 miles or more	164	6	72

take a representative farm state in which rural schools are more evenly distributed than in many states, data for non-transported children constituting 83 percent of the entire school group show that the median days attended by children living less than one mile from school

TABLE IV.—ATTENDANCE OF CHILDREN TRANSPORTED AT PUBLIC EXPENSE
LIVING AT STATED DISTANCES FROM SCHOOL

DISTANCE	MEDIAN DAYS ATTENDED	PERCENT ATTENDING	
		70 days or fewer	151 days or more
California:			
Less than 2 miles............	165	11	70
2–4 miles..................	158	16	71
4–6 miles..................	171	21	73
6–8 miles..................	172	21	86
8–10 miles.................	162	3	83
10 miles or more.............	162	3	96
Colorado:			
Less than 2 miles............	159	12	64
2–4 miles..................	152	19	55
4–6 miles..................	151	11	53
6–8 miles..................	151	15	50
8–10 miles.................	154	12	53
10 miles or more.............	142	26	45
Iowa:			
Less than 2 miles............	171	2	82
2–4 miles..................	166	4	80
4–6 miles..................	165	5	82
6–8 miles..................	164	6	82
8–10 miles.................	162	9	73
10 miles or more.............	—	—	—
Kentucky:			
Less than 2 miles............	140	8	35
2–4 miles..................	132	6	25
4–6 miles..................	136	9	31
6–8 miles..................	134	14	30
8–10 miles.................	—	—	—
10 miles or more.............	—	—	—
Wisconsin:			
Less than 2 miles............	161	15	63
2–4 miles..................	163	14	57
4–6 miles..................	132	13	32
6–8 miles..................	—	—	—
8–10 miles.................	—	—	—
10 miles or more.............	—	—	—
Five States:			
Less than 2 miles............	163	7	69
2–4 miles..................	160	10	65
4–6 miles..................	158	9	63
6–8 miles..................	155	11	57
8–10 miles.................	158	6	69
10 miles or more.............	157	16	69

TABLE V.—CHILDREN NOT ENROLLED IN SCHOOL, DISTRIBUTED ACCORDING TO AGE, IN FIVE STATES

AGES	PERCENTAGE WITHIN THE STATES				
	Colorado (1,205 children)	California (848 children)	Wisconsin (1,367 children)	Kentucky (1,348 children)	Iowa (5,023 children)
5 years	14	27	9	—	4
6–8 years	5	8	6	13	4
9–12 years	5	5	8	12	6
13–14 years	6	5	11	16	11
15–16 years	22	14	25	34	25
17–20 years	47	40	41	24	51

is 162; one to two miles, 150 days; two to three miles 153 days; three to four miles 169 days; more than four miles, 170 days. The nearest-to-school group apparently has an advantage over the two next nearest groups; children in the two longest-distance groups seem to overcome the disadvantage of distance. This is probably partly explained by the fact that more older children attend school from long-distance areas; and by the probability that there is more self-transportation from long distances.

Among transported children in the same state (see Table IV) the median days attended apparently increased slightly but progressively as distance decreased, as follows: children living eight to ten miles from school attended 162 days; six to eight miles, 164 days; four to six miles, 165 days; two to four miles, 166 days; less than two miles, 171 days. The percentage attending 151 or more days shows a less regular improvement for the given distance intervals.

Among non-transported children in the other states, Table III shows that the number of days attended by the median child and the percentages of children attending 151 days or more bear an inverse relationship to distance throughout in Wisconsin and Colorado, and up to the group living from three to four miles from the schoolhouse in Kentucky and Iowa. In Kentucky the children living four miles or more from school, in Iowa the children living three to four miles and those living four miles or more attend better than the children living nearest the schoolhouse. In California the group with the highest attendance record is that in which children live from one to two miles from school.

Comparison of data in Table III with those in Table IV indicates that distance is not so important a factor in attendance when children are transported at public expense, as when they must walk or be transported at their own expense; but that it influences somewhat the number of days attended and the percentage attending the long-term period in all states studied except California.

Dr. O. L. Troxel recently made an extensive examination of available literature for this report for the purpose of discovering objective material showing what relationship exists between transportation and school availability. He found that comparisons of enrollment and attendance showing a causal relationship with transportation are lacking; that there is little objective evidence showing the effect of transportation on the provision of more education or better schools. Studies on transportation costs are more complete than studies of other phases of the question.

Children Not Enrolled in Any School. Studies of rural-school conditions generally show an unsatisfactory school enrollment based on scholastic population. Though objective data are not always presented to substantiate it, the implication is that distance from school is a significant cause. Following is one example:

The survey staff have found that a considerable proportion of the children between the ages of six and fourteen is not in any school. If there is no school within easy reach of these children, the compulsory attendance law is not applied to them. Some of the children are not in school because there is no room for them (24:12).

Considerable information was gathered in the special studies made for this report concerning children not in school. Attention has previously been called to the high percentage of out-of-school children, averaging for the 22 counties studied, 16 percent of children five to twenty years old; and to the fact that a disproportionately high percentage of non-enrolled as compared with enrolled children live long distances from school. This indicated relationship between distance and failure to enroll in school suggests a need of further study.

Again it is shown in Table V that a high percentage of the children not enrolled in school are six to fourteen years of age. The percentages by states are: Iowa, 20; Wisconsin, 25; Kentucky, 41; Colorado, 17; California, 18—averaging 25 percent for the 22 counties studied. Since this is the usual compulsory-attendance, as well as the important elementary-school, period, further study of this situation is needed.

TABLE VI.—HIGHEST GRADE REACHED BEFORE ELIMINATION—CHILDREN TEN
TO TWENTY YEARS OF AGE NOT IN SCHOOL

ESTIMATED GRADE OF ELIMINATION	PERCENTAGE WITHIN THE STATES					
	Colorado (841 children)	California (546 children)	Wisconsin (1,131 children)	Kentucky (977 children)	Iowa (4,059 children)	Total for these States (7,554 children)
Between I and IV..........	6	2	2	30	1	6
Between V and VI.........	15	7	9	26	5	10
From Grade VII...........	13	12	14	12	10	11
From Grade VIII..........	41	41	56	19	51	46
Between IX and X.........	16	23	12	12	15	15
Between XI and XII.......	8	13	6	2	17	12
Between XIII and XIV.....	1	2	2	—	1	1
Percent reaching Grade IX or higher...........	26	37	19	14	33	27
Percent reaching Grade XI or higher...........	10	15	7	2	18	12

Grades at Which Elimination Occurs. Table VI concerns the highest grade reached before elimination of children ten to twenty years
of age. It may be read for all states as in the following manner for
Iowa: The record shows the approximate grade of elimination of over
four thousand children. Of these 10 percent had reached the seventh
grade when they last attended school. Approximately 5 percent had
reached the fifth or sixth grade, and one percent were eliminated before reaching the fourth grade. Approximately 33 percent of the
children not now attending any school in the Iowa counties had entered high school before being eliminated. Many of these were eliminated before reaching the eleventh grade.

The percentages of children out of school eliminated at each of
the grade levels indicated for the five states included in the study
are shown in the last column of Table VI. More than one-fourth of
the children do not reach the eighth grade. High elimination from
school—46 percent—during or at the close of the eighth grade is another striking disclosure. To what extent inaccessibility of secondary
schools is responsible for this situation, probably reasonably representative of conditions in rural communities throughout the country,
is a pertinent question.

If one can judge conditions in rural communities in the country
at large from these samplings, and if they are indicative of the amount

of education which children who drop out of rural school on the average obtain, one may expect to find that approximately 14 percent of the children five to twenty years old will be found eliminated from school at any one time, and that they will be distributed (as to highest grade reached before elimination) about as follows: fourth grade, approximately 6 percent; sixth grade, approximately 10 percent; seventh grade, approximately 11 percent; eighth grade, approximately 46 percent; ninth or tenth grade, 14 percent; eleventh or twelfth grade, 12 percent; thirteenth or fourteenth grade, 7 percent.

Young Children and School Accessibility. Higher percentages of the older than of the younger age groups are enrolled from long distance areas;[4] number of days attended increases as children grow older; a lower percentage of the younger children attend 151 days or more; the loss in days attended compared to the term offered is greater among the younger children. This statement is based on data from the special studies some of which are shown in tables which follow. Table VIII shows that fewer median days are attended by young than by older children, and that a relatively smaller percentage of young children attend through a 151-day term. In Iowa, where the data are most apt to be representative of a state-wide condition, the improvement in attendance as children grow older is progressive and consistent.

In Table VII the loss in days attended as compared with the average term offered is shown according to an age-grouping of children. The young children are again at a disadvantage. In rural districts it is not uncommon for five-year-old children to enroll in school regardless of legal entrance age or provision for their care and education. There were reported from the ten counties studied in Iowa 1,958 rural children five years of age. Of these, 1,779 were in school and about one-third (617) were in kindergarten classes. The remaining two-thirds were presumably placed in the first grade. In the California counties, 524 children five years of age were reported; approximately 56 percent were in school, 78 percent of whom were in kindergartens. In the Wisconsin counties 300 five-year-olds were reported, 60 percent

---

[4] Blankenship found that children under twelve cannot walk so far as those over twelve years of age; and Reavis that the influence of distance on attendance decreases as age increases. The correlation is .60 for five to seven-year-old children; .45 for the eight to eleven-year-olds, and .25 for those twelve years of age and over.

TABLE VII.—LENGTH OF TERM AND LOSS IN DAYS ATTENDED BY THE MEDIAN CHILD IN EACH OF THE VARIOUS AGE GROUPS IN FIVE STATES

	Colorado	California	Wisconsin	Kentucky	Iowa
Average term, rural schools.............	170	174	173	162	172
Loss in days 6-year-olds	35	19	31	113	20
7–10-year-olds........	21	9	21	58	12
11–14-year-olds........	22	11	19	32	10
15–16-year-olds........	32	19	39	39	—
17–18-year-olds........	12	2	—	4	—

of whom were in school. No kindergartens were reported. Presumably the five-year-old rural children enrolled were placed in the first grade. Legal school age in Wisconsin includes children four years of age. In Colorado 303 five-year-olds were reported; here the legal school age is six to twenty-one years. Forty-five percent were in school, 12 percent of whom were reported in kindergarten classes. Kentucky reported no five-year-olds. This information seems to indicate that the educational welfare of young children in the country offers a serious problem under present conditions. Where one-teacher schools prevail, education suited to their age and needs is rarely provided.

Other Important Considerations. That distance is a decisive factor in school enrollment, attendance, and attenuation, and that it works a special hardship on young children, but that it affects thousands of rural children at all the different age-levels is believed to be a reasonable conclusion from the data presented.

Space forbids presentation of the data concerning, or the full discussion of, many important aspects of school accessibility. Considerable numbers of rural children live away from home to attend school —2.5 percent of all the children from five to twenty years of age in counties studied in one state. More than half of such children (54 to 80 percent) live five miles or more from the schoolhouse. Many of them are ten years of age or younger.

Many rural children attend school in districts other than their residence district. For the majority of such children reported in the special study provisions for tuition and transportation are inadequate

TABLE VIII.—SCHOOL ATTENDANCE OF NON-TRANSPORTED CHILDREN; DISTRIBUTION ACCORDING TO CERTAIN AGE GROUPS

AGES OF PUPILS	MEDIAN DAYS ATTENDED	PERCENT ATTENDING	
		70 days or fewer	151 days or more
California			
6 years or younger	155	22	30
7–10 years	165	11	73
11–14 years	163	9	79
15–16 years	155	9	74
17–18 years	172	9	81
Colorado:			
6 years or younger	135	21	35
7–10 years	149	14	49
11–14 years	148	16	48
15–16 years	138	24	42
17–18 years	158	11	62
Iowa:			
6 years or younger	152	13	54
7–10 years	160	6	66
11–14 years	162	6	68
15–16 years	172	6	78
17–18 years	174	2	88
Kentucky:			
6 years or younger	49	60	4
7–10 years	104	28	11
11–14 years	130	23	16
15–16 years	123	23	36
17–18 years	158	9	71
Wisconsin:			
6 years or younger	142	15	42
7–10 years	152	6	55
11–14 years	154	6	58
15–16 years	134	13	40
17–18 years	—	—	—
Five States:			
6 years or younger	137	18	52
7–10 years	155	11	59
11–14 years	157	10	62
15–16 years	163	11	71
17–18 years	172	4	93

or wholly lacking. Inaccessibility of schools of proper grade appears to be the cause.

Reavis (26:13 ff.) found that "distance causes absence; absence lowers quality of work; lower quality of work increases failures; and failures retard progress of children through the grades. These factors have a cumulative effect." Cooper (9:180) found, "As attendance increases or decreases promotion increases or decreases in all types of schools, for both sexes, for promoted or non-promoted pupils, all enrollment groups, all age-grade subdivisions, all parental groups, and all distance groups." He found also that "weather absence" increases as distance increases.

Distance and exposure as possible causes of fatigue; the influence of fatigue on the spirit and degree of participation in school activities, particularly of the less robust though physically normal children; their effect on undernourished, anaemic, and pretubercular children, of whom there are a larger percentage in rural than in urban communities (18:146 and 27:309, 377) are problems seriously in need of investigation.

So far research has failed to attack in any adequate way problems concerned with the availability of education adapted to physically and mentally handicapped children in rural communities. Dr. Charles Scott Berry estimates that there are at least two hundred thousand such children enrolled in the one-teacher rural schools of the United States alone. The number of handicapped children in rural communities in school and out of school and possible means of providing adequately for their care and education are immediately pressing problems for investigation.

There are striking indications that fewer schools are available for Negro children than for white children in rural communities. Data collected in the Office of Education show the following: The percentage of all children five to seventeen years old enrolled in public schools in fifteen southern states in 1928 was 84.2 for white children and 71 for colored; the percentage of enrollment in high school, 14.6 for white, 3.7 for colored; the average length of term was 25 days shorter, and the average child enrolled in colored schools attended 24 days fewer than one enrolled in white schools. In the same states the percentages of rural children seven to twenty years of age enrolled in school, as computed from the *United States Census Report,* 1920, are 68.8 for white and 56.2 for colored, respectively. In a recent study Cooke (6) says: "It is clearly apparent from the literature reviewed that the Negro pupils are not provided for adequately either in type of buildings or training and salary of teachers in schools in the southern states."

Material prepared in the Office of Education discloses serious problems concerned with providing educational opportunities for local and migratory rural children who work in seasonal industries, or whose parents are employed in seasonal labor. California has probably established a more extensive state program for the education of migratory children than any other state, yet according to Mrs. Lillian Hill,[5] even the number of such children in that state is still uncertain and the program only partially effective. There is considerable evidence to show that many migratory children do not stay in one place long enough to enter school or do not fit into the schools available, and that those in school are far more retarded than other rural children. The situation offers serious problems demanding careful investigation.

III. Types of Schools Available to Rural Children

When children in rural communities cover the long distances (thousands of them by walking) between home and school, what quality of education is then available? While the main factors in school efficiency are treated elsewhere in this Yearbook, certain outstanding features indicating the degree to which the rural schools meet certain generally accepted standards or those set up within their respective states are presented here.

1. Types of Rural Schools in Five Representative States

Tables IX, X, XI, and XII present facts concerning these features in the rural schools of the sampling counties in the five states studied. They are not presented to offer comparisons among the states; but to picture a situation varying in kind and degree, but deemed reasonably representative of educational conditions common in rural communities throughout the country. Table IX shows the total number of children enrolled and the percentage in each of several types of rural schools. It is apparent that a high percentage of children in rural communities in these states are still receiving their education in one-teacher schools, and that the quality of education available is conditioned by the limitations inherent in this type of school as conducted under present conditions. The percentages of enrolled children attending one-teacher schools vary among the states from 13 to 77, averaging for all the territory studied approximately 45 percent. The schools having four

---

[5] Study on file in United States Office of Education.

or more teachers, many of which represent centralization, enroll the next larger proportion, while the schools with two and three teachers, particularly in Colorado and Kentucky, enroll smaller but still considerable percentages of rural children.

There are large differentials between median annual salaries paid in one-teacher schools and in the four-teacher and larger schools (Table X), averaging for the five states approximately $212. Considering the four types of schools included, Table X shows that, with few exceptions, salaries increase as the size of school increases, that there is a fairly consistent premium on size of school as a means of salary promotion. This table shows also the average annual salaries of elementary teachers in cities of over one hundred thousand population in the respective states. The differentials between these two types of schools range from $723 to $1,511.

Table XI presents certain other facts which condition the quality of instruction available to rural children. Thus, in percentage of relatively inexperienced teachers employed, in stability of the teaching force, and in qualifications of teachers as measured by education and professional preparation, the one-teacher schools consistently suffer by comparison with the average of all types of rural schools studied. The data concerning professional preparation of teachers as shown in this table are believed to be particularly significant. The percentage of untrained and relatively untrained teachers is higher, and the percentage of teachers with standard preparation—namely, 72 weeks or more above high school—is uniformly lower in the one-teacher schools. The minimum prerequisite for state certification equals or ex-

TABLE IX.—PERCENTAGE OF CHILDREN ENROLLED IN EACH OF FOUR TYPES OF RURAL SCHOOLS

STATE	TOTAL NUMBER	PERCENTAGE OF CHILDREN IN:			
		One-Teacher Schools	Two-Teacher Schools	Three-Teacher Schools	Four or More Teacher Schools
Colorado.......	6,100	28	22	18	32
California.......	10,267	13	12	9	66
Wisconsin......	4,788	77	10	6	7
Kentucky......	8,058	50	20	6	24
Iowa...........	20,516	58	3	4	35

TABLE X.—MEDIAN ANNUAL SALARIES OF TEACHERS IN FOUR TYPES OF RURAL SCHOOLS

STATE	ONE-TEACHER	TWO-TEACHER	THREE-TEACHER	FOUR OR MORE TEACHERS	ALL FOUR TYPES	CITIES*	SALARY DIFFERENTIALS BETWEEN:	
							One- and Four-Teacher Schools	One-Teacher and City Schools
Colorado............	$950	$1,029	$1,050	$1,188	$1,000	$2,203	$238	$1,253
California..........	1,408	1,550	1,629	1,570	1,543	2,131	162	723
Wisconsin..........	891	1,125	1,099	1,050	1,013	2,402	159	1,511
Kentucky...........	526	609	750	771	594	1,489	250	963
Iowa..............	713	860	808	963	766	1,835	250	1,122

*Median salaries (averaged by states) of elementary teachers in cities of over one hundred thousand in population. "Salary scales in city school systems." *Research Bulletin of the N. E. A.*, 7:1929, 115.

TABLE XI.—CERTAIN FACTORS CONCERNED WITH THE QUALIFICATIONS
OF RURAL SCHOOL TEACHERS

	PERCENT OF TEACHERS				
	Colorado	California	Wisconsin	Kentucky	Iowa
EXPERIENCE: Relatively inexperienced, 16 months or less (excluding present year):					
One-teacher schools.............	34	37	48	51	34
All schools studied..............	33	25	42	47	30
TENURE: Percent teaching 8 months or less in present position (excluding present year):					
One-teacher schools.............	67	47	55	67	66
All schools studied..............	49	36	45	59	57
TRAINING: Percent with not more than 6 weeks of training beyond high school:					
One-teacher schools.............	22	43	21	30	33
All schools studied..............	19	15	21	25	26
Percent reporting training between 7 weeks and 36 weeks in length:					
One-teacher schools.............	35	9	53	38	47
All schools studied..............	21	9	46	27	41
Percent reporting training between 37 and 72 weeks in length:					
One-teacher schools.............	22	9	21	18	13
All schools studied..............	31	10	21	28	20
Percent reporting training of more than 72 weeks:					
One-teacher schools.............	21	40	5	13	7
All schools studied..............	29	66	12	21	13

ceeds the minimum shown in the table—that is, six weeks training beyond high school—in four of the states studied, Kentucky being the
exception. It must be inferred, therefore, that a high percentage of
the teachers in the rural schools studied fail to meet legal standards
set up by the respective states for novitiates in teaching as well as
standards generally considered acceptable from a professional point
of view.

TABLE XII.—THE SCHOOL TERM, IN DAYS, REPORTED FROM CITIES AND THE
SELECTED COUNTIES IN THE FIVE STATES STUDIED

	Colorado	California	Wisconsin	Kentucky	Iowa	Average for Five States
AVERAGE LENGTH OF SCHOOL TERM IN DAYS:						
Cities* of two thousand five hundred or more population............	180	185	171	177	175	178
Rural schools (sampling counties)..............	170	174	173	162	171	170
One-teacher rural schools	169	174	172	142	171	166
Two-teacher rural schools	171	174	173	153	168	168
Three-teacher rural schools...............	170	177	175	163	178	173
Rural schools employing four or more teachers...	175	175	176	190	177	179

*Computed from Frank M. Phillips, *Statistics of City School Systems, 1927-28* (United States Office of Education Bulletin, 1929, No. 34).

In school term offered, as shown in Table XII, Wisconsin rural schools average a few days longer than schools in cities. In the other states the rural term is shorter. For all counties studied the average rural term is eight days shorter than the average for cities in the same states; the average term in one-teacher schools is twelve days shorter.

2. Types of Rural Schools Available in the United States as a Whole

For the United States as a whole the situation resembles in the main that indicated in the five states studied. Table XIII shows an estimated distribution of children among five different types of rural schools. Of approximately eleven million white and colored pupils enrolled, 33 percent are in one-teacher schools, 18 percent in consolidated schools, and 27 percent in schools in small towns and villages. In the two-teacher schools and the schools employing three or more teachers in the open country, 12 percent and 10 percent respectively are enrolled. If one segregates white and colored rural children for further consideration, it appears that a higher percentage of Negro than of white children are in the one- and two-teacher schools and a lower percentage in the consolidated and village schools. We know, of course, that many children living in rural communities attend schools in towns and cities of twenty-five hundred and more population because of distance from any school or from one of proper grade level. We have no information as to the number. Many farm families move to towns and cities in order to educate their children. Galpin (13:8) states that "this reason ranks high as an inducement with both owners and tenants."

The one-teacher schools still enroll a far higher percentage of rural children than any other one type of school, notwithstanding the fact that the average one-teacher school for white children enrolls approximately only 19 pupils. Probably there are from sixty-five thousand to seventy thousand such schools in the country with an enrollment of fewer than 19 children each. Average enrollments in one-teacher schools in Minnesota, California, Iowa, and Colorado—reasonably representative of conditions in farm communities—are 16, 16, 14, and 15, respectively; in Wisconsin, 24; and in Kentucky, 36. In Missouri 60 percent of all rural districts enroll fewer than 20 pupils each (22:121).

In the two-teacher schools and in those non-consolidated schools in the open country having three or more teachers, approximately 20 percent of rural white children and 22 percent of all rural children, colored and white, are enrolled. The two-teacher schools for white children appear to enroll an average of about 50; those for colored, an average of 70 pupils. The three or more teacher schools in the open country, both white and colored, average 120 children. A canvass of research studies made in connection with this report indicates that the two- and three-teacher schools have received less study as to organization, instruction, educational achievement, and curriculum reorganization than either the one-teacher or the consolidated type. In the generally neglected field of research in rural education, probably the two- and three-teacher schools are those most neglected.

Median annual salaries of teachers in each of the different types of schools, as of 1925, are presented also in Table XIII. Median salaries in five classes of cities, based on population, for the same year show the following differentials when compared to average salaries in rural schools. City schools: twenty-five hundred to five thousand population, $237; five thousand to ten thousand, $333; ten thousand to twenty thousand, $418; thirty thousand to one hundred thousand, $591; over one hundred thousand, $1,000 (15:36).

The average term in rural schools (all types) in the United States was 27 days shorter in 1925-26 than in urban schools. The cost per pupil in average daily attendance in urban schools was $130; in rural

TABLE XIII.—CERTAIN ESTIMATES CONCERNING RURAL SCHOOLS IN THE UNITED STATES, 1928–29

	TOTAL NUMBER	PERCENTAGES OF TOTAL				
		One-Teacher	Two-Teacher	Three or More Teacher Schools in Open Country	Consolidated Schools	Three or More Teacher Schools in Villages and Towns
		Schools				
White schools	190,343	73	10	4	5	8
Colored schools	26,539	66	21	5	3	5
Total	216,882	72	11	4	5	8
		Enrollment				
White pupils	9,001,092	30	10	10	20	30
Colored pupils	1,706,676	43	25	10	7	15
Total	10,707,768	33	12	10	18	27
Median annual salaries of rural teachers, 1925	$871	$761	$754	$834	$996	$1,124

schools, $75, a difference of $45 per pupil. The average value of school property was $299 in urban communities, and $99 in rural, a difference of $200 in per pupil investment (16 : 4f.).

Of the total number of children five to twenty years of age in urban communities 79.8 percent are enrolled in schools, public and private. Of the corresponding group in rural communities 73.9 percent are enrolled in such schools, a differential of almost 6 percent in favor of urban enrollment.

3. The General Picture

The general picture of educational facilities, elementary and secondary, available to children in rural communities of the United States presented is one of a multiplicity of small, relatively ineffective schools, inequitably distributed, and still more inequitably supported. Numerous studies and surveys indicate that the teachers are itinerant, undertrained, and underpaid when compared with state standards and particularly when compared with standards prevailing in cities. The situation in one-teacher schools is less favorable than in any other type or than the average for all rural schools.

The school term for the country as a whole is more than 5 weeks shorter in rural than in urban schools; the percentage of children five to twenty years of age enrolled in school is considerably lower; the investment in buildings and equipment is much less. For approximately 25 percent of the non-transported rural children, the distance between their homes and the schools of their residence districts is three times as great as is considered reasonable for urban children. Undoubtedly, distance and allied accessibility factors render regular attendance impossible or constitute a severe hardship for many thousands of rural children.

In 1926 slightly over half the public-school enrollment was in rural schools. It is estimated that the percentage will be somewhat lower when the figures for the 1930 census are available, as the exodus from farm to city continues.

IV. AVAILABILITY OF SECONDARY EDUCATION IN RURAL COMMUNITIES[6]

Numerous investigations have shown that comparatively few of the rural children of high-school age are actually obtaining a high-

---

[6] Mr. Gaumnitz is primarily responsible for this section on secondary education.

school education. A recent study by Gaumnitz (14:5) shows that in 1926 there were in the United States approximately 4,191,522 children between the ages of fifteen and eighteen who lived either on farms or in villages and towns of twenty-five hundred or fewer population. During the same year 1,079,086 of these children were enrolled in the public high schools located in these same population centers. These figures indicate that only about 26 percent of the rural children fifteen to eighteen years of age are enrolled in high school. When it is considered that there are in these schools a good many boys and girls who are either younger than fifteen years of age or older than eighteen, it is probable that this percentage is too high. Of course there are some rural children who are attending city high schools, but the study argues that the proportion so attending is comparatively small. By way of a comparison, estimates by Gaumnitz show that in urban communities more than 70 percent of the children of the group fifteen to eighteen years of age are enrolled in the high school.

Looking at the situation in another way, it is found that fully 53 percent of all children of this age-group and about 29 percent of those attending public secondary schools reside in these rural communities. It may, therefore, be seen that, although more than half of those of high-school age live in rural centers, less than a third of the high-school enrollment is recruited from these areas.

Another study by Gaumnitz (17:50f.) shows that for the United States as a whole only about 9.01 rural children are enjoying the benefits of a secondary education for each 100 children in rural elementary schools. In urban communities the ratio is 29.4 to 100, or more than three times as great. When the data for the individual states are considered, many show proportions of rural children in the high school much smaller than for the nation as a whole. Disparities between rural and urban communities also are found to be much greater. This is especially true in some of the southern states.

Windes (32:4) gathered data from six selected states to show the extent to which farm children and non-farm children attend the high school, and found the figures quoted in Table XIV.

He summarizes (32:5) as follows:

> In North Dakota and South Carolina, however, the differences in the percentages of farm and nonfarm groups enrolled [in high school] are so great that when all [the] States studied are thrown together the percentage of the farm groups enrolled is 15.5 less than for the non-

TABLE XIV.—COMPARISON OF PERCENTAGES OF FARM AND NON-FARM CHILDREN ENROLLED IN THE HIGH SCHOOL

	North Dakota	South Carolina	Montana	Oregon	Maine	New Hampshire
Percent of farm population fifteen to nineteen years of age enrolled.............	12.0	22.1	31.9	50.5	49.3	51.1
Percent of non-farm population fifteen to nineteen years of age enrolled......	42.8	33.7	32.6	46.5	42.3	49.0

farm group . . . on the whole, [they] are not participating in public high-school education to the extent that nonfarm children are; . . . farm boys, particularly, are not reached by high schools to the extent that other children are. . . Apparently we have a serious problem in providing high-school education for farm children, but we have a more serious problem of reaching the boy and especially the farm boy.

Of any given 100 children living in rural communities, about 26 were in the high school. Of these, about 16 continued to graduation, and 5 went to college. Similar estimates for urban communties show that about 71 of a given 100 children attended the high school. Of these, about 40 were retained until graduation and 13 went to college.

A study of Adams (1) of the enrollment and retention in the high school of rural children living in a community high-school district showed that, of 100 children enrolled in the first grade, 50 entered and 39 graduated from the eighth grade; 26 entered and 14 graduated from the high school; and 1.6 entered college. By comparison the study showed that, of 100 urban children living in the same school district, 61 entered and 52 graduated from the eighth grade; 44 entered and 40 graduated from high school; and 9.9 entered college. The community high-school district from which these data were gathered does not furnish transportation, although many of the children live from eight to ten miles from the school. The rural area was found to supply half the taxes to run the community high school and to have potentially about half of the high-school students.

A study by Burdge involving 245,000 employed boys in New York State shows (3:65) that large proportions of farm boys are eliminated from school from the grades, and very few complete the high school. Table XV presents comparative data for urban and farm boys. All

TABLE XV.—LAST GRADE COMPLETED, PERCENTAGE COMPLETING EACH GRADE

Types of Communities	Grade IV or under	Grade V	Grade VI	Grade VII	Grade VIII	High School Grades			
						IX	X	XI	XII
Cities over 2,500 population....	100	96.6	92.6	77.4	55.6	24.2	11.2	4.0	1.3
Villages under 5,000 population.	100	95.8	89.4	71.8	47.9	21.0	10.1	3.9	2.0
Farms, open country..........	100	96.8	89.3	71.0	41.5	12.4	5.6	1.9	0.7

these data tend to show that rural children are not reached by, or if reached do not continue to enjoy, the benefits of secondary education. This fact becomes strikingly apparent when comparisons are made between urban and rural situations. It is reasonable to believe that one of the chief reasons for this condition is the inaccessibility of high schools to children living in rural communities. Although there are no extensive studies to show adequately the status of rural children with regard to the accessibility of schools offering opportunities for secondary education, those available support the general observation that inaccessibility is one of the chief causes why these children are not attending the high school.

Vaughn (31: 30) studied the several factors which influence entrance into high school of rural elementary-school graduates. He found that, of 177 children graduating from the eighth grade in 1926, 66 entered the high school, but many of these did not remain long. The county from which these data were gathered was thirty miles across in its extreme diameter. There was but one high school in the county, and this was located near the mid-point of the eastern boundary. Many points in the county were fully thirty miles from the high school, and no transportation was furnished. Of the country children attending, the median child traveled 12.57 miles, and the average distance was 13.2 miles. The nearest 25 percent lived within 6.5 miles of the school, and the homes of the 25 percent living most remote were 17.7 or more miles away. The homes of children not in school were on an average 14.8 miles away. An arc 11.5 miles in radius had to be drawn to include the nearest 25 percent of the eighth-grade graduates not in school; the 25 percent of the non-attending group most remote from school lived beyond 17.4 miles from the school. Vaughn concludes that distance is one of the most important factors conditioning the enrollment and retention of rural children in high school.

Recent studies of representative counties in five states[7] gathered data to show the effect of distance upon the attendance of rural chil-

[7] United States Office of Education, Bulletin, 1930, No. 34.

dren in school. Data for 12,496 rural school children thirteen to twenty years of age were included in this study. It may be assumed that the majority of the children of this age group are attending schools of secondary grade. Of the 9,671 children of this age group who were not transported at public expense, 2,848, or 29.3 percent, lived one and one-half miles or more from the schools they attended, and 1,003, or 10.4 percent, lived three miles away or farther. Of the 2,825 children of this age group who were transported at public expense, 585, or 23 percent, lived five miles or more away, and 122 children, or 5 percent, lived ten miles or more away. If these conditions are representative of the nation as a whole, about eighty thousand of the non-transported children attending the rural high schools in the United States must travel three miles or more to school, and more than ten thousand of those transported at public expense must travel more than ten miles in order to attend these schools.

When non-transported children attending school and those not attending are compared with respect to the distances their homes are from school, data from 10 representative counties in Iowa showed that 20.5 percent of the former lived one and one-half or more miles from schools, whereas of the latter group 30.3 percent lived beyond this distance; 4.4 percent of those attending live more than three miles away, whereas 6.8 percent of those not in school lived beyond this distance. The data just cited include children of elementary-school age as well as those of secondary age. Indications are that, if data for secondary schools could be presented separately, the disparities between the distance enrolled and non-enrolled children live from their high schools would be much higher than those shown. The studies just referred to also show that among the children enrolled in rural high schools there are large numbers of high-school age who are living away from home in order to attend school. Indeed, a number of states are resorting to dormitory and boarding facilities as a means of bringing children in sparsely settled areas into contact with secondary education (20: 18ff.).

In order to get a concrete picture of the long distances between schools offering secondary work in rural communities for the nation as a whole, it will be of interest to cite data showing how many of these schools there are per given population unit. Generally speaking, in any home in which there are children of elementary-school age there also are apt to be children of high-school age. Rural children eligible for high school are probably scattered over as wide an area as are those attending elementary schools. Since rural schools must, by and large, be established and maintained with regard to distance rather than population, it may be argued that, unless transportation or other special provisions obtain, there should, to insure accessibility, be about as many rural high schools as elementary schools. Statistics show, however, that for the United States as a whole there are approximately 167 rural elementary schools for each ten thousand children in attendance in elementary schools, and another part of this study established the fact that, despite this large ratio, there are many rural elementary children who, if school attendance and retention are made the criteria, live excessive distances from their schools. If, then, for the nation we find only 12 schools offering work of a secondary level for each ten thousand attending elementary schools, we get some idea of the extreme distances rural children live from their secondary schools. Computations for individual states show that in some of the states only 4 or 5 schools offer high-school work for each ten thousand rural elementary children, while other states report as many as 35. Just what proportion of the rural high-school children are transported is not known. According to Drewes (9:5), however, a larger number of states have legislation compelling the transportation of elementary-school children living excessive distances from school than those making similar provisions for children attending secondary schools. States seem to feel a greater obligation in the matter of transporting elementary-school children, and in consequence it may be assumed that larger proportions of them are transported

Generally speaking, the states which rank high in the proportionate number of high schools provided in rural areas also rank high in the proportion of rural children attending secondary schools. When this relationship is computed statistically for the nation as a whole, a positive correlation of .724 is found with a probable error of ±.045. Troxel (29:175) studying this relationship for 13 selected states found a correlation of +.94. He concludes that "evidently the way to secure attendance of rural children at high school is to provide high schools near to the children's homes."

The Indiana Rural Education Survey Committee (19:26) attempted to find out whether "the provision of a greater number of high schools [in rural areas] results in a greater percent of the prospective high school population being enrolled in the school." It will be noted from Table XVI that, with one exception, as the average area and the average number of children of school age per high-school

TABLE XVI.—RELATION OF SIZE OF HIGH SCHOOL TO PERCENT OF ENROLLMENT IN INDIANA

Ratio of Twelfth-grade Enrollment to Eligibles	Number of Counties	Average Enumeration per High School	Average Square Miles per High School
Below 26.0...........................	9	955	85.30
26.0–37.99...........................	19	794	53.99
38.0–45.99...........................	19	669	45.46
46.0–56.99...........................	15	595	49.41
57.0 and above.......................	12	483	36.38

decrease, the enrollment in the twelfth grades increases. The report of the committee concludes as follows:

> Summarizing the results of the study, it should be pointed out that the rural counties of Indiana show a substantial relationship between this attendance factor and the adequacy with which high schools are provided when measured either on the basis of population or area.

The data thus far adduced seem to show beyond a reasonable doubt that comparatively few rural children of high-school age are enjoying the benefits of secondary education because schools of this level of education are either not available or so remote from their homes that large proportions of them are not reached. It has been shown that many of those who are reached do not remain in school. It is probable that the expense, effort, and hardships involved in overcoming the distance factor are so great as to discourage any desire to continue in school.

Methods of Meeting the Difficulties

The data just presented would leave the impression that the solution to the problem of bringing more of the rural children into contact with secondary education hinges upon the establishment of additional high schools nearer to the homes of the children. It seems to be an established fact that to bring the high schools closer to the rural child does result in attracting more of the educables. But many data are now also available to show that the type and quality of education provided in this way falls greatly short of our ideals for secondary education and that such as is thus provided is inordinately expensive. Generally speaking, the problem of providing a high grade of secondary education in sparsely settled communities is still unsolved.

A great many experiments are being tried. Larger units of high-school control, with complex schemes for providing special state aid and free tuition, are being experimented with on a wide scale. Investigations show that some form of consolidation or centralization of local school districts for purposes of effecting secondary education in rural communities is found in every state of the Union. But consolidation without a system of free transportation may actually become a hindrance to availability. Consolidation means fewer high schools placed farther apart, and if children must depend upon themselves or their parents for means of covering the distance to and from these schools, those living remotely will naturally find the school provided more rather than less inaccessible. The building of good roads and the prevalence of motor vehicles among rural folk may not safely be taken as reasons for locating high schools farther apart. In order to be truly accessible schools must be placed with regard to those children living in the area in question who must travel by the unimproved road and those whose parents either have no automobile or are unwilling or unable to transport their children. A great many errors have been committed in locating secondary schools on the assumption that all children have access to good roads and automobile transportation. Indeed, these errors have probably been an important factor in creating inaccessibility.

Provisions for transporting rural children to high schools, if the distances involved are excessive, are widespread. Troxel (29:22) found laws and regulations obtaining in 41 states definitely providing for the transportation of high-school children in consolidated and other districts; 12 states were found to have provisions for transporting those pupils who lived in one district and attended school in another. Of these, 3 states made transportation compulsory under certain conditions; 14 states granted state aid for transportation of high-school pupils; and 10 were reported as having provisions for board and lodging for high-school pupils attending in a district other than the one in which their homes are located.

Troxel also investigated the extent to which free tuition is being provided in the several states. He found (29:16) that over four-fifths of the states make definite provisions for the payment of tuition of pupils attending high schools from areas not in a high-school district; the pupils' home districts are most commonly required to assume the burden of paying tuition, but state aid for this purpose is provided in over a fifth of the states; completion of the elementary school by pupils is necessary in over one-fourth of the states to make him eligible to have tuition paid; in one-third of the states the amount of tuition is set by law or the limits are set by law; in one-fourth, the amount is determined by the cost of high-school education; and in approximately one-fifth of the states the amount is definitely left for local decision.

Provisions for the transportation of high-school pupils not living in a unit maintaining a high school obviously lag behind the provisions for paying tuition. There can be no doubt that the extension of transportation provisions would increase high-school availability. It is certain, however, that there are at present many areas where transportation is not feasible. Board and dormitory provisions or a system of correspondence lessons supplemented with a system of itinerant teachers seems the only solution for many of the most isolated rural children.

The Type and Quality of Rural Secondary Education

Turning our attention now to the type and quality of secondary education provided for rural children, it will be pertinent to consider the number and size of the high schools obtaining in rural communities and the implications of these findings for the quality of education provided. In a study already referred to, Gaumnitz showed the distribution of 14,143 schools of the United States located in centers of twenty-five hundred or fewer population and offering some work of secondary grade by enrollment and size of teaching staff. It was found that 3.6 percent of the rural high schools offering four years of high-school work enroll fewer than 20 children, and 22 precent enroll between 1 and 40 pupils each. The median enrollment of these schools was 65.3 and the average 79.9. Of the same four-year schools, 130 employ but one teacher each, and 1,195 employ but two teachers. The data clearly show that large numbers of the schools offering high-school work in rural communities are very small, both with respect to the number of children enrolled and the number of teachers employed. The same study also points out the weaknesses resulting from this smallness and some of the ways and means resorted to by communities in overcoming these weaknesses.

Two further factors must be considered as an index of the type of secondary-school opportunities made available to rural children. These are the amount of secondary education provided in terms of the length of the course in years and the length of the annual school term in days. The study just cited shows that nearly 78 percent of all America's high schools are located in rural communities. Of these, 9,926 operate as four-year high schools and 1,418 more as junior-senior high schools. Twenty percent offer either one-, two-, or three-year courses. It must be concluded that, of the schools made available to rural children, about one-fifth do not permit in the same school the completion of the four-year course—implying, of course, that the children attending these schools must travel longer distances if they wish to complete the secondary-school program.

TABLE XVII.—LENGTH OF TERM FOR WHICH STUDENTS ARE ENROLLED

LENGTH OF TERM	URBAN		RURAL	
	Number	Percent	Number	Percent
Students enrolled in schools with term of 160 days or less................	7,449	0.3	117,754	10.9
Students enrolled in schools with term of 161-180 days...................	1,074,206	40.3	824,057	76.4
Students enrolled in schools with term of 180 days or more...............	1,580,709	59.4	137,275	12.7
Total enrollment.................	2,662,364	100.0	1,079,086	100.0

Statistics presented in Table XVII show clearly that much larger percentages of rural than urban children attend high schools which are in session 160 days or fewer, and conversely much smaller percentages of rural children attend schools in session 180 days or more. Data regarding the length of term establish definitely that a smaller amount of secondary education is available to the rural child than to the city child.

SUMMARY FOR SECONDARY EDUCATION

This section dealing with the availability of high-school opportunities in rural communities has cited data to show that comparatively small proportions of rural children enter secondary schools and that still smaller proportions are retained to graduation; it has shown that one of the major reasons for their non-attendance is the inaccessibility of the high schools in rural areas; it has called attention to the fact that many of the rural high schools are very small and are thereby greatly limited in the quality of educational opportunity they can provide; and it has shown that term lengths are by and large shorter. It is clear that the country child is not now enjoying the benefits of secondary education to anywhere near the degree true of the city child. If we believe in equal educational opportunities for all American children, the problem of providing a satisfactory type of secondary education in sparsely settled communities is a challenging one, demanding much more study than has been given to it.

BIBLIOGRAPHY

1. ADAMS, JESSE B. *A Study of Rural Education in Harvard Community, McHenry County, Illinois, 1927.* (Master's Thesis on file in the Library of University of Wisconsin.)

2. BLANKENSHIP, ALBERT S. *Accessibility of Rural School Houses in Texas.* New York, 1926, 61 pp. (Teachers College, Columbia Univ. Contr. to Educ., No. 229.)

3. BURDGE, HOWARD G. *Our Boys: A Study of 245,000, Sixteen, Seventeen and Eighteen-year Old Employed Boys of New York State.* Albany, 1921, p. 65.

4. BURNHAM, ERNEST. *Two Types of Rural Schools.* New York, 1912. 23 pp. (Teachers College, Columbia Univ. Contr. to Education, No. 51.)

5. CAVINS, L. V., *et al. Survey of Education in West Virginia; Organization, Administration, and Finance.* Charleston, 1928. Vol. I.

6. COOKE, DENNIS H. "Availability of schools to Negro rural children in the southern states." (To appear in *Bull. Dept. Rural Educ., Nat. Educ. Assoc.* 1931.)

7. COOPER, RICHARD WATSON and COOPER, HERMAN. *Negro School Attendance in Delaware.* Newark, 1923. (Bureau of Education, Service Citizens of Delaware.)

8. COOPER, RICHARD WATSON and COOPER, HERMAN. *The One-Teacher School in Delaware; a Study in Attendance.* Newark, 1925. (Bureau of Education, Service Citizens of Delaware.)

9. DREWES, ARNOLD W. *Legal Status of Transportation of School Children in Forty-Eight States.* (Master's Thesis on file in the Library at Ohio State University.)

10. EELLS, WALTER CROSBY. "Graphic representation of distances children must walk to school." *American Sch. Board Jour.*, 77: 1928, p. 42.

11. FOOTE, J. M., and GRIFFITH, P. H. *The Schools of LaSalle Parish. Educational Survey Report.* Baton Rouge, 1929. (Bull. of the State Dept. of Educ., Louisiana, No. 155.)

12. FOOTE, J. M. and LEWIS, A. C. *An Administrative and Financial Study of the Tangipahoa Parish School System.* Baton Rouge, 1928. (Bull. of the State Dept. of Educ., Louisiana, No. 133.)

13. GALPIN, C. J. *Analysis of Migration of Population to and from Farms.* Washington, 1927. (U. S. Dept. of Agriculture Bur. of Agricultural Economics Circular, October, 1927.)

14. GAUMNITZ, W. H. *Comparative Status of Secondary Education in Rural and Urban Communities.* Washington, 1928. (U. S. Office of Education Rural School Leaflet, No. 44.)

15. GAUMNITZ, W. H. *Salaries and Salary Trends of Teachers in Rural Schools. Washington,* 1929, p. 36. (U. S. Office of Education Bulletin, No. 6.)

16. GAUMNITZ, W. H. *Some Comparative Statistics of Public School Education in Urban and Rural Communities.* Washington, 1928. (U. S. Office of Educ. Rural School Circular, No. 27.)

17. GAUMNITZ, W. H. *The Smallness of America's Rural High Schools.* Washington, 1930. On the press. (U. S. Office of Education Bulletin, No. 13.)

18. GILLETTE, JOHN MORRIS. *Rural Sociology.* New York, 1928, p. 146.

19. Indiana. *Report of the Indiana Rural Education Survey Committee.* Indianapolis, 1926, pp. 26-32.

20. LATHROP, EDITH A. *Dormitories in Connection with Public Secondary Schools.* Washington, 1922, p. 18. (U. S. Bureau of Educ. Bull., No. 12.)

21. McGILL, NETTIE P. *Children in Agriculture.* Washington, 1929, p. 417. (U. S. Dept. of Labor, Children's Bureau Publication, No. 187.)

22. Missouri. *Report of State Survey Commission.* Jefferson City, 1929.

23. National Education Association. "Salary scales in city school systems." *Research Bulletin of the N.E.A.,* 7:1929, 115.

24. O'SHEA, M. V. *Public Education in Virginia.* Richmond, 1928.

25. PHILLIPS, FRANK M. *Statistics of City School Systems,* 1927-28. Washington, 1929. (U. S. Office of Educ. Bull. No. 34.)

26. REAVIS, GEORGE H. *Factors Controlling Attendance in Rural Schools.* New York, 1920, 69 pp. (Teachers College, Columbia Univ. Contri. to Educ., No. 108.)

27. REEDER, WARD G. *The Fundamentals of Public School Administration.* New York, 1930, pp. 309, 377.

28. Texas. *Texas Educational Survey,* 1924-25. Austin, 1925. (Texas Educational Survey Commission, Vol. I.)

29. TROXEL, O. L. *State Control of Secondary Education.* Baltimore, 1928, pp. 170-179. (Univ. Research Monographs, No. 4.)

30. U. S. Department of Labor. *The Welfare of Children in the Cotton-Growing Areas of Texas.* p. 8. (Children's Bureau Publication, No. 134.)

31. VAUGHN, W. H. Lawrence County, Kentucky. *Rural School Graduates in High School.* 1927. (Master's Thesis on file in the Library of George Peabody College for Teachers.)

32. WINDES, E. E. *High School Education of the Farm Population in Selected States.* Washington, 1925. 24 pp. (U. S. Bur. of Educ. Bull. No. 6.)

33. WORKS, GEORGE A. *Texas Educational Survey Report; Organization and Administration.* Austin, 1925. Vol. I, p. 224.

CHAPTER IV

THE RURAL ELEMENTARY CURRICULUM

FANNIE W. DUNN
Associate Professor of Education
Teachers College, Columbia University, New York City

Any curriculum in fact, whatever it may be in print, is the product of three factors, or sets of factors: the philosophy upon which it is based; the abilities and interests, native or acquired, of the pupils to be educated; and the conditions, within or without the school, which postitively or negatively affect the realization of desired ends. Characteristic differences in any of these respects inevitably result in corresponding differences in the actual curriculum, and call for appropriate differences in the printed curriculum. This chapter attempts: (1) to summarize available information on the rural status in respect to these three factors; (2) to indicate the type of curriculum provision which is being made for rural schools; and (3) to suggest investigations and curriculum revision which appear to be needed.

I. THE RURAL STATUS

1. As to the Philosophy Underlying the Rural Curriculum

a. With Regard to the Aim of Education. National attention was focussed upon the rural school as a distinct educational situation by the report of President Roosevelt's Commission on Country Life in 1909. But the fact that country children were being increasingly disadvantaged by the growing difference between educational provision for country and city had been recognized for at least ten years before that time by rural educational leaders of the day, outstanding among whom was Kern. The dominant purpose which controlled him and his followers and co-workers may be gathered from his own statements in his book, *Among Country Schools* (17),[1] the first book ever written on the rural school in this country.

---

[1] Numbers in parentheses conjoined with citations refer to the references, by number and pages, listed at the end of this chapter.

"My educational decalogue for school officers and teachers" he declared, "may be reduced to one simple commandment, namely, Thou shalt enrich and enlarge the life of the country child." He quoted Hanus to express his idea of education: "Education cannot be limited to the school arts—reading, writing, ciphering. It must acquaint the pupil with the material and social environment in order that every avenue of knowledge may be opened to him, and every incipient power receive appropriate cultivation"; and in accord with this theory he attempted to provide for his country children opportunity for participation in a rich variety of educational experiences, through the school garden, indoor art and decoration, school socials, school libraries, excursions, manual training, and his farm boys' experimental club. It seemed to him a distressing thing that farm people should find it necessary to move to the city in order to secure such educational opportunities for their children.

The Country Life Commission, which reported in 1909, called attention to the economic handicaps and deficiencies of agriculture as an occupation, as well as the inadequancy of the schools available for farmers' children, stated the underlying problem of country life to be "to develop and maintain on our farms a civilization in full harmony with the best American ideals," and declared that

> upon the development of this distinctly rural civilization rests ultimately our ability, by methods of farming requiring the highest intelligence, to continue to feed and clothe the hungry nations; to supply the city and metropolis with fresh blood, clean bodies, and clear brains that can endure the strain of modern urban life; and to preserve a race of men in the open country that, in the future as in the past, will be the stay and strength of the nation in time of war and its guiding and controlling spirit in time of peace.[2]

Here is to be seen a distinct change of emphasis. The conception expressed by Kern and Hanus focussed upon the child, and sought primarily the development of his personality, with spiritual values set high. But in this statement of the Commission the chief concern was with the adult society of rural America, and with this society not primarily as an end to be served, but as a means to the welfare of the nation in general, and of the metropolitan sections in particular.

---

[2] For a reprint of the Report of the Commission of Country Life, and of President Roosevelt's Message transmitting it to the Congress, see *Rural America*, January, 1929.

Thus, during the second decade of the century, there developed
and prevailed a strong sentiment, with its roots partly in genuine love
and appreciation of country life, and partly in a belief that the nation's economic well-being was threatened by a decrease in the pro-
ducers of raw materials, that farm children should remain on the
farm, for their own sake and that of the nation as well; and it was
accordingly held to be an outstanding purpose of rural education,
elementary as well as secondary, to predispose farm children to farm
life and prepare them specifically for it.

As early as 1916, however, strong reactions against this philosophy
began to be uttered; and for the past decade the position more commonly held, by rural and urban educators alike, is, as stated by Brim,
that "the rural elementary-school problem is merely one phase of
the problem of education in a democracy" (4:27).

Thus, in 1921, the Department of Rural Education of the National
Education Association declared, in its adopted 'platform' (24:41f.)
that "the standard of educational product is the same, country, and
city"; that "the general ends of public school education are the same
everywhere"; and that, since "the school is an educational institution, supplementing the natural education provided by home experiences,....rural and urban schools, based on different home experiences,
will require some differentiation in content to meet their common
ends."

This point of view, expressed by the rural education group, was
subsequently stated by the Department of Superintendence of the
National Education Association in the *Third Yearbook* (23:23):

> In rural districts, the objectives of elementary education are not
> different from those in the city, but the means of reaching them and
> materials available differ from those in large centers of population.
> . . . The ultimate purpose of elementary education is the same every-
> where, but the content and method through which it is achieved varies.

Another statement, by the rural group, of the same position, was
made in 1926 in the preliminary report of the subcommittee of the
Rural Department of the N. E. A., the Committee on Rural School
Curricula (23a:197ff.):

> The principal difference between rural and urban curricula is one
> of environment. . . The curriculum must draw freely upon the ex-
> periences of the child, upon the educational resources of the community,
> and must supply whatever the environment lacks to round out the life

experiences of an American child. The elementary rural curriculum will differ, therefore, in content, in point of approach, and in method somewhat from the urban curriculum, but it should be emphasized that its aim is identical, viz., to make the highest type of American citizen.

The earlier position, however, is still more or less an influential determiner of the curriculum in certain situations, whether because the conviction is explicitly held or because it persists as an uncritical mind set.

b. With Regard to the Nature and Means of the Educative Process. Undemocratic and mistaken as the effort to predispose all rural children to the agricultural vocation may have been (and the present economic situation clearly indicates that it was mistaken), nevertheless, owing to the persistence of the liberal concept of rural education which Kern had first expressed, certain educational practices which it fostered were in definite harmony with the "foundations of curriculum making" of this Society. The beliefs "that country children be taught in terms of their own lives"; that "the course of study... should conform more closely to the environment of the child;" that farm-life experience should be made "the starting point of elementary rural education;" that we should "begin with the child's world ... and use the common objects, phenomena, and activities as means of education" (4:7-23), led to the development in numerous scattered rural schools, between 1910 and 1920, of genuinely social and dynamic education. It was not in the use of the environment, but in overstressing the immediate environment, and overemphasizing the vocational aspects and the adult, economic interests, that evil lay.

In recent years a philosophy of vital education has begun to find expression in state surveys and in state courses of study, which in general furnish the curriculum used by rural schools. According to an unpublished study by Miss Langvick, of the Federal Office of Education:

> Statements of philosophy of education and principles basic to construction of curriculum are given in the prefaces or introductory chapterms of seven courses. An analysis of these statements reveals the fact that education is . . . conceived of as a dynamic process. Children are no longer regarded as passive recipients but as "dynamic, self-reacting, self-determining individuals." Growth is the accepted end of education.

This statement indicates that comparatively few state educational departments have as yet avowed the philosophy it expresses. It may, in fact, be said with little fear of contravention that the conception of education underlying the majority of even the recent state courses of study is the mastery of subject matter specifically set out to be learned. There appears, however, to be increasing recognition, or at least verbal avowal, of varied activities as a means of learning and of child interest, rather than the logic of the subject matter, as the organizing principle.

2. As to the Abilities and Interests of the Pupils to Be Educated

a. Abilities. Not only educational aims and ideals, but educational potentialities as well, affect the curriculum. A belief that the rural child is mentally inferior to the national average has been widely held and frequently voiced in recent years. An important basis for this belief has been found in the scores made on standard tests. Sorokin and Zimmerman (30: 234ff.), summarizing the conclusions from "more than thirty of the best studies in the field," from both the United States and England, involving all ages and grades of school children, and all types of farming and city population, state that "the greater proportion of the tests place the rural children below the urban;" that, with a few minor exceptions, "all these studies agree that the intelligence of farmer-peasants and their children is lower than the urban averages;" and that "the greater proportion of the investigators seem convinced that the differences in results is due to difference in native ability of the two populations."

These two authors, however, do not accept these conclusions at their face value, criticizing them on the grounds of lack of clear demarcation of schools, bias in the tests, failure to take into consideration "the enormous differences in educational and cultural opportunities," and other items.

Studies of retardation and acceleration in school, of persistence in school, and of men of eminence are also carefully and critically summarized in relation to this question, after which the authors state (30: 261):

> This study will have achieved its purpose if it has shown the doubt and unreliability which exist concerning the methods, the tools, and the results of most of these studies of comparative rural and urban intelligence. We are not yet ready to reach sure and definite conclusions. . . Last, but not least, whatever may be the [operation] of urban selection upon the native intelligence of rural people, or the farmer-peasant class, the rural groups are holding and maintaining their in-

telligence with much greater persistence than the lower urban classes. If there is any validity to the theories that the declines of civilization are functionally connected with the process of draining and exploitation of the intelligence of the masses by the upper urban groups, the farmer-peasant class responds much more slowly to this process, is more persistent in keeping its leaders, and hence operates to slow down this process and to maintain the stability and position of a society for a much longer period. Here, as in many other social phenomena, the position of the farmer-peasant class is considerably better than it is credited in popular and pseudo-scientific beliefs.

The conclusion of Sorokin and Zimmerman as to the indeterminateness of the question of relative rural-urban intelligence is similar to that reached by Shimberg (29), who compared the scores of rural children on an information test standardized for classification purposes on urban children, with scores of urban children on a closely similar test standardized on rural children; and found the inferiority of rural children as indicated by the former to be matched by a corresponding showing of inferiority for urban children as indicated by the latter. Her conclusions were that our test returns to date prove, not the superiority of one group or the other, but merely that the groups are different; and that so far we have devised no measures whereby we can make valid comparisons between distinctly different groups.

A study begun by Baldwin and finished by his associates (2a: 232ff.) in the Child Welfare Research Station of Iowa University points to the probable effect of nurture on intelligence as measured by our tests. According to this study, no significant difference was found when rural and city babies, matched in age, were compared. At ages five and six, however, the farm children began to show inferiority to the city groups. The discussion of the possible causes of this deficiency emphasizes in particular the factor of language, but suggests other factors in the rural environment or experience.

Indications from the studies here reported all point in the same direction. Rural children generally make poorer showing on intelligence tests than do urban. This, however, may be due to an amount still in debate to factors other than native ability, as, for example, differences in experience, especially differences in language experiences and stimuli, and more especially deficiencies in the one-teacher schools in provision for language development.

Since certain of the differences, notably those in language, may be said to indicate definite mental malnutrition, clear implications for curriculum-making appear, because whether the condition is attributed to nature or nurture, the child who comes to school with a language deficiency is not equipped for content or rate of learning identical with the child of normal language abilities. Prescription of a specified number of books to be read in the first grade, if the number prescribed has been determined through experience with normally equipped children, must set an impossible goal for the under-equipped. Oral language appears to require an important place in the primary program, and Rugg's suggested factor for a child-centered school, ''Remove the ban from speech,'' appears especially desirable to follow in the rural school.

b. Interests of Rural Elementary-School Pupils. It has been said that the steps necessary in moving toward educational goals are ''dictated by the character of the child's interests, needs,....and experience, as well as by the larger demands of society'' (2:12). If the rural child's interests, needs, and experiences are to any extent different from those of the urban child, to that extent differentiation of the steps by which the two groups reach a common education goal would appear to be required.

Statements cited in this chapter from both the Department of Rural Education and the Department of Superintendence of the National Education Association show that each of these bodies recognizes a sufficient degree of difference in experiences to warrant the opinion that the curricula in the two situations will require some differentiation in both content and method.

Various statements of the nature of the differences believed to exist have been made. Brim (3:52-63) listed the following as handicaps of the rural child: the tendency, which Galpin has termed 'ruralism,' to class consciousness and a spirit of group isolation on the part of the rural population; the limited opportunity of the rural child for number, variety, and equality of social contacts; the conservatism of the rural social group of which the child is a part, its critical attitude toward the new, and its tendency to resist change; the retarded nature of rural standards and practices in the realm of sanitation and hygiene; deficient appreciation on the part of rural people of the place of play and recreation in normal living, and corresponding inadequacies in provision; shortages in reading material in homes and communities, little stimulus for rural children to read in the practice of parents and friends, and unsatisfactory provision for reading in the way of a suitable place, sufficient light, warmth, quietness, leisure time, and reserve energy; and poverty of the rural situation in opportunities for the development of artistic and musical taste and ability and for intelligent vocational choice.

Few significant studies are available. Most studies, as might be expected, are limited as to the area sampled, so that it is impossible to tell whether their findings are true of rural situations in general. Evidence cited by Brim, besides certain statements from rural specialists, Galpin, H. P. Douglass, Gillette, Vogt, and W. H. Wilson, includes a study by J. O. Rankin, on "Reading-Matter in Nebraska Farm Homes," covering 1,338 homes in eight selected counties. Brim (3:61) summarized the pertinent results as follows:

> Newspapers reached approximately 92 percent of the rural homes studied. No figures are given to indicate the quality. The author states, however, that the great bulk of those found were (1) county weeklies, or (2) dailies published in Omaha, Lincoln, or Kansas City. About 76 percent of the rural homes receive farm papers. . . . Women's magazines came next in the list, but are found in only approximately 24 percent of the homes. General magazines found their way into a still smaller number of homes, only 18 percent reporting such reading-matter. Concerning literature for children the writer says: "Perhaps the most startling fact revealed by this study is the almost total absence of periodicals intended primarily for the younger members of the household." The juvenile periodical is reaching only 4 percent of the Nebraska farm owner's homes and about half that proportion of tenants. Library service to rural people in Nebraska is meager. Less than two-fifths have access to public library facilities. Even such facilities are evidently not fully used because not over 5 percent of the rural population report the use of library books.

That the condition with regard to library service in Nebraska is at least as favorable as in the majority of predominantly agricultural states is indicated by a report on *People without Public Library Service,* made public by the American Library Association in 1926. The total number of persons lacking this service was given as 45,069,897, of which 42,152,291 were rural. A total of 1,135 counties were unprovided with library facilities. Eight states had library provision in every county, including all the New England States and all the North Atlantic except Maryland, with two counties unprovided, and Pennsylvania, with five. Outside these two groups, Iowa alone had no counties without this service, though Indiana had only one.

Other studies of reading facilities and habits in rural homes are so scattering as to be of little general significance, but studies of periodical reading in farm homes in Oklahoma (11), of reading matter in two Connecticut rural towns, of reading material in rural areas of South Carolina (14), and of the magazines found in rural homes of Calloway County, in western Kentucky (16), all agree in substance with the Nebraska study, especially as to the lack of adequate provision for children's reading. Minor though each of them is, their total evidence definitely points to an important lack widely found in rural children's out-of-school educational opportunities, and to the especial necessity for the provision of reading suited to their age, interests, and abilities.

However, in spite of the fact, according to Edith A. Lathrop, that more emphasis than ever before is being placed upon the improvement of library facilities in rural schools, in only a few states as yet do they approximate adequacy, and in some the lack is very great (18). Where libraries are found, they are often ill-selected and serve neither the ages and abilities of the children in the schools nor the important purposes of the curriculum.

According to the bulletin just referred to, there is lack of research studies dealing with the subject of libraries for rural schools and definite information is needed regarding the type of library books available and the extent to which they are used. It is impossible to make authenticated generalizations on this matter. What data are available indicate that conditions vary greatly from state to state, county to county, and probably often from school to school.

Besides library provision, the field of health has been more extensively investigated than any other phase of farm life importantly related to the rural elementary curriculum. These studies, too, are scattered and fragmentary, and those which are available seldom reveal types of conditions to which the curriculum must be adjusted. Physicians and hospital facilities are recognized to be inadequate in numbers in rural communities, but what can the elementary school do to meet this lack? Surveys commonly reveal greater incidence of physical defects, such as malnutrition, spinal curvature, eye-defects, defective tonsils, and heart disease, among rural children than among urban, but better systems of health service, rather than differences in curriculum, appear to be indicated here. Although city children's defects may be less in number, they are alike in kind, and such education as will develop preventive or protective knowledge, habits, and attitudes, is required in both urban and rural curricula.

Little genuine knowledge is available as to habits, attitudes, or information which may characteristically need improving among rural people, and more specifically among rural children. A few investigations which do seek such information as this are summarized in the paragraphs which follow.

A South Carolina study (14) points out lack of understanding, or unsatisfactory practice, with regard to fresh air and sunshine, sleep requirements for children, care of the teeth, regularity of meal hours, and especially with regard to diet, including general adequacy, consumption of milk, use of white potatoes, vegetables, and fruits, and provision for necessary vitamins.

A field study of the elementary-school children of two rural Massachusetts towns (9) showed only 15 percent in the one town and 24 percent in the other to have diets suited to their needs.

According to information assembled by the American Child Health Association, in 142 small towns and cities in three states and one Canadian province surveyed between January, 1926, and July, 1927, grave potential dangers lurk in the milk supply of these communities. The "problem of the small town" was stated (8) to be "to awaken its citizens to the need for the production of clean milk rendered safe by pasteurization." Here is place for the development in the school children of the small town of appropriate knowledge and attitudes.

That the facts here presented are meager is readily granted. That they are the type of facts which are essential to the best adjustment of health curricula to rural school children will probably not be disputed.

In the use of leisure time many observers see a shortage in the rural child's environment. That this shortage is a fact in the field of reading has been demonstrated, at least in so far as library availability is concerned. A condition and attitude with regard to play, which if not general, is at least very common, has been expressed by Carl Taylor (31: 361) in the following words:

> The work attitude which makes all play negative and wasteful activity, and the Puritan attitude which makes all pleasure sin, have slowed up the play movement in the country more than any other thing. Their lingering pressure still keeps many rural communities negative,

or at best passive, on the problem of introducing organized recreation into rural life.

On the other hand, the same sociologist says (31:196) :

The child on the farm can have its pets, its own playground, its own small work projects, and the range of the open fields . . . The opportunity of the rural child to get the joy of being discoverer, explorer, and inventor during childhood is unique. . . The range of the farm is his, the tools, implements, and animals are his to use, and observe, and handle. If all these things can be given meaning to him as he experiences contact with them, the opportunity for personality development is unexcelled elsewhere in life.

These, however appear to Taylor to be as yet only potentialities, for he states (31:372) :

The problems of the rural home in the field of play are: (a) the gaining of more leisure time; (b) the development of an appreciation on the part of parents of the values of play in developing the character habits and personality of their children; (c) supplying good reading; (d) the necessity for relieving the monotony and restricted contacts of isolated farm home life; and (e) the equipment of the home and yard with play and game equipments.

Here is clear intimation of a duty of the school, through its curriculum, to supply serious lacks if Taylor is correct in his estimation of the recreatory provision in rural homes. That this lack does exist, and that leadership by the school is important if the lack is to be supplied, at least so far as children old enough to require group recreation are concerned, is confirmed by several studies. According to Brunner (6: 200-214), the necessary leadership is not yet afforded in agricultural villages. A two-year survey, May, 1923, to May, 1925, secured information for about 140 such villages, with population ranging between two hundred fifty and twenty-five hundred, in the Middle Atlantic, South, Far West, and Middle West states, and also for the open country area immediately surrounding these villages. It was found that the villages appeared to have provided adequately in the way of social organizations of various types for their adults, but that "only the exceptional village has taken its young people seriously into account."

Excluding the church and school organizations, the former negligible, only 7 percent of the membership of the social organizations of the communities were minors, although boys and girls from ten to twenty make up one-fifth of the population of these villages. . . . For all the young people in vacation time there was 'nothing doing' in the average village (5:92).

In 1926 the Institute of Social and Religious Research undertook a study of the rural work of the Y.M.C.A., Y.W.C.A., Boy Scouts, Girl Scouts, and Campfire Girls. As a result of the investigation (10) it was frankly acknowledged that the genuinely rural and especially open-country areas were receiving very meager attention.

> The field as a whole is not really occupied. . . Much of the work labelled 'rural' is really suburban, and when the option is present, the agencies show a strong tendency to cultivate the suburban at the expense of rural communities in the same area. . . The rural communities frequently present the tragical spectacle of an impoverished life for youth. . . Their need of something for boys and girls and their inability to provide a satisfactory solution is the most outstanding and pathetic revelation of the study.

Several interesting investigations of play interests or activities of rural children have been made by Lehman, who compared 15,061 children in four Kansas cities, and 2,175 children in one-teacher schools of three Kansas counties by the method of submitting to them lists of play activities to be checked.

On the basis of one investigation (19) Lehman states:

> The rural districts included in this study were not found to be so barren of play opportunity as might have been imagined. The play behavior of the country children was found to differ from that of town children, but the number of play activities engaged in does not differ by any great amount. In general, it was found that the younger country children, those of ages eight and a half to ten and a half, engage in slightly fewer play activities than town children, but that the older country children, those of ages fourteen and a half to fifteen and a half, engage in slightly more play activities than town children of the same chronological age and sex. . . The conclusion seems to be that town life offers certain recreative opportunities to the child that rural life does not offer, but that country life likewise offers its own peculiar opportunities, including certain opportunity for natural, spontaneous self-expression that tends to be eliminated by town life.

The fairly consistent tendency also found by Lehman (19, 20, 21) for certain expressive activities, as carpentering, drawing, paper-cutting, singing, and whistling, to persist to a later age level in rural than in urban children may perhaps be explicable by competition, in the case of the city children, from a range of other potential leisure-time occupations. On the other hand, there is a possibility that we have here a sad commentary on the type of instruction offered by the city schools, in which, for a number of years, drawing, singing, and manual arts have rather generally been taught, whereas little if any attention has been given to these subjects in the rural schools. Since there is some tendency to-day to extend the rural curriculum to make definite provision for these arts, it would seem opportune to examine critically the content and methods employed in the city schools of Lehman's study before adopting them without modification in the rural schools.

Another study indicative of difference in interests of rural and urban children has been made by Professor Palmer, who during the past ten years, through the *Cornell Rural School Leaflets,* has collected the questions which rural children ask in the field of science. During the four-year period, 1922-25, slightly more than 60 percent of the questions he received were in the field of zoölogy; about 22 percent in botany; 6 percent in inanimate nature; and 7 percent in agriculture. Studies by Pollock and Washburne which Palmer cites appear to indicate that the interests of urban children lie rather in the field of the physical sciences, with physics leading in each case, and with zoölogy and botany at the end of each list. Recognizing certain possible unduly influencing factors in each of the studies, including his own, Palmer (26) says:

> The quotation of any number of authorities would not settle the question as to whether or not there were appreciable differences in the science interests of rural and urban children. It only emphasizes the fact that those who have written on the matter do not agree. . . This matter would seem worthy of more attention than it has received. . . My experience with rural children indicates that their interests are much more strongly in the field of biology than are the interests of city children as indicated by the records of others.

This statement of Palmer might well be applied to all the items of interest, rural and urban, discussed in the preceding pages. The evidence there presented is neither intensive nor particularly extensive. If it suggests possibilities deserving investigation, of differences between rural and urban children in interests, needs, and experiences, it will have served its purpose in this chapter. As matters now stand, although practical observation and experience have built up a widespread conviction among rural educators that significant differences in these respects do exist, scientific research has not made a respectable beginning of validating this conviction or of affording guidance for its expression through curricula.

3. As to Conditions, Within and Without the School, Which Affect Realization of Desired Ends

Certain environmental conditions, which affect the possibility of realizing ends desired of the curriculum or the means whereby these ends may be realized, have been included for economy of space in the preceding section. Opportunities of rural children for first-hand experience with animals, wild and domestic; plants useful, beautiful, or injurious; rocks; soils; machines; tools of many kinds; a variety of household occupations; and for genuine responsibilities not too burdensome, in the affairs of home and farm, afford a highly favorable condition for the employment of the school. The existence of such activities is fairly obvious. No more data can be given to prove it than has already been presented. Whether its potentialities are realized by the school depends to a large extent upon the adjustment of curriculum, including in some cases selection and in others sequence of educational units and of activities within units.

The provision of educational materials, illustrated in the preceding section in respect to school-library facilities, is an inevitably limiting factor. Little information is available as to the nature and extent of educative equipment in rural schools in general. All rural educators have seen some schools practically barren, and others with generous supplies of books, play equipment, musical instruments, and materials and tools for a variety of constructive activities. In recent years 'standard school' requirements issued by state educational departments have shown distinct advance in the increased emphasis given to educative equipment. The Foreword of a recent bulletin from the State Education Department of New York (25) sets a high standard:

> A standard teaching plant is one that provides for the full development of the child—his mind, his body and his spirit. . . Our school buildings and grounds should be as attractive as those of the best rural homes, designed for health, beauty, and comfort. In each school we want a well-trained teacher provided with every teaching help that will keep pupils happy, healthy and profitably busy; we want this teacher to use modern methods and modern tools.

This bulletin, besides the traditional maps, globe, and dictionary, lists as 'Desirable Equipment' phonographs; arithmetic practice sets; library equipment, including among other items a reading table, vertical file, library supplies; a library of reference material, general and recreatory reading, periodicals, and supplementary readers; and "a well-chosen supply of material for educative seatwork;'' and provides an additional list of 'Other Desirable Equipment,' including ''hot lunch equipment ($20 up); science equipment ($5 up); and playground equipment ($15 up).'' Doubtless numerous rural schools in New York State will shortly, if not already, be equipped with practically all the materials recommended in this bulletin. Others will possess useful equipment not here listed. One rural county in the state is said to have equipped all its schools with radios, which are to-day found in other states also in an increasing number even of one-teacher schools.

It is evident that the type and richness of curriculum possible in schools thus supplied far exceeds that which can be offered where the only books are the single texts in the children's hands, where materials and tools are limited to those which children and teachers can beg, borrow, or raise money to purchase, and the schoolroom is crowded to the walls with desks and seats. Yet the potentiality, already mentioned, of the rural environment and the rural home-life still remains. Curricula for rural schools desirably should be adjusted to all the educational experiences and materials available, whether within or without the school. Other important conditions, characteristic of many rural schools, are short terms and the one-teacher organization. These are further discussed in the next section.

II. The Present Rural Curriculum

Whereas cities in increasing numbers make their own courses of study, the state course is still the chief, and usually the only, curriculum provided for rural schools. Occasionally counties issue courses. These may be as elaborate as any city course, as in the case of Baltimore County, Maryland, or of Cuyahoga County, Ohio; or they may be only a prescriptive outline to be used in preparation for the county superintendent's monthly examinations. It is in the main to the state courses, however, that we must go to discover the printed curriculum of the rural schools.

On the other hand, the printed curriculum may not be followed in its entirety, either because individual schools or groups of schools adjust and enrich it in terms of the 'interests, needs, and experiences' of their pupils, or because the teacher is unable to provide all the instruction it outlines. It is necessary, therefore, to consider also notable variations from the printed course, in either direction, if we are to apprehend the real curriculum of the schools.

1. The Nature of State Courses of Study, and Their Adjustment to Rural Schools

State courses of study can be found representing practically every level, from the bare prescription of textbook material to be covered, to a type of organization equalling that of superior city courses. The following more detailed statements are based upon examination of practically every state course published in the United States in the last five years—no course cited is dated prior to 1925.

To a notable extent the textbook is still a chief curriculum determiner. One state course, for example, declares specifically: "The elementary course and teachers' manual is as a matter of fact based primarily on the textbooks selected for use in the elementary schools." Another states, "This revision is made necessary because of recent new adoptions of textbooks in some subjects." Several other courses consist of monthly outlines, by pages and by topics, of a specified textbook.

In practically all the courses, as was stated in the first section of this chapter, mastery of information and skills appears to be the dominating aim. Occasionally, the desired items of information are specified to an amazing detail, as in a certain state course which prescribes the following: "New Jersey. Simply teach *the sentence* 'New Jersey was at first part of New Netherlands, then of New York, then it was purchased by the Quakers, and finally became a separate colony'." Yet the foreword to teachers in this course states: "The principal feature of the course is the attempt to vitalize the work in each subject." Thus does practice lag behind principle.

It has not been possible to make a sufficiently exhaustive study of state courses of study to determine accurately or completely the nature and extent of their specific adaptations in content or approach to the interests, experiences, and needs characteristic of the state and especially to those of the rural sections and rural children of the state. The investigation that was possible has discovered little of either type, except in the obviously distinctive subject of state history and civics, and to a somewhat less extent in home geography. The general impression received was that the courses are but little better adjusted to specific conditions than are the textbooks, which have been shown practically to constitute the curriculum in many instances.

Six county courses and six courses from states with a large rural population, selected because of high rankings assigned to them by a curriculum research bureau, were carefully examined for particular adaptations to rural schools. In choice of subject matter or approach to subject matter very little such adaptation was found in most of them. This is frankly recognized in the preface to the *Baltimore County Course:* "Although this course is prepared mainly for the suburban schools, it will also prove a valuable aid to the rural schools, after certain eliminations and additions are worked out in the rural-school groups with the supervisor during the Institute and in group meetings."

An example of differentiation between courses for rural and urban schools is found in Minnesota in the case of the course in agriculture. The differentiation in this case is basically one of aim. The first aim stated for the 'graded' schools is "to develop an understanding and appreciation of agriculture as an industry," the corresponding aim for the 'ungraded' schools being "To develop an interest in and appreciation of farming and farm life so that children may come to realize the possibilities and opportunities of farming as an occupation." The emphasis for farm children is stated to be upon "improved methods in production and distribution of farm products." The city course stresses appreciation and consumption; the rural, vocational skills. The differentiation is a clear illustration of the philosophy which has been described above as more or less dominant between 1910 and 1920. To one who to-day repudiates this philosophy, the 'graded' course here outlined is superior for the 'ungraded' schools to that prescribed for them, in that it is more nearly based upon interests and needs of children of elementary-grade age, while it utilizes their experience as much as the other course.

Both because of its unusual provision for local adaptation, and because of its suggestive nature, a bulletin *Teaching Wyoming History by Counties,* written by a professor in the state university and published in 1926 by the Wyoming Education Department, deserves especial mention. This bulletin does not attempt to outline a course of study, but gives lists of reference books, methods of obtaining historical material, and for each county, items of especial interest and significance. With this information it becomes practical for a wide-awake teacher, or even a group of wide-awake children, to develop units of curriculum appropriate to their own interests and needs. Similar bulletins might be provided in other subjects, geography, arithmetic, elementary science, and perhaps even literature. With a basis of expert guidance of this type in a variety of fields, state and county courses could be developed which in adaptation of content and approach would be outstandingly superior to practically all that are now available.

Some states adapt their courses to the poorly trained teacher and to deficient provision of supervision, by the lockstep device of month-by-month prescription of subject matter to be covered, and by 'monthly reviews' or examinations, sent out from the county superintendent's office, to check on the prescribed work. This is specifically stated in one state course, which claims to be "arranged with special reference to the needs of the rural schools," and which describes these needs in terms of pupils moving about and teachers frequently changed, frequently untrained, and often having never attended a rural school, so that "without a plan of organization definitely worked out, the schools are in a chaotic condition." A 'fixed and definite course' is provided, organized by months, and the schools are tested as just indicated. The monthly review is declared to be "one of the best means" of supervision at the superintendent's command. With the present rapidly rising standards for certification and the present surplus of teachers, it seems worth considering whether other and better means may not be devised of protecting the rural child's educational opportunity.

A common characteristic of rural schools, obviously demanding curriculum adjustment, is the short school term, averaging 156 days for the rural schools of the United States, and frequently no more than six months in many states. Yet not a single state has adjusted its course of study for the six months' school; most states, on the contrary, organize the work upon the length of term common in their city schools. A few organize it for an eight months' term, and then offer the schools with shorter terms such helpful suggestions as:

> Schools that do not have an eight months' term can easily arrange the work to fit conditions. Schools that have only seven months' terms

may by doing extra work complete the work of a grade in the school year.

It is hoped that schools with shorter terms may be able to abbreviate the work more, or to spread over two terms the work outlined for one year. The latter policy is recommended.

Even with this short term [eight months] the majority of the pupils should complete the work requirements [nine months] of the grade.

Another state with a nine months' curriculum provides for seven months' schools that 'credit' for two additional months may be received by pupils completing a seven months' term and in addition completing required work in a boys' and girls' club, completing at home during vacation a prescribed course in agriculture and home economics, or completing during vacation a prescribed reading-circle course and passing an examination.

Of the first of these four suggested adaptations it may be asked, if the work can easily be arranged, why does not the state course provide that arrangement? Of the second, could not the state offer helpful plans for abbreviation, or a more economical adjustment than spending two years on every grade-level? Of the third, if a *bare* 'majority' is meant, will not tremendous waste in retardation result; and what, moreover, of the six months' schools in the same state? And of the fourth, what of children too young for boys' and girls' club work, for "a prescribed course in home economics and agriculture," or for "a prescribed reading-circle course?" And, if so drastic a plan as allotting two-ninths of the whole elementary-school course to agriculture and home economics must be adopted, should not the course for the seven months in school be definitely organized to make of the total nine months' work an integrated whole?

It is certainly conceivable that by careful differentiation of minimal essentials and supplementary units, a course might be prepared for six months' or seven months' schools that would be immeasurably superior to what the individual teachers of such schools could select from the nine-months' courses provided. It might prove necessary to allow nine years for the elementary school instead of eight, but an added year in eight is less expensive of time than "spreading over two terms" the work outlined for each year.

Still another rural condition crying for an adjusted curriculum is the one-teacher school. Applying to it opprobrious epithets and hoping for a future of complete consolidation will not educate the present approximately four million children annually in approximately one hundred fifty thousand such schools in the United States. Their handicaps are heavy enough without the added problem of fitting on a curriculum organized, grade by grade, for the city type of school. This fact was recognized by the committee which recently reorganized the curriculum for Iowa, as a statement in the introduction to this course shows:

> The difficulty of making a course of study to serve both rural and graded schools arises not so much out of differences in the subject matter which should be taught in these two types of schools as out of the differences in administrative problems involved in teaching the two types of schools. . . It is the belief of the executive committee that those making the course of study which succeeds this one should consider seriously the plan of issuing a separate course of study for rural school teachers and one for teachers in graded schools.

The 'administrative problems' here mentioned are interpreted to mean the class organization and daily program whereby one teacher may effectively instruct eight grade-levels in all the subjects of the elementary curriculum. The device almost universally employed for meeting this difficulty is 'alternation and combination.'

> Briefly stated, this means that the course is outlined by grades and subjects, as for a 'graded' school, and the teacher of the 'ungraded' school is instructed to 'combine' certain grades, alternating their outlines by years, and occasionally also to 'combine' or 'correlate' certain subjects. Thus seventh and eighth grades may combine in history, being taught as one class, and studying together one year the course as outlined for seventh grade and the alternate year that outlined for eighth grade. History, geography, civics, agriculture, hygiene, and English and reading above primary grades are subjects often combined and alternated, arithmetic and primary reading very seldom, if at all.

> It is often recommended that the school be "taught as a whole" in some subjects, as for example, in music, writing, nature study, and art. Combinations or correlations of two subjects in one class usually include language or reading as one of the two. Thus language and nature study, language and reading, language and number, or reading and history may be suggested combinations.

The objection to alternation and combination is that the two years of work that are combined are often on different levels of difficulty, or one of them is to some extent prerequisite to the other. It is possible to arrange for alternation two years' work, of equal difficulty, but this is not a feature of the plan as worked out in most state courses of study. For this reason the plan has met with much objection, and some courses of study advise that it be not used. They offer no substitute plan, however. One state, after definitely warning against its use by "teachers with poor organizing ability," in the next paragraph declares, "It is absolutely essential to combine classes in the one- and two-teacher schools if satisfactory work is done."

The objection to combining or correlating two subjects in one is that the whole task of thus reorganizing and adjusting the printed curriculum falls upon the teacher. If the combinations suggested are practical, it would seem that they might be incorporated in the curriculum as sent out by the state. As it is, some quite impossible suggestions are offered.

Thus one course directs that nature study, literature, and history be 'correlated' with language in first to third grades, and hygiene with language in first to fourth. The only time allotted to primary language on the sample program given in this course for a school of eight grades, is ten minutes daily for language and numbers in first and second grades, and fifteen minutes daily for third, fourth, and fifth-grade language, all together. In this total of twenty-five minutes daily, therefore, there is supposed to be included the entire provision for first-grade numbers, language in the first five grades, literature in the first three, history in the first three, and nature study and hygiene in the first four. Suggestions for combining all grades in music are equally impossible for the teacher who is provided only with a curriculum offering eight sequential years of music instruction.

Combinations which would be not only practicable, but fruitful, are sometimes unnecessarily made impossible. For example, in a recent superior state course, separate outlines are provided for geography and industrial arts. In fourth-grade geography, one of the objectives is a knowledge of the state's products, and two of the units outlined are "How houses are built" and "Lumbering." It is in fifth and sixth grades, however, that in industrial arts "shelter study" is outlined, including the subtopics "How is lumber made?" "What lumber has our state?" "Where in our state do we get building material?" "Where get those not available here?" It is difficult to see what principle of sequence would have been violated by putting the two outlines in one grade, say the fourth.

The failures to utilize potentialities for useful combinations which are noted in various state courses perhaps indicate that courses in separate subjects are being made quite independently, by subject-matter committees, with weak coördinating organization.

In spite of the fact that Reinoehl (28) in 1922 made a number of very definite and useful suggestions for a curriculum organization especially helpful to one-teacher schools, only a few states have advanced beyond the provision of the customarily graded outline, with directions to alternate and combine as just described. The most serviceably organized courses at present available appear to be those of Montana, Nebraska, and Wyoming. Promising enterprises in curriculum revision to fit small rural schools are on foot in New York and New Jersey. Several states have begun the development of music courses for ungraded schools; California, Alabama, and Indiana have issued special bulletins on this subject. Washington has a particularly helpful section on art, which although not entirely organized for ungraded schools, has many suggestions which promote its adaptation to their conditions.

Another means recommended in a few states for meeting the administrative difficulties of the one-teacher school is individual instruction, which obviously is especially easy of application with the small enrollments frequently found in such schools. That it is a serviceable means for promoting the mastery of certain minimal essentials of information and skill is widely recognized. As a general measure, however, it has been severely criticised as exaggerating rather than remedying some of the very important lacks characteristic of the rural child's environment, such as those in socialization and language; and it is not in rural schools ordinarily counterbalanced by a variety of enriching and socialized activities. So far, only one state has materially recognized this plan in its curriculum.

2. The Curriculum Actually in Use

The curriculum actually in use in rural schools is both worse and better than that shown in the printed courses. It is worse, because time is not adequate to teach all the separate classes in 'ungraded' schools, and consequently the actual program of instruction is seriously limited, with the special subjects, particularly art and music, almost omitted, and with hurried and infrequent recitations of textbook assignments, interspersed with long periods of unsupervised study. Covert (7) reported in 1930 for 49 cities 33.9 percent of total time allotted to 'special subjects,' including physical training, recess and supervised play exclusive of the noon hour, industrial arts, drawing, music, opening exercises, and miscellaneous; and for 80 consolidated schools 26.4 percent of time for the same subjects. Reinoehl (28) found 10 percent of the school day given to these subjects in one-teacher schools in 1922, a proportion little improved in the programs offered by superior state courses to-day. Thus one recent course, specifically for one-teacher schools, allows in its proposed program 10 minutes daily for opening exercises, 5 minutes for physical exercise, 20 minutes for recesses, and 10 minutes for music, a total of only 45 minutes, or 12.5 percent of the six-hour school day; and a recent and especially good state course provides 10 minutes for opening exercises, 20 minutes for recesses, and 80 minutes, one day weekly, for industrial and fine arts and home economics.

Reinoehl reported also an average daily allotment, for all subjects, of only 56 minutes of class time to first and second grades together, 78 minutes to third and fourth, 90 minutes to fifth and sixth, and 105 to seventh and eighth. The difficulty of offering a whole curriculum in such brief periods of instruction is manifest.

The rural curriculum to-day, however, is also better than the printed courses, because here and there, in both one-teacher and consolidated rural schools, usually in well-supervised states and counties, work of very high type is being done. California through its 'demonstration schools' is developing a program of 'progressive education' in rural schools. Numerous very fine units of work have been carried out in several North Carolina counties, notably in Wake County. Vermont has issued a bulletin describing the genuinely vital activities carried on by some of the superior teachers of that state. Rural supervisors in Maryland are incorporating modern ideals and practices in county courses of study. Connecticut has promoted a very free type of curriculum in certain of its small rural schools. New York is developing 'child-centered' education in many one-teacher schools, and has committees of rural teachers and supervisors at work on a rural curriculum, of which one part has been issued in tentative form. The helping teachers of New Jersey are building a social-studies course for rural primary grades which will enrich both content and activities.

Several rural curriculum experiments are on foot. Delaware has a rural demonstration school which is attempting to work out a curriculum and organization desirable for imitation throughout the state. The Ballard school, some ten miles from Louisville, Kentucky, with

Elsie Clapp as principal, is carrying on progressive education in a rural public-school situation. Collings' experiment in a school in the Missouri Ozarks has been described in his book, *An Experiment with a Project Curriculum.* Teachers College, Columbia University, has reported, in *Four Years in a Country School,* the experimental organization of a one-teacher school in New Jersey in three groups instead of eight grades, has since that time further tested the same organization, with a considerably extended activity program, in the rural schools of a Connecticut town, and is preparing a bulletin of curriculum materials as an outcome of that experiment. The Southern Women's Educational Alliance is promoting a program of educational guidance in a mission school in the Appalachian region of southwestern Virginia. The progressive movement is being advanced by no one group exclusively. Wherever there is leadership, whether in a state department, a county, an individual, a community back of a school, or a state-wide or national organization of some type, there constructive work on the rural curriculum is being done.

III. CONCLUSIONS AND RECOMMENDATIONS

Studies of rural children's interests, experiences, and needs are insufficient in number and extent to afford basis for extensive generalizations. It is to be expected that few such generalizations will ever be reached, for the reason that rural children are not a separate genus. Certain features more or less characteristic of an agricultural rather than an industrial background and of sparse rather than dense population groups will always be important determiners of their education, but even these features vary from state to state and some of them from one section of a state to another. It is not important, therefore, that we are unable to generalize extensively with regard to rural curriculum factors for the nation as a whole.

It is, however, extremely important that each responsible curriculum-developing unit, which means ordinarily each state, and to a lesser extent each county, should be informed as to the distinctive characteristics of its rural population and the conditions under which its rural elementary schools are conducted, and should organize its curriculum to be of maximal helpfulness to the teachers of these schools as well as to those of its city schools. That two or more different organizations for the same state may be needed is highly probable. The Texas survey commission recommended several, for rural and urban, and for Mexican and Negro, yet that commission was committed to the policy of common educational aims for all groups. The peculiar difficulties of the short-term and of the one-teacher schools appear especially to require the assistance which an adapted state curriculum could give.

On the whole, the states are not facing squarely the curriculum problem of the rural schools; they are organizing their courses of study primarily for city educational conditions and leaving the brunt of the burden of adjustment for the rural teachers and supervisors to carry. The assumption appears to be that the adjustments required are unimportant and readily made. If this be true, it is suggested that the curriculum be organized very specifically for six-month, one-teacher rural schools, leaving it to better-staffed consolidated schools and to the well-qualified teachers and fairly adequate supervisory force of cities to make the minor necessary adjustments.

Just what adaptations or adjustments each state needs to make can be determined only by studies within that state, made in the light of the philosophy of education which that state accepts. No state can make all the needed adjustments without a knowledge of the level of mental ability, the health needs, and the social and cultural opportunities and experiences of its rural children. Studies along lines indicated in Section I, Subtopics 2 and 3, of this Chapter, are suggested as desirable.

That rural curriculum development is proceeding under quite different lines in a number of independent situations is an especially hopeful fact. A variety of suggestions for solving the very difficult curriculum problems of rural schools promises a better eventual answer than would premature selection of one solution for general development. It is not probably to be recommended that any one plan as yet advanced be universally adopted, but rather that the problem of the rural curriculum be squarely faced and constructively attacked in each state and also in each county which can command the necessary personnel for the undertaking.

REFERENCES

1. American Library Association. *People without Library Service.* 1926.
2. BAGLEY, WM., and others. "Foundations of curriculum-making." *The Twenty-Sixth Yearbook* of this Society. Part II. Bloomington, 1926. P. 12.
2a. BALDWIN, B. T., and others. *Farm Children.* New York, 1930.
3. BRIM, O. G. "Handicaps of the rural child." *Jour. of Rural Educ.,* 2 : 1922, 52-63.
4. BRIM, O. G. *Rural Education.* New York, 1923. Pp. 7-23, 27.
5. BRUNNER, E. DE S. *Village Communities.* New York, 1927. P. 92.
6. BRUNNER, HUGHES PATTEN. *American Agricultural Villages.* New York, 1927. Pp. 200-214.
7. COVERT, TIMON. *Time Allotments in Selected Consolidated Schools.* Washington, 1930. (Office of Educ., Rural School Leaflet, No. 46.)
8. CRUMBINE, SAMUEL J., and HOLLAND, DOROTHY F. "Small farm milk supplies." *Rural America,* October, 1928.
9. DAVIES, ESTHER S. *The Food Consumption of Rural School Children in Relation to Their Health.* Amherst, 1928. (Bulletin No. 241.)
10. DOUGLASS, H. PAUL. *How Shall Country Youth be Served?* New York, 1926. Pp. 164, 183, 235.
11. FERNANDES, GRACE. *A Critical Study of Periodical Reading in Farm Homes.* Stillwater, 1928. (Agri. Expt. Station Bull., No. 176.)
12. FOGHT, HAROLD W. "Report of the Committee of One Hundred on Rural Teachers Problems." *Nat. Educ. Assoc. Proc.* Washington, 1926. Pp. 197-199.
13. FRAYSER, MARY E. *The Use of Leisure in Selected Rural Areas of South Carolina.* Anderson, 1930. (Bulletin No. 263.)
14. FRAYSER, MARY E. *Children of Pre-School Age in Selected Areas of South Carolina.* Anderson, 1929. (Bulletin No. 260.)
15. HEYL, HELEN H. *Differentiation in Curricula to Meet the Life and Needs of Rural Children.* Washington, 1927. Pp. 43-46. (U. S. Bur. Educ. Bull. No. 24.)
16. JORDAN, PEARL T. "Factors Relating to Reading Progress in Rural Schools." Nashville, 1929. (On file in library of George Peabody College for Teachers.)
17. KERN, O. J. *Among Country Schools.* New York, 1906.
18. LATHROP, EDITH A. *State Direction of Rural Library Service.* Washington, 1930. (Office of Educ. Bull. No. 6.)
19. LEHMAN, HARVEY C. "Comparison of play activities of town and country children." *Jour. of Rural Educ.,* 5 : 1926, 253-259.
20. LEHMAN, HARVEY C. "Environmental influence upon drawing 'just for fun.'" *Jour. of Rural Educ.,* 5 : 1926, 425-429.
21. LEHMAN, HARVEY C. "Identifying the rural child's play activities." *Jour. of Rural Educ.,* 5 : 1926, 430-432.
22. LEWIS, CHARLES D. "The advantages of the rural child." *Jour. of Rural Educ.,* 4 : 1925, 452-453.

23. National Education Association. "Possible variations in curricula to meet community and individual needs." *Third Yearbook. Department of Superintendence.* Washington, 1925. P. 23.

23a. *National Education Association, Proceedings.* July, 1926.

24. "News, notes, and editorials." *Jour. of Rural Educ.,* 1 : 1921, 41-42.

25. New York. *Standard Equipment Recommended for Rural Schools.* Albany, 1929. (Univ. of State of New York Bull. No. 934.)

26. PALMER, E. L. "Are the nature interests of rural children and urban children the same?" *Cornell Rural School Leaflet 19.* Ithaca, 1925. Pp. 16-30.

27. President Roosevelt's Message. "Report of Commission of Country Life." Reprinted in *Rural America.* January, 1929.

28. REINOEHL, C. M. *Analytic Survey of State Courses of Study for Rural Elementary Schools.* Washington, 1923. Pp. 47-52. (U. S. Bur. of Educ. Bull. No. 42.)

29. SHIMBERG, MYRA E. "An Investigation into the Validity of Norms, with Special Reference to Urban Rural Groups." New York, 1929. Reviewed in *Archives of Psychology,* 104.

30. SOROKIN, PETERIN, and ZIMMERMAN, CARL C. *Principles of Rural-Urban Sociology.* New York, 1929. Pp. 234-236, 261.

31. TAYLOR, CARL. *Rural Sociology.* New York, 1926. Pp. 196, 361, 372.

CHAPTER V

THE CURRICULUM OF THE RURAL SECONDARY SCHOOL[1]

WILLIAM H. BRISTOW, EMERY N. FERRISS, AND R. M. STEWART

The contributors to this chapter present their discussion of the rural secondary-school curriculum in four sections: I, Programs of Studies in Junior and Junior-Senior High Schools; II, The Curriculum of the Rural Four-Year High School; III, Progress in Curriculum-Making for Vocational Agriculture in Rural Secondary Schools; and IV, Some Important Curricular Problems in Rural Secondary Education.

SECTION I
PROGRAMS OF STUDIES IN JUNIOR AND JUNIOR-SENIOR HIGH SCHOOLS

WILLIAM H. BRISTOW
Assistant Director of Secondary Education
Department of Public Instruction, Harrisburg, Pennsylvania

I. SECONDARY-SCHOOL REORGANIZATION IN RURAL COMMUNITIES

The development of practices and procedures, as they affect rural secondary education, is generally formulated by the state departments of public instruction. Some of the special formulations suggested for the programs of rural junior and junior-senior high schools by representative state departments will be summarized in this section.

Of the essential characteristics of the junior high school Judd (9:12f.)[2] says:

> The junior high school is an organized effort to give the type of training that shall not be a mere repetition of arithmetic, nor a mere

---

[1] Professor Ferriss, who is responsible for the general organization of this chapter, acknowledges the coöperation of various representatives of state departments of education who supplied material pertaining to the programs of study in the small and the rural secondary schools in their several states, and in particular the coöperation of Helen Heffernan, Chief of the Division of Rural Education, State Department of Education, Sacramento, California, for supplying extensive material pertaining to the rural high schools in that state.

[2] Numbers in parentheses conjoined with citations refer by number and page to the references listed at the end of this chapter.

repetition of geography, . . . the essential core of this new curriculum is social study. . . . A junior high school which is nothing but a departmentalized elementary school must be described as a sham. . . . The real business of the junior high school is to organize a new curriculum, organize a new body of constructive material which shall be richer and broader and better for the children. That is the only legitimate motive for this organization.

Studying the phases of the junior-high-school movement in Indiana, H. G. Child (3) found that the four factors listed as most important were: a reorganized course of study, an opportunity for pupils to take more extensive offerings in prevocational studies, a provision for greater differentiation of curricula than under old conditions, and the opportunity for some pupils to take some high-school subjects, such as foreign languages and algebra, earlier. Other investigators have found substantially the same results.

Since the curriculum is a significant index of the effectiveness of this movement, one regrets, in making an evaluation of junior-high-school development in rural communities, the difficulty of securing accurate information regarding the extent to which the content of the program of studies has been reorganized. Full information can be secured only by analyzing curricular materials, a task beyond the scope of the present study.

Failure on the part of those working in the rural secondary school to bring about this reorganization has led many leaders to be skeptical of the possibilities of the junior high school in rural and small communities. Spaulding (22:210) concludes that "the need of a new type of organization is, however, clearly evident. It is only to some plan, apparently undeveloped, that we must look for possibilities of achievement in the small junior high school.

The program of studies in the junior high schools of Nebraska is indicated by a study made by Greene (6:143f., 154) in which he concludes:

> In examining the curricula of the junior high schools under consideration, the observation is justified that they have made only a beginning at accomplishing the desired ends which a program of studies is supposed to achieve. Since 94 percent of the thirty-eight schools of the state belong to systems which are accredited to the North Central Association, it is not unexpected that they largely meet the recommendations of that accrediting agency. Davis reports that of the 293 junior high schools of the North Central territory, 34.8 percent have definitely outlined curricula, 25.3 percent allow election by curricula,

and 48.5 percent allow election by subject. On the other hand, the Nebraska data show that 42.1 percent of the schools offer a single curriculum. Not a school, however, offers multiple curricula, while 57.9 percent offer constants with variables.

The kinds of industrial work offered are practically limited to manual training and domestic science. These are found in every school we have examined. Yet the absence of variety in this regard shows a lack of understanding of one of the chief functions of the junior-high-school organization, namely, the exploratory function. There is every appearance here that the greater number of these junior high schools do not differ markedly in their curriculum organization from the traditional type.

At present, it seems justifiable to state that many of the junior high schools of Nebraska are that in name only, and that they profess to be that reorganized unit mainly because of 'paper changes' in both organization and curricula. . . The principal change, as evidenced, is a grouping together of two or three of the grades under departmental plans and assuming the new name.

There are varying opinions concerning the feasibility and value of the junior high school in rural communities. Virginia officials (24:4) deem it impractical except in communities which have large school populations and ample school revenues. Arkansas (17:8f.) favors it as a means of bringing some high-school opportunities to its scattered pupils. West Virginia (25:35f.) proposes several forms to meet varying conditions. OBrien, of Kansas, (13) urges it as an improvement over the work for seventh and eighth grades in one-teacher schools. On the actual status Mrs. Cook (5:44) reports as follows:

Establishment of junior high schools as a means of improving secondary education in rural areas is growing in favor. According to a recent check, twenty-six states have passed laws relating specifically to the junior high school and thirty-two state departments of public instruction encourage this type of organization within their respective states. Recent statistics show that 12 percent of the high schools in population centers of 2,500 or fewer are organized under the junior-high-school system enrolling 21.6 percent of the pupils attending high school in such centers. Most of these schools are organized as junior-senior high schools under the 2-4 or the 3-3 plan. The junior high school, as an independent unit or associated with the elementary school only, is comparatively infrequent in rural areas, but is showing growth in favorable sentiment.

TABLE I.—PERCENTAGE OF FIFTY-NINE THREE-YEAR AND FORTY-FIVE TWO-YEAR RURAL JUNIOR HIGH SCHOOLS OFFERING SUBJECTS AS REQUIRED OR ELECTIVE COURSES

(From U. S. Bur. Educ. Bull., 1928. No. 28)

| | Three-Year Schools | | | | | | Two-Year Schools | | | |
| | Grade VII | | Grade VIII | | Grade IX | | Grade VII | | Grade VIII | |
	Required	Elective	Required	Elective	Required	Elective	Required	Elective	Required	Elective
English	100	...	100	...	100	...	100	...	100	...
Spelling (separate)	37	2	34	2	9	3	67	...	64	...
Foreign language	...	9	5	10	2	64	...	2	...	4
Social science and history	95	...	100	...	59	20	96	...	100	...
Mathematics	100	...	100	...	76	24	100	...	100	...
Geography	88	...	29	2	3	16	89	...	36	...
Science	22	3	51	12	22	44	31	...	60	2
Health	76	3	65	3	41	10	69	...	49	...
Art	34	15	27	22	8	32	42	7	40	9
Music	56	22	49	24	31	41	53	13	53	13
Industrial arts and agriculture	54	12	49	17	22	47	38	9	60	13
Home economics	56	9	56	14	25	49	56	9	64	11
Junior business training	...	3	7	3	...	7	...	...	2	2
Commercial mathematics	2	...	2	2	...	22	...	...	2	...
Bookkeeping	2	...	2	2	...	7	...	...	...	...
Business practice	...	...	...	...	...	2	...	...	...	...
Typewriting	31	...	31	2	7	2	...	...	...	2
Penmanship	8	...	7	...	5	3	44	...	42	...
Guidance	15	5	15	5	17	3	4	7	4	7
School activities	...	...	...	...	...	...	4	...	...	...
Unit try-out courses	...	...	...	...	...	3+	...	...	...	...

II. THE OFFERINGS OF THE RURAL JUNIOR HIGH SCHOOL

In a recent yearbook of the Department of Superintendence, Briggs (1: 199) has emphasized the exploratory function as one of the special characteristics of the secondary school. In dealing with this exploratory function the emphasis has been placed largely upon differentiated curricula, practical arts, vocational courses, commercial education, and home-making, but extended programs of this sort are generally to be found only in large junior high schools. Nevertheless, experience has proved that a program of practical arts can be carried out in a limited and worth-while fashion even in the smallest secondary schools. Likewise, we are coming to realize that exploration is by no means confined to the practical arts, commercial subjects, or vocational education. English, science, mathematics, music and art, health and physical education, geography, and guidance courses may also contribute to the development of this important function of the junior high school.

A study made by a subcommittee of the National Committee on Research in Secondary Education summarizes the curricula of 104 representative two-year and three-year junior high schools in rural communities distributed throughout thirty states. The percentages of the schools offering the different subjects, as required or elective courses, according to this study (20: 43) are quoted in Table I herewith.

III. THE SIX-YEAR HIGH SCHOOL IN RURAL SECONDARY-SCHOOL ORGANIZATION

In the development of a program of reorganization, the junior-senior high school should play an increasingly important part in bringing to rural boys and girls a more effective secondary-school program. Rule (19: 90) suggests certain principles of organization which, in his opinion, offer distinctive advantages. Space does not permit their inclusion in this article. The advantages enumerated, however, vitally affect the development of the program of studies in rural secondary schools.

The danger involved in the encouragement of too many small high schools of the old type is indicated in a survey made at the University of Kansas. In the light of the findings, which cannot be reproduced here, the authors (14: 8) conclude:

> Briefly stated, a goodly number of these small [rural high] schools are so handicapped . . . that they are providing an inferior grade of in-

struction at an excessive cost. By far the larger portion of these two hundred and more rural high schools are still classified by the State Department of Education as in either the unapproved class or the lowest class approved by the state for doing high-school work. As a consequence the rural boy and girl may frequently be getting a spurious article labeled as modern high-school advantages. The exercise of more intelligence and foresight in the organization of the district and the school will be required, first of all, to change this deplorable situation. Certainly, a rural high school may be made one of the best high schools in the state.

An outstanding study of the six-year high school in Indiana was made by Simon (21) in 1928. A number of the findings and conclusions in the seventh chapter of his thesis indicate in a specific manner the problems which arise relative to the junior-senior high-school program of studies in small schools. Of these the following are significant:

> The median school corporation [in Indiana] maintaining a six-year high school has a population of 1,516. The chief occupation of the people of the community is farming. The median school has an enrollment of 125 pupils, 62 of whom are boys and 63 are girls. There are 25 pupils in the seventh grade, 24 in the eighth, 24 in the ninth, 20 in the tenth, 17 in the eleventh, and 15 in the twelfth.
>
> The courses offered in the school are those required by the State Board of Education in Indiana and some elective courses approved by the State Board. About one-fourth of the work in Grades VII and VIII is elective and about one-half of the work for the other grades is elective. The median number of subjects offered in the school is eleven. The subjects mentioned most frequently are English, history, and social science, mathematics, Latin, home economics, music, art, physics, industrial arts, agriculture, and biology. . .
>
> The courses offered in the six-year high schools are largely of the academic type with some deviation into the fields of commerce and practical arts. The course of study outlined by the State Board of Education is used by all high schools of the State regardless of location. However, the schools are given a great amount of liberty in regard to the work which may be offered. Although they are free from restrictions, the six-year high schools of Indiana are limited in some cases in the number of courses they may offer by the pupil enrollment, size of teaching staff, and equipment.

The subjects offered in the six-year junior-senior high schools of Indiana as reported by Simon are listed in Table II.

IV. Programs of Studies Developed by State Departments

Trends in the curriculum development of rural junior and junior-senior high schools may be observed in the programs of studies pre-

TABLE II.—NUMBER OF JUNIOR-SENIOR-HIGH SCHOOLS OF CLASSIFIED ENROLL-
MENTS IN INDIANA OFFERING THE SUBJECTS LISTED
(From Simon)

SUBJECTS	SCHOOLS CLASSIFIED BY TOTAL ENROLLMENT				
	100 or fewer	101-150	151-200	201 and over	Total
English	70	108	44	35	257
History and social science	70	108	44	35	257
Mathematics	70	108	44	35	257
Latin	65	102	44	34	245
Home economics	59	106	41	35	241
Music	59	93	42	34	228
Art	39	76	37	30	182
Physics	38	75	34	29	176
Industrial arts	30	61	32	32	155
Agriculture	32	53	20	13	118
Biology	20	51	21	20	112
Commercial subjects	14	35	25	28	102
Physical training	21	35	18	21	95
Botany	23	25	10	13	71
Physical geography	19	26	14	9	68
Commercial geography	19	22	9	7	57
Physiology	14	23	3	10	50
Band and orchestra	9	14	10	11	44
Chemistry	2	2	2	11	17
Public speaking	3	7	1	6	17
Bible	...	3	3	3	9
Hygiene	2	2	2	3	9
French	...	2	1	4	7
Penmanship	4	...	2	1	7

pared by state departments of public instruction. These programs
of study are often the result of a careful survey of the field, and
embody standards chosen for the type of school for which they are
prepared. Because these programs indicate what is being attempted
in the small schools, programs from certain states are reproduced;
most of the valuable suggestions regarding objectives and adaptations
of the programs to the school and the community are, of necessity,
omitted. The programs of studies prepared by the state department
of Indiana (Table III), New York (Table IV), and West Virginia
(Table V) supply typical examples of the different sorts which are
found.

It is highly important to the progress of this reorganization movement that each state act as a directing force to insure the development of a coördinated program of study. Enthusiasm for the reorganization movement or the need of temporary adjustments should not result in setting up ineffective organizations which might be improved through a system of consolidation using larger units of administration. On the other hand, there is a place for junior and junior-senior high schools, offering a modified program, in small centers of population and rural communities. But before organizing a small junior

TABLE III.—THE INDIANA JUNIOR-HIGH-SCHOOL PROGRAM OF STUDIES, SHOWING MAXIMAL AND MINIMAL PERIODS*

	GRADE VII		GRADE VIII		GRADE IX	
	Min-imum	Max-imum	Min-imum	Max-imum	Min-imum	Max-imum
Required						
English...................	5	7	5	7	5	...
Social studies†..............	5	5	5	5	...	...
Mathematics................	5	5	4	5	5	...
Geography.................	3	5	...	...	...	...
Physical education..........	2	3	2	2	2	...
Practical arts‡..............	2	3	3	3	...	...
Music.....................	1	2	...	...	...	...
Art.......................	1	2	...	...	...	...
General science.............	...	...	4	5	...	...
Electives:						
Music.....................	...	...	1	3	1	5
Art.......................	...	...	1	3	1	5
Foreign language............	...	...	2	5	5	...
Commercial arts.............	...	...	2	5	1	5
Citizenship vocations........	...	...	...	...	5	...
Biology....................	...	...	...	...	5	7
Practical arts...............	...	...	...	...	5	10

*From *Administrative Handbook for Indiana High Schools*. Indianapolis, 1928. Pp. 43-44.

†Social studies in Grade VII include Indiana history, community civics, and United States history; in Grade VIII, United States history and constitutional civics.

‡Practical arts in Grade VII include general shop and home economics; agriculture is added in Grade VIII, and trade and industry takes the place of general shop in Grade IX.

high school, consideration should be given to the advisability of reorganizing existing 8-4 or 7-4 units in the development of a junior-senior high school.

The offering of a satisfactory program of studies in small junior and junior-senior schools closely concerns such administrative features

TABLE IV.—A NEW YORK PROGRAM OF STUDIES FOR THE SMALL JUNIOR HIGH SCHOOL SHOWING PERIODS PER WEEK*

	GRADE VII		GRADE VIII		GRADE IX	
	First Term	Second Term	First Term	Second Term	First Term	Second Term
English	5	5	5	5	5	5
Social studies	5	5	5	5	5†	5†
Mathematics	5	5	5	5	5	5
Science	2	2	3	3	5	5
Health	2	2	2	2	2	2
Music	2	2	2‡		5‡	5‡
Art	2	2	2‡ }4	4	5‡	5‡
Practical arts§	2	2	2‡		5‡	5‡
Library instruction	1	1	...	...	...	...
Home room:						
Assembly	1	1	1	1	1	1
Clubs	...	1	1	1	1‡	1‡
Guidance	1	...	...	1	...	...
Home-room business	0.5	0.5	0.5	0.5	0.5	0.5
Reading	0.5	0.5	0.5	...	...	...
Spelling	0.5	0.5	0.5	0.5	...	...
Writing	0.5	0.5	0.5	...	...	...
Language	...	...	2‡ }2	2‡ }2	5‡	5‡
Commercial subjects	...	...	2‡	2‡	5‡	5‡

*From *The Junior High School in New York State.* Albany, 1928. P. 87.
†Becomes a variable for different groups.
‡Is an elective.
§This title includes home-making for girls and industrial arts or agriculture for the boys.

as 'individual instruction,' 'grouping of subjects,' 'alternation of subjects,' 'part-time or itinerant teachers,' 'teachers with preparation in a number of fields,' and 'building adjustments.' These phases of administration offer a profitable field for research in rural secondary education.

The principle of 'adaptation,' rather than the 'adoption' of curriculum materials and procedures found helpful in larger schools, should characterize the administration of small rural junior and junior-senior high schools.

The teachers, principals, and superintendents should be encouraged to experiment with new procedures and policies which promise aid in the enrichment of the programs of studies in small secondary schools. State departments of education and other educational agencies

TABLE V.—SUGGESTED WEST VIRGINIA CURRICULUM FOR SIX-YEAR HIGH SCHOOLS EMPLOYING SIX TEACHERS*

	Seventh Year	Eighth Year	Ninth Year	Tenth Year‡	Eleventh Year‡	Twelfth Year‡
English..........................	5	5	5	5	5	5
Geography......................	5	...	...	5	...	...
Elementary Science...............	3	3	3	...	...	...
Health and physical education.....	2	2	2	2	2	2
Elementary mathematics..........	5	5	5†	...	...	...
Home Economics—girls; or Industrial arts or agriculture—boys...	3	3	3	*5*	...	...
Fine arts.......................	2	2	...	...	...	...
Guidance and student activities....	5	5	5	...	...	...
American history.................	...	5	...	...	5	...
Citizenship and occupations.......	...	5	5	...	...	...
Biology.........................	...	...	...	5	...	...
Modern world history.............	...	...	...	*5*	...	...
Commercial studies...............	...	...	...	*5*	...	...
Algebra.........................	...	...	...	...	*5*	...
Chemistry.......................	...	...	...	...	*5*	...
Latin or French (not both)........	...	...	...	...	*5*	*5*
Geometry.......................	...	...	...	...	...	*5*
Elementary economics or sociology	...	...	...	...	...	*5*
Physics.........................	...	...	...	...	...	*5*
Fine arts§......................	...	...	...	...	...	...

*From *Manual for Secondary Schools.* Charleston, 1926. Pp. 35f.
†Mathematics in ninth year includes algebra, composite mathematics, or advanced arithmetic.
‡The hours of electives are set in italics. Any two are to be chosen for the tenth, eleventh, and twelfth years.
§Fine Arts may be offered in the eleventh and twelfth years in place of either Latin or French.

can make outstanding contributions through the promulgation of programs which will make it possible to carry these studies on over long enough a period to make the results valid. At the present time the heavy turnover of the teachers and the members of the administrative personnel in rural communities make such studies difficult.

V. SUMMARY

1. Some evidence of the reorganization of courses of study and of the development of curricular materials to meet the needs of rural communities has been assembled here. For the most part, however, little has been done in this field.

2. A status study of the offerings in small junior and junior-senior schools gives important information concerning the programs of studies in these schools. It does not, however, reveal the nature of courses of study. Further study is needed with reference to objectives and curricula for rural and small high schools.

SECTION II

THE CURRICULUM OF THE RURAL FOUR-YEAR HIGH SCHOOL

EMERY N. FERRISS
Professor of Rural Education
Cornell University, Ithaca, New York

Approximately seventy percent of the secondary schools in rural areas are of the traditional four-year type. They enroll about 75 percent of the children attending rural secondary schools. Whatever may be the future development of rural secondary education, at the present time, so far as curriculum offerings are an index, the subjects in the programs of studies of rural four-year high schools probably give most adequately an indication of the educational opportunities afforded to the young people living in rural communities.

In this section the purpose is to give a composite picture of the significant features of the curriculum of the rural four-year high school from several angles. Because of the limitation of space and the view that subjects offered by fewer than one-fourth of any group of schools studied are not of particular significance in a picture of status, such subjects are omitted from consideration. Though extra-class activities are recognized as being increasingly important in any portrayal of educational opportunities afforded children, they are also omitted, save for incidental mention.

I. SUBJECTS OFFERED IN REPRESENTATIVE SMALL HIGH SCHOOLS

The subjects offered by 196 representative small high schools distributed over 44 states were listed in a study of the senior-high-school curriculum by J. N. Rule included in the *Sixth Yearbook of the Department of Superintendence.* This probably contains (19: 95ff.) the most recent data of nation-wide scope on the programs of studies of rural high schools.

The subjects included in the programs of at least 25 percent of these 196 schools, with the percentage of schools offering each, are:

Subject	Percent of Schools
English 1	94
English 2	94
English 3	74
English 4	68

Latin 1 57
Latin 2 52
French 1 26

Elementary algebra 91
Advanced algebra 44
Plane geometry 78

American history 62
Ancient history 39
Medieval and modern history 35
World history 27
Civics and citizenship 1 and 2 49

General science 60
Biology 42
Physics 43
Chemistry 31
Agriculture 30
Physical education and physical training 29

Bookkeeping 1 31
Typewriting 1 28
Home economics 41

Examination of this list shows that the subjects offered by one-half or more of the schools are English, Latin, algebra, geometry, American history, and general science. If all the subjects included in the programs of 25 to 49 percent of the schools are added, this list is increased by one year of a second foreign language, French 1; three courses in history and a course in civics; three courses in science; one year each of agriculture, home economics, typewriting, and bookkeeping; and physical education and physical training.

II. An Ohio Study

A study by Clifton (4) of fifty representative small first-grade high schools of Ohio, each enrolling fewer than fifty pupils, probably indicates rather accurately the status of the program of studies in schools of this type, of which there are approximately four hundred in the state of Ohio. The subjects offered by 25 percent or more of these small high schools in Ohio are (4: 78f.) :

English 1	Elementary algebra	Geography
English 2	Advanced algebra	Economics
English 3	Plane geometry	Sociology
English 4	Arithmetic	Modern history
Latin 1	General science	Occupations
Latin 2	Biology	Bookkeeping
Latin 3	Physics	Manual training
Latin 4	American history	Home economics
French 1	Civics	Physical education
		Music

If only the subjects that are found in the programs of at least 50 percent of the schools are considered, the offerings are algebra, plane geometry, and arithmetic; four years of English; four years of Latin; two years of science; two of history and civics; two of home economics; and two of manual training. If the subjects offered by 25 to 49 percent of the schools are also included, eleven subjects are added to the list. By including all the subjects offered by any school and by less than 25 percent of the schools, a considerable number of subjects, diverse in character, are added. Clifton says (4:80):

> There is little uniformity in the curricular offerings of these schools outside of that dictated by college-entrance requirements and tradition. This is indicated by the fact that twelve subjects in the ninth grade, nineteen in the tenth, twenty in the eleventh, and twenty-three in the twelfth are offered by less than 25 percent of the schools.

III. OFFERINGS IN THE RURAL HIGH SCHOOLS OF CALIFORNIA

Since California holds the unique position of having a small percentage of rural high schools with enrollments of fewer than fifty students and a large percentage with enrollments over one hundred, an analysis of the curriculum status of the rural high schools of that state should offer the basis for interesting comparisons. Miss Heffernan in her study of the rural high schools of California (7) gives complete data on the subjects offered by those schools. Only data for the 180 schools with enrollments of three hundred or less are reproduced here in Table VI, since four-year rural high schools with enrollments of more than three hundred are exceedingly rare in practically all other states. As would undoubtedly be expected, since the California schools are as a group much larger than those represented in other studies, the range and number of subjects offered is much larger. The most surprising features, perhaps, are the predominant

Table VI.—Subjects Offered By 25 Percent or More of the Small Rural
High Schools of California as Reported by Heffernan
(180 Rural High Schools with Enrollments of 300 or Less)

	Size of Enrollment	
	Under 100	101–300
English 1	100	100
English 2	100	100
English 3	100	100
English 4	76	89
Public speaking	...	34
Latin 1	44	80
Latin 2	39	77
French 1	...	29
French 2	...	25
Spanish 1	85	94
Spanish 2	77	92
Spanish 3	43	46
Elementary algebra	100	100
Advanced algebra	76	89
Plane geometry	100	100
Solid geometry	...	49
Trigonometry	35	55
General science	75	74
Biology	40	76
Chemistry	61	86
Physics	55	81
American history	100	100
American government	100	100
World history	61	67
Ancient history	...	31
Modern history	...	33
Economics	44	56
Typewriting 1	92	97
Typewriting 2	69	86
Elementary bookkeeping	76	91
Advanced bookkeeping	33	56
Shorthand 1	64	89
Shorthand 2	39	71
Commercial arithmetic	...	26
Business methods	...	28
Elementary mechanical drawing	67	73
Advanced mechanical drawing	...	25
Woodwork 1	39	56
Woodwork 2	...	33
Machine shop	31	45

TABLE VI.—*Continued*

	SIZE OF ENROLLMENT	
	Under 100	101–300
Homemaking 1...	76	92
Homemaking 2...	45	59
Elementary art..	33	73
Advanced art..	...	38
Agriculture 1...	29	44
Agriculture 2...	...	34
Farm mechanics.......................................	25	40
Physical education....................................	100	100
Orchestra...	37	65
Glee club...	29	62
Theory and sight singing..............................	...	47
Instrumental music...................................	...	30

attention given to the traditional academic departments of learning, the relatively small proportion of schools offering instruction in practical arts and vocational activities, and the relatively large place given to commercial subjects. Another striking feature is the relatively small amount of emphasis in these larger rural high schools upon such fields of study as health education, music, and art. While a somewhat larger percentage of the California rural high schools provide, in their programs of studies, for work in special practical and vocational fields (with the exception of agriculture), the most noticeable characteristic is the increased number of offerings in such strictly academic fields as languages, mathematics, and history.

It should be noted that among the courses listed by fewer than 25 percent of these California schools—facts not included in Table VII—a considerable number of additional electives are offered many of them representative of the newer subjects.

Dramatics, journalism, and stagecraft are included in the field of English; Latin 3 and 4, French 3 and 4, Spanish 4, and two years of German in languages; general mathematics; physical geography; sociology; community civics, medieval history, occupations, medieval and modern history, and English history; commercial law, commercial English, commercial geography, and salesmanship; home-making 3 and 4; band and chorus; health education; agriculture 3 and 4; aeronautics; military science; and library methods.

Some of Miss Heffernan's comments on the present status of the curriculum of the California rural high schools, which are of wide application to rural high-school curricula, are quoted here:

The smaller schools offer a surprising number of mathematics electives. Over 54 percent offer advanced algebra and over 54 percent offer trigonometry. The composite mathematics course has shown little progress in California high schools. The college-entrance requirements of algebra and geometry keep them firmly entrenched in the high-school curriculum.

The curriculum shows the effect of the growing conviction that the task of education is to prepare citizens to cope with modern social problems. Although history is still the predominating subject, economics has reached second place and sociology fifth place in the curricular offerings in the social-science field.

The commercial curriculum is the most flourishing vocational curriculum in the high schools included in the study. Small schools are frequently offering more commercial subjects than the opportunity for graduates of the commercial curriculum would warrant.

Industrial arts occupy no very significant place in the high-school curriculum. In the smaller schools due to lack of equipment and small faculties, these non-academic fields have not received the development that the strong movement toward vocational education would lead us to anticipate. Only in schools enrolling over two hundred students are any differentiated industrial-arts curricula provided.

The home-making courses occupy a strong, but in no sense dominant, position in the high-school curriculum. It is easy to argue the desirability of these courses but more difficult to make the high-school girl elect them. . . An effort should probably be made to direct the home-making courses into an analysis of the responsibilities which will probably belong to the homemaker of the future. Processes which were the common home duties of a generation ago have been taken over and performed more satisfactorily by industry. The homemaking course of the future will probably concern itself with giving the student, (1) an appreciation of the place of the home in the social order, (2) a realization of the responsibility of the members of the family to each other and to the social group, and (3) a sense of responsibility for those community problems which affect the position of the home in society.

Music is just emerging from the extra-curricular status in our smaller secondary schools. The avocational and vocational values of music have not been fully appreciated in the construction of secondary curricula.

Although we have enunciated the health objective of secondary education for over ten years, little of this objective is found translated into direct health teaching. . . Definite health instruction is afforded in the curriculum of only 15 percent of the courses of study examined.

For a commonwealth that bases its industrial life on agriculture, agricultural education has not received the emphasis in the secondary-school curriculum to be expected. Only about 43 percent of the schools offer any courses in agriculture and an even smaller percentage offer a complete agriculture curriculum. Causes may probably be found in the serious economic conditions with which the farm group have been confronted in recent years.

IV. General Status of the Rural High-School Curriculum

A critical examination of the several groups of data on the programs of studies of rural high schools indicates clearly that the core of the rural high-school curriculum is still largely composed of college-preparatory subjects. It is academic in its most common features. It lacks balance, whether viewed from the angle of the common developmental needs of the adolescent, or from the angle of individual differences in interests and aptitudes, not to mention purposes, or from the angle of the social adjustments commonly needed by the great mass of people in modern life. As far as any dominant aim is apparent, it is the preparatory aim. All other aims are secondary, and they gradually but surely yield to this dominant aim, as the groups considered represent schools of smaller enrollments.

Comparison of recent statistics with those of approximately a decade ago indicate little change in the general features of the rural high-school curriculum. In a minor way, however, encouraging changes seem to be taking place. Latin and other foreign languages have apparently decreased in importance as required subjects; mathematics has lost some ground as a common requirement for all pupils; ancient history and certain special courses in history, such as English history, have somewhat declined in importance. Such social studies as community civics and courses dealing with social and economic problems and general science as an introductory course in science have gained in frequency in the rural high-school curriculum. Practical arts, other than manual training, and agriculture and home-making have become more common in programs of studies. Commercial subjects are receiving much emphasis.

V. State Departments of Education and the Curriculum of
the Rural Four-Year High School

Rural high schools are much influenced in their programs of studies and curriculum organization by regulations and recommendations of

TABLE VII.—SUBJECTS IN PROGRAMS OF STUDIES FOR SMALL AND RURAL HIGH SCHOOLS SUGGESTED BY 21 STATE DEPARTMENTS OF EDUCATION

	NINTH YEAR		TENTH YEAR		ELEVENTH YEAR		TWELFTH YEAR		NUMBER OF PROGRAMS IN WHICH OFFERED
	Required	Elective	Required	Elective	Required	Elective	Required	Elective	
Latin 1	4	3	1	6	1	7			21
Latin 2			4	2	1	6	1	7	20
Latin 3					1	4	1	3	9
French 1	1	2	2	4		6		6	14
French 2			1	2	2	4		4	14
French 3						3			7
Spanish 1		2		2		4		4	7
Spanish 2				2		2			7
German 1		2		2		6		6	8
German 2				2		2			8
English	21		21		21		18	3	21
General mathematics	6*	1	1						7
Elementary algebra	16	4	2	2	2	4	3	5	21
Advanced algebra					1	2	4		10
Plane geometry			5	4	6	2	1	5	21
Solid geometry					2	2	1	2	10
Advanced arithmetic		3		3	2	1		1	5
Commercial or business arithmetic			2		1	3			10
Civics	14†	1	1		1		2	1	19
American history			1		14		4		19
Modern European or modern world history	1		6	3					11

TABLE VII.—*Continued*

	Ninth Year		Tenth Year		Eleventh Year		Twelfth Year		Number of Programs in Which Offered
	Required	Elective	Required	Elective	Required	Elective	Required	Elective	
Ancient or early European or early world history		3	1	1					8
Political science or problems of democracy					1		5	3	9
Elementary economics or sociology						1	2	7	10
Occupations	7†	1					1		7
Industrial and commercial geography	1	1	3	5	1				11
Physical geography	2			2					5
General science	14	3		5					17
Biology			8		2	5	1	1	19
Physics					1	5	1	12	20
Chemistry						8	3	6	18
Zoology			1			1		1	3
Agriculture	1	15‡		15		8		6	18
Home economics		15	2	18		9		3	20
Manual training and manual arts		9		8		3		2	10
Bookkeeping and accounting				1	1	8		4	10
Typewriting		1	1	1	1	5	1	6	8
Art	1	3		2		3		3	6
Music		3		2	1	3	1	3	6
Health and physical education	8		8		7		7		8

* In four cases either general mathematics or algebra is required in the ninth year.
† In four cases occupations is taught in connection with the course in civics.
‡ In some states several curricula are suggested for small and rural high schools, and certain subjects are required in certain curricula only. In the table just given all subjects are classed as elective if not required in all curricula.

state departments of education.   Rule (19:85) gives the following summary of state requirements for high-school graduation by subjects in 1925-1926.

> *English*—20 states require three years; and 20 states require four years.
> *Language*—8 states require two years.
> *Mathematics*—25 states require one year of algebra; 16 states require geometry; and 3 states require general mathematics.
> *History*—38 states require American history.
> *Social science*—17 states require some social science other than history and civics.
> *Science*—30 states require at least one year of science; nine of them name general science; 6, biology; and 5, either physics or chemistry.

The most significant items in these requirements, as they affect rural high schools, would appear to be that in 8 states all pupils are required to take two years of a foreign language, and that in 25 states and 15 states, respectively, algebra and geometry are necessary for graduation.   Other interesting items are the absence of health and physical education as subject requirements, and the fact that in 10 states no work in science is required for graduation.   A critical analysis of these requirements raises the question regarding the aims of public secondary education and the common needs of the great mass of secondary-school pupils in meeting the demands of everyday life.

State departments of education have in many states prepared programs of studies and curricula for small and rural high schools.   Table VII shows an analysis of the programs of studies for small and rural high schools suggested by 21 state departments of education.   Subjects offered in fewer than five programs are not given.

Comparison of the subjects offered in these suggested programs of 21 states with the preceding tables of subjects offered by rural high schools reveals the close similarity.   There is the same emphasis upon the traditional academic subjects, the same lack of emphasis upon such subjects as art, music, industrial arts, and physical and health education.   It is probably true, however, that the percentage of state programs of studies for small and rural high schools in which one or more of this last-mentioned group of subjects are suggested has increased within the last decade.

VI. The Curriculum of the Rural Junior College

Inquiries addressed to the several states in regard to adaptations made in public junior colleges to meet the specific educational needs of rural communities resulted almost without exception in negative replies. A notable example of a variant development, in which definite adaptation of the work of a junior college to the peculiar educational needs of rural people is made (2), is the Chaffee Junior College, of Ontario, California. Agriculture is offered in the two-year junior certificate curriculum and in the two-year non-collegiate diploma curriculum. Six one-year vocational curricula are offered, among which are an inspector's course containing the subjects of botany, entomology, pomology, plant pathology, citriculture, and field practice; and a homemaker's course containing the subjects of home activities, clothing, textiles, interior decorating, arts and crafts, foods, and household accounting.

One of the significant features of the program of the Chaffee Junior College is its short unit courses for adults. These courses as offered in 1929 are listed in Table VIII. The work in the Chaffee Junior College represents, it would seem, a significant development in the direction of meeting rural needs and indicates some of the possibilities in rural secondary education on the junior-college level.

VII. State Educational Surveys and the Rural Secondary Curriculum

State educational surveys have pointed out time and again the characteristics and weaknesses of rural high-school curricula. The Virginia survey (16:179), one of the more recent state surveys, in regard to the curricula of the rural high school, embodies the following typical characterization and recommendations:

> It appears, therefore, that both of these schools—typical of the small rural high schools of the state, are essentially college-preparatory schools. Youths attending them head for college because, forsooth, they know of no other route to traverse and have no opportunities to travel in any other direction even though they desired to do so.
>
> There is need in Virginia for a revision of the program of studies for rural high schools, . . . for making all work that is offered function more vitally than it does at present. . . Specifically the survey staff recommends that the two-year course in ancient and modern European history give place to a single year of European history; that a course

TABLE VIII.—CHAFFEE JUNIOR COLLEGE UNIT CURRICULA: SHORT COURSES
FOR ADULTS

	Clock Hours		Clock Hours
Agriculture:		Education:	
Citriculture	10	Parent education	60
Deciduous fruits	10	Teacher-training lectures	30
Poultry husbandry	10	Extension courses, each	32
Project visitation	20		
		English:	
Astronomy	60	Contemporaneous literature	30
		The drama	30
California history	30		
		Language:	
Commercial subjects:		Spanish	120
Business law	60		
Salesmanship	30	Music:	
Commercial English	60	Orchestra	60
Typing	120	Chorus—community	60
Shorthand	120		
		Public speaking	30
		Scout leadership training:	
		Men	30
		Women	30

in occupations and in community and vocational civics be established;
that the science courses be articulated more closely with the interests
and needs of rural life; that at least an introductory course in business
practices and bookkeeping be provided; that only one foreign language
be offered in the very small schools—and that preferably this language
be Latin; that home economics be offered for at least two years in
every school; that a course in farm and home mechanics be introduced;
that some attention be given to drawing and music; and that the
courses in English be vitalized by the introduction of more of the
features that relate to the practical experience of the pupils pursuing
them. There is, of course, no justice in depriving those who honestly
desire to prepare for college of the opportunities to do so. Contrari-
wise, however, there is no justice in guiding all toward college doors,
when clearly only a portion of the pupils will ever enter therein.

SECTION III

PROGRESS IN CURRICULUM-MAKING FOR VOCATIONAL AGRICULTURE IN RURAL SECONDARY SCHOOLS

R. M. STEWART
Professor of Rural Education
Cornell University, Ithaca, New York

Those interested in the organization and methods of handling the content of agriculture, its supporting sciences, and the vehicular subjects needed for its adequate use and dissemination in the education of youth for farming vocations have during the last decade or more shared in the general agitation for the reconstruction of the curriculum. In addition they have carried on collaborative experimentation in the schools. In fact, no little credit is due the leaders in agricultural education who have been responsible for giving form and impetus to the movement for a curriculum that will not only conserve the best of past experience, but will at the same time make vivid and dynamic the school programs that reflect present-day experiences and that integrate the best of these experiences with the traditional subjects into a curriculum which is consonant with the needs of the new day.

In 1917, agricultural education, though dependent upon the extant forms of general education and upon experiments in industrial education, was faced with the problems of formulating a curriculum based upon the needs of persons engaged in farming occupations. The short time available, after the passage of the National Vocational Education Act, for constructing the program of vocational agriculture for secondary schools, made it necessary to prepare a program based largely on experience gained in other fields. It was logical, therefore, that the first steps in making a curriculum for agriculture in secondary schools should be empirical in character and based essentially upon experience in the colleges.

The programs set up by the several states reflected this general conception. It soon became evident that the practical experience gained on the home farm was to become pivotal in the arrangement of the curriculum. It was evident also that no curriculum of studies could be set up that would have universal validity for all the schools in any given region of the state, to say nothing of the schools of a whole state. This situation presented a most difficult problem, that of setting up a dynamic curriculum sufficiently definite for use by either the relatively untrained teacher or by the teacher of science who may have been called upon to teach the new courses. That the less competent the teacher, the more dynamic the teaching material should be is perhaps true; but, in general, the less competent the teacher, the greater the need also for the fixed curriculum as a means of controlling the instruction.

The point just emphasized is included in this discussion because in the rapid development in curriculum construction it has been necessary to provide an extensive program of teacher training that would make the teacher specifically competent, not only in teaching classes from an outline of studies already provided, but also in discovering the type of farming in the area served, the pupils' experiences, the conditions under which the pupils get their education, and the practices of the best farmers.

This type of training and competency was forced upon teachers from another angle. From the beginning of the program in agricultural education, it was provided that each pupil should have six months of supervised farm practice in connection with his school instruction. It soon became evident that not only did the curriculum have to conform to the farming needs of the region, but that the local curriculum should also first be based upon situations presented by the home farms in the area, and, finally, upon the farms of the region and of the state. A recent study by Kiltz (10) showing to what extent the kinds of supervised farm practice carried on by the pupils reflected the major farm enterprises of the home farms and to what extent the teachers taught in terms of these farms and these farm practices is indicative of a rapidly developing point of view.

In a study made by the writer (23) covering nineteen representative states located in the four regional areas of the United States and representing 987 teachers of vocational agriculture, it was shown, on the question of the teacher's studying the agricultural resources of the school community, that:

1. 81 percent (by median of states) made animal surveys for school use.
2. 82.6 percent made crop surveys for school use.
3. 34.9 percent made service appliance surveys.
4. 58.3 percent used census reports for studying the community.
5. 65.7 percent received help from the county agricultural agent.

6. 69.9 percent received information from grain dealers, stock buyers, merchants, bankers, or other local citizens.
7. 73.3 percent used bulletins from the college of agriculture for assistance in the study of the local community.
8. 52.8 percent used bulletins from other states for that purpose.
9. 55.0 percent used specialists from the college to assist in carrying out the local program.

In this same study, certain activities regarding the construction of curricula and courses of study were noted. In this connection the study showed that:

1. 89.2 percent of the teachers made their own curricula.
2. 80.9 percent submitted their proposed curricula to the state supervisor for approval.
3. 96. 2 percent assumed the responsibility for the selection of content for the various agricultural courses that they taught.
4. 96 percent based the content of their courses upon an analysis of the activities of the farmers in the community.
5. 53.8 percent were working coöperatively with other agencies on a long-time agricultural program for the community.
6. 84 percent attempted to correlate their work with the non-vocational work in the high school.
7. 23.5 percent set up special curricula for pupils who did not take the four-year curriculum.

Similar results were found concerning the methods of teaching used and the character of the activities in the supervised farm-practice program. This shows rather conclusively that the teachers of agriculture are committed to the responsibility of constructing a curriculum which reflects the local needs of the pupils in the selection and organization of materials of instruction.

The following excerpts from a state bulletin typify the aims of the majority of the states, and also their actual practices:

> In any community, therefore, the course objectives are determined by (a) the type or types of farming in which the farmers are engaging and (b) the local related agricultural occupations such as herdsman, farm manager, milk tester. . . Such courses [as teachers prepare] should be organized so as to make the fullest possible use of the pupils' experience gained on the home farm as well as the experience of the

successful farmers in the community. . . In the preparation of the courses of study consideration should be had for the following:

1. Study the local types of farming, and related occupations in order to determine the course objective.

2. Summarize the facts as suggested above and assign to each year's work the enterprises that may be most appropriately and effectively studied that year.

3. Break down the enterprises to be taught in any given year into the component jobs which the farmers need to perform during the year in carrying on the enterprises.

4. Arrange the enterprises and farm jobs in accordance with the seasonal sequence operations on the farm.

5. Get acquainted with the pupils who have enrolled or who are likely to enroll for vocational instruction . . . Make a systematic study of their individual interests and aptitudes, general intelligence, farm and school experience, ages and ambitions with respect to a vocation.

6. As the work progresses, memoranda of the desired changes should be made, to the end that the actual experience of teaching the various lessons may result in the preparation of a better course of study and teaching plan for the following year.

In carrying out such suggestions as those already given, the following points will appear as valuable:

1. The part of the curriculum in any one year would be varied to suit the needs of pupils and to provide for a continuity of enterprises in keeping with a long-time program of study.

2. Unifying and integrating content would be related to the enterprises, according to significance and difficulty.

3. The most important crop and animal enterprises would come in the first years and specialities and specialized study would follow.

4. Service subjects such as soils and fertilizers, shop exercises, etc., would be introduced gradually in relation to enterprises and their organization in the farm business, taking on management emphasis toward the end of the high-school period.

5. Integrating and unifying subjects would come in the last year or years as the basis of organizing and evaluating the principles that were operating in the enterprises taught.

SECTION IV
SOME IMPORTANT CURRICULAR PROBLEMS IN RURAL SECONDARY EDUCATION

EMERY N. FERRISS

After an analysis of state surveys and other data Dr. Roemer (18) concludes that the small high school means "limited curricula, poorly arranged and ill-balanced curricula, unjustifiable subject requirements of pupils, and practically no vocational offerings. Miss Heffernan in her study of the curricula of the rural high schools of California (7) points out that in the small high school "college prescription is the outstanding curricular determinant." In her study of courses of study she concludes that we are "hardly curriculum conscious" in the small high school. She states that in the 239 rural high schools studied "only 12 percent had the curriculum in mechanical form to be studied by students, teachers, or parents." The implication appears to be that the textbook used largely determines the content and organization of the course of study in the subjects taught in the rural high school. Among other studies supporting the latter statement is the *Report of the Survey Staff in the Virginia Survey,* which states: "On the other hand, the ancient history work, as observed, was registering no worthwhile values; the science work was unapplied to the problems of life; and, the language work was formal and stilted" (16:179). Practically all these conclusions are directly supported or implied in the results of the present study.

Some salient problems of the rural secondary curriculum which need careful study may be set forth in concluding this chapter.

First, in view of the various limitations of the rural secondary school and in accord with a sound educational philosophy of secondary education like that implied in the 'Cardinal Principles' or other adequate modern statements of the aims and purposes of secondary education, what is the primary and what is the secondary responsibility of the rural secondary school? At present college preparation is undoubtedly observed in practice as the primary responsibility. In view of the character of the rural secondary-school population in school and particularly in view of the potential school population, is this practice defensible? Also, should the primary responsibility of the rural secondary school be to help the great mass of rural children to make the best possible individual and social adjustments to the common practical and cultural needs of modern life? If an affirmative answer to the last question is the correct interpretation of the rural secondary school, what should be the content of its basic or 'constant curriculum'? Furthermore, if the provision for the differentiated needs of important pupil groups, especially vocational, is the secondary responsibility of the rural high schools, should the college-preparatory group be regarded as one of the special groups, and its special needs, as with other special groups, be met so far as the school facilities permit, only after the school has adequately fulfilled its primary responsibility?

Second, there is a group of problems which may be embodied in one question, as they are needed for rural high schools, what provision can be made for developing and revising in a scientific manner objectives and curricula, and courses of study in the various subjects, including their adaptation to regional and local needs?

Large urban centers are able to carry on programs of curriculum development and revision providing the necessary expert assistance. They have been able to analyze local needs and provide for them through curricula. Rural secondary schools, with the exception of vocational agriculture and more rarely of home economics, have either had no definite courses of study or else have had only state syllabi in which, from the very nature of the case, no local or regional adaptations are provided. In rural secondary schools there is neither the personnel nor the means for carrying out a continuing program of scientific curriculum-building suited to discovering and making the desirable local and regional adaptations. What organization of state, regional, and local educational institutions and personnel can be effected for providing rural secondary schools with modern curricula and courses of study?

Third, what are the material and social (including institutional) educational resources of rural environments that can and should be utilized in providing for rural youth the most effective and worthwhile curricular materials and exercises? Can these be discovered by the analysis of certain type localities and regions?

Fourth, what must be the range and variety of curricular elements in the rural secondary-school curriculum to provide adequately for the developmental needs of adolescent youth, the desirable common social adjustments, the desirable exploratory experiences, and the desirable vocational information, training, and appreciation? Since in many rural schools the number of pupils enrolled is insufficient to make local provision for special vocational preferences either practicable or effective, how shall these special curricular needs be met in rural secondary schools? Also, what are the educational needs of rural boys and girls not in attendance in rural high schools and of adults in rural communities for whom educational opportunities should be afforded by the rural high school? What type of curricula are needed to supply these needs and what should be the content of these curricula?

Fifth, administrative routine presents the final problem: What is the applicability of 'new plans' of curriculum organization and method to the rural secondary school, especially as regards their values in making possible more varied and richer curriculum offerings in the smaller schools without increasing the size of teaching staff? Within the scope of this problem there is need of careful study of such methods of individualized instruction as the Dalton plan and the 'unit' plan.

BIBLIOGRAPHY

1. BRIGGS, THOMAS H. "The special functions of secondary schools." *Seventh Yearbook. Department of Superintendence.* Washington, 1929.

2. CHAFFEE JUNIOR COLLEGE. *Curriculum Bulletin.* Ontario, California. 1929.

3. CHILD, H. A. "An Investigation of Certain Phases of the Reorganization Movement in the Grammar Grades of Indiana Public Schools."

4. CLIFTON, JOHN L. *The Small Secondary School in Ohio.* Columbus, 1929.

5. COOK, KATHERINE M. *Rural Education in 1926-28.* Washington, 1929. (U. S. Bur. Educ. Bull., No. 18).

6. GREENE, RHUE E. "A Study of the Distinguishing Characteristics of the Junior High Schools of Nebraska." (Unpublished master's dissertation on file in the University of Nebraska Library).

7. HEFFERNAN, HELEN. *Some Problems Suggested by a Study of Curricula in 239 California Rural High Schools.* 1929.

8. Indiana. *Administrative Handbook for Indiana High Schools.* Indianapolis, 1928. (State Dep. of Public Instr. Bull., No. 100).

9. JUDD, CHARLES H. "The development of the junior high school movement." *Course of Lectures on the Junior High School.* Chicago, 1924.

10. KILTZ, K. W. "Study of a Local Area at Crawfordsville, Indiana." (Unpublished study).

11. New York. *The Junior High School in New York State.* Albany, 1928.

12. North Dakota. *Twenty-first Annual Report of the Inspector of High Schools.* Bismarck, 1928.

13. OBRIEN, F. P., and KELLY, VICTOR H. "An improved organization affecting small high schools." *Univ. of Kansas Bull. of Educ.,* 1:1928, 3-9.

14. OBRIEN, F. P. and SMART, T. J. *The Organization and Distinctive Features of the Shawnee-Mission Rural High School, Johnson County, Kansas.* Lawrence, 1923. (Kansas Studies in Educ., No. 1).

15. Oklahoma. *Annual High School Bulletin.* Guthrie, 1929. Pp. 17-41.

16. O'SHEA, M. V. (Director). *Public Education in Virginia.* Richmond, 1928. P. 179.

17. OWENS, MORGAN R. "Arkansas high-school program." *Arkansas Jour. of Educ.,* 8:1930, 8-9.

18. ROEMER, JOSEPH. "The weakness of the small high school." *Peabody Jour. of Educ.,* 6:1928, 37-43.

19. RULE, JAMES N. "Influence of state departments of education upon curriculums of small high schools." *Sixth Yearbook. Department of Superintendence.* Washington, 1928.

20. *Rural Junior High School, The.* Washington, 1929. (U. S. Bur. Educ. Bull. 1928, No. 28.)

21. SIMON, DONALD LIONEL. "The Six-Year High School in Indiana." (Unpublished thesis on file in the Library of the University of Chicago).

22. SPAULDING, F. T. *The Small Junior High School.* Cambridge, 1927.

23. STEWART, R. M. *An Analysis of the Activities of Teachers of Vocational Agriculture in Nineteen States.*

24. Virginia. *Manual of Administration for High Schools of Virginia No. 4.* Richmond, 1928.

25. West Virginia. *Manual for Secondary Schools.* Charleston, 1926.

CHAPTER VI

THE PREPARATION OF TEACHERS FOR RURAL SCHOOLS

MABEL CARNEY
Associate Professor of Education
Teachers College, Columbia University, New York City

The term *rural teachers* as employed in this chapter relates to the teachers of farm-dwelling children. Included here are 153,300 teachers in one-room schools, 47,000 in two-teacher schools, and 100,000 in consolidated schools, making an approximate total of 300,000. These 300,000 rural teachers constituted nearly half of the 642,712 elementary teachers in the United States in 1928 and occupied 36 percent of the 831,934 total teaching positions recorded for the same year. Of the entire group, the 200,000 working in one- and two-teacher schools and responsible for the instruction of over five million country children will be held particularly in mind throughout this discussion.

Contrary to impression, one-teacher schools, which represent the problem of rural teacher training at its worst, are not only numerous still, but also widely distributed. Only six states have fewer than five hundred schools each of this type, while six other states—Illinois, Iowa, Pennsylvania, New York, Missouri, and Kansas—have over seven thousand each, and twenty-one states have over three thousand each. Regionally the great majority of one-teacher schools are in the Mid-West, while most two-teacher schools are in the South.

I. THE PRESENT STATUS OF RURAL TEACHERS

No comprehensive study of the general status of rural teachers has yet been made. Information on this subject is, therefore, restricted to various state surveys and special studies made recently and to personal judgments collected from well-informed persons in the different state departments of education as hereinafter described.

1. Present Status as Revealed by State Surveys and Special Studies

Data presented here have been selected from studies conducted in eleven widely distributed states during the last seven years, or since 1923. For comparative purposes these eleven states have been classifid both by regions and by the unit of school organization employed: (1) Midwestern states (and also New York) under district organization; namely, Wisconsin, Missouri, and North Dakota; (2) Western states, Texas, and California, under the semi-county unit; and (3) Southern states under the county unit; namely, Alabama, Arkansas, Florida, Maryland, and North Carolina.

a. In New York and Mid-Western States under District Organization.—Teacher training being a state function, those states with the least centralized control have the greatest difficulty in raising qualifications. This makes the problem of rural-teacher improvement particularly difficult in the Wid-West and also in New York where the district unit of organization is employed.

The *Rural School Survey of New York State* published in 1923, in which Professor W. C. Bagley was responsible for the study of teaching personnel, gives the most vivid and comprehensive portrayal of the typical rural teacher ever drawn. According to this picture (4 : 96)[1] the median rural teacher of New York at this time was a young woman between twenty-three and twenty-four years of age who had been teaching three or four years. She came from a farm family and had completed a four-year high school, taking the teacher-training course in the last year. Her salary was $800 to $850 for a term of nine months. By 1929, however, New York, according to records in the State Department of Education, had increased standards until the average rural teacher was a high-school graduate with one year of advanced preparation, four years' experience, and a salary of $1,250 to $1,300.

Wisconsin, Missouri, and North Dakota, all under district organization, represent the present status in the Midwest with fair accuracy. In Wisconsin, in 1926, 6.5 percent of the teachers in one-room schools had had two or more years of professional preparation, and 85 percent were high-school graduates with one year of training

---

[1] Figures in parentheses conjoined with citations from the literature refer by number and page to the bibliography at the end of this chapter.

acquired chiefly in the county normal schools; but 7 percent had finished the high school only and 2 percent less than the high school (2:162f.). In Missouri, the recent state survey (1929) shows most of the 8500 rural teachers of the state to be four-year high-school graduates with a little professional training embodied in the high-school curriculum. In North Dakota, according to the study by W. E. Peik (14), only 1.6 percent of the rural teachers of the state are less than high-school graduates, while 30 percent have had one or two years of normal-school training.

b. *In Western States under the Semi-County Unit.*—Texas with a state survey in 1925 and California from a special study by Margaret Elizabeth Siggins in 1927 furnish good illustrations of rural-teacher status in western states under semi-county administration. The typical one-room rural-school teacher in Texas in 1925 was a young woman between twenty-two and twenty-three years of age with 34 months, or approximately four years, of high-school education and a median of 1.7 months, or one summer term, of professional training. She came from a farm home, remained only one year in the same school, and received a median rural salary of $608 (20:151ff.).

Elementary teachers in California are now supposed to have had three years of training beyond the high school, but nearly 70 percent of the 1652 one-room rural teachers of the state fail to meet this standard, while 21 percent are not high-school graduates, and 7 percent have had no schooling beyond the elementary grades. The average preparation of rural teachers, as shown by 30 percent of the total number, is high-school graduation with one or two years of normal-school training (8).

c. *In Southern States Under the County Unit.*—In the South, the extensive use of the county unit, when combined with aggressive leadership by state departments of education, has contributed greatly to higher qualifications for rural teachers, notably in Alabama, Maryland, and North Carolina, though Arkansas and Florida show much lower status. In Florida 60 percent of all schools are of the one-, two-, and three-teacher type, and many of the rural teachers have completed only the seven elementary grades (18), while Arkansas in 1923 had only common-school graduates in 22 percent of the rural schools (19).

In Alabama, the State Department of Education has made careful studies of teacher status, one of which, conducted in a typical county, reveals the median rural teacher as follows (1:136):

She is unmarried, 23 years of age; possesses less than two years of education above high-school level; has had 3.8 years of teaching experience, but is new to her teaching job this school session, and teaches seven different subjects, hearing daily sixteen recitations, each twenty minutes in length. She walks daily over a sand-clay road to and from school a total distance of 5.6 miles. She pays $21.11 a month for board and room where she has a roommate. She receives a salary of $85.50 a month for 7.44 months in the year, which amounts to $636.12 per annum, or $1.74 a day, calculated on a 365-day year. When her annual board bill is paid, her net income is $1.04 per day for the year.

Of all states, however, North Carolina and Maryland furnish the most striking illustrations of rapid improvement in the preparation of teachers. In the former, the average training of white teachers in 1922-23 was only one year of college, whereas in 1929-30 the average was two and three-fourths years. Even at this, the training of city white teachers is on the average slightly more than a year above that for rural white teachers. In Maryland, only 54 percent of all white elementary teachers were normal-school graduates or the equivalent in 1923, but 93.3 percent had attained this rank in 1929-30. Of the white teachers in one-teacher schools, 89 percent were normal-school graduates in 1929, their average salary being $1,118 and their median experience three years.

2. Status as Revealed by Personal Inquiry of State Departments of Education

To gather some idea of trends in this field, the writer addressed a brief inquiry in June, 1930, to one or more well-informed persons in each state department of education. This letter requested scientific data, when available, or when not, personal estimates regarding: (a) the scholarship and training, (b) the present average salary, (c) the tenure, and (d) the surplus, of rural teachers. The replies, received from all states, were in some cases supported by accurate data, but represented only personal opinion in other cases.

a. *Scholarship and Training.* Only two states, Arkansas and Florida, admit that the general average scholarship for rural teachers is below high-school graduation. Two other states, Georgia and Missouri, reply that high-school graduation is their average level, but all the others claim that the average teacher in one-room rural schools under their jurisdiction is more advanced professionally than a high-school graduate. Fourteen states; namely, Colorado, Illinois, Iowa, Kansas, Kentucky, Nebraska, New Mexico, North Dakota, Oklahoma, South Carolina, South Dakota, Tennessee, Vermont, and West Virginia, report their typical rural teacher as a four-year high-school graduate with some additional training—usually six to twelve weeks, but not so much as a full year. Seventeen states, on the other hand, stipulated high-school graduation and one full year of additional training as their most universal standard. These are Alabama, Indiana, Louisiana, Michigan, Minnesota, Mississippi, Montana, New Hampshire, New Jersey, New York, Ohio, Pennsylvania, Rhode Island, Texas, Virginia, Wisconsin, and Wyoming. Above these come the thirteen remaining states where the majority of teachers in one-teacher rural schools, as in other elementary schools, are four-year high-school graduates with two full years of professional training. This list includes Arizona, California, Connecticut, Delaware, Idaho, Maine, Maryland, Massachusetts, Nevada, Ohio, Rhode Island, Utah, and Washington.

b. Salaries. In the matter of annual salary for teachers in one-teacher schools, three states, Arkansas, Georgia, and North Carolina, reply that the actual or estimated figure for this item falls below $500. Fifteen states place it from $500 to $750; seventeen states, from $750 to $1,000; and thirteen, above $1,000. The highest salaries indicated are $1,485 in Arizona and $1,385 in California, while the lowest is $392 in Georgia. All states show recent increases in salary, except Indiana, Missouri, New Mexico, Oklahoma, Washington, and West Virginia, where there have been slight decreases. Except for Delaware, where the median salary of this type increased over $300 during the last five years, there has been little change in most of the states, indicating that the national median for one-teacher schools is still not far above $761, as computed by W. H. Gaumnitz (9:41) for 1924-25.

c. Tenure. This question, asking how long the average rural teacher remains in country schools, was not satisfactorily answered. Eleven states had no information on the subject; others could offer only loose estimates. Of 37 state representatives responding, 7 put the average tenure of rural teachers in their state as two years; 18 say three years; 4, four years; and 8, five years. This indication of three years as the usual tenure of rural teachers is verified by most surveys and other studies touching this subject.

d. *Surplus and Its Effects Upon Rural Schools.* Five states failed to answer this question. Of the 43 replying, 35 report a surplus of elementary-school teachers, while 8 states: namely, California, Idaho, Maine, Maryland, Michigan, Rhode Island, Vermont, and Wyoming, declare they have no oversupply in this field (though California has a surplus of high-school teachers). Maryland and Rhode Island are apparently the only states which have adopted the commendable practice of preventing a surplus by requiring two years of preparation and then restricting enrollment in their teacher-training institutions. All states but three, Iowa, Missouri, and West Virginia, report that the present surplus has benefited rural schools by making better qualified teachers available for their service. The present surplus seems greatest and most inimical to rural schools in Missouri and Iowa, where the recent farm depression has been marked and where large numbers of high-school graduates are being turned out every year and allowed to compete for one-teacher schools under rather lax certificate requirements. From the data, it is quite clear that there is no surplus of fully trained teachers for the United States as a whole. The surplus existing to-day is largely a surplus of half-prepared or unprepared teachers which could be immediately relieved by increasing standards.

e. *Median Rural Teacher of the United States.* Summarizing the foregoing estimates and such other data as are available, it appears that the typical one-room rural teacher of the United States to-day (1930) is a young woman about twenty-three years of age, of native American stock, and of farm or small-town background. Her preparation includes four years of high-school education with apparently 12 to 18 weeks of professional training secured frequently in summer sessions or in the graduate year of high-school training classes. She teaches from 20 to 25 children through the eight grades of the elementary curriculum for a school term of 7.8 months, and remains only one or two years in the same school. Her median annual salary is $761, and her total service in rural schools averages about three years, after which she is married or transfers to grade teaching or continues her education, usually in a state teachers' college.[2]

---

[2] The foregoing discussion relates wholly to white teachers. Unfortunately, the status of Negro rural teachers, involving the most deplorable situation in the whole field of teacher training, must be entirely omitted here for lack of space.

II. The Specialized Preparation of Rural Teachers

1. Historical Statement

The oldest system of formal teacher training in the United States is associated with the preparation of rural teachers. This refers to normal training in high schools, which was established in New York in 1834, five years prior to the founding of the first American normal school. Though gradually disappearing, this system is still employed in 19 states; 1,491 such departments were maintained in 1928-29, enrolling 21,308 students and certificating 12,584 (10). Notwithstanding its present disfavor, the secondary system of teacher training has given rural schools more teachers, at least partially prepared, than has any other agency, and was first in initiating two notable contributions to the general field of teacher training; namely, graded practice and professionalized subject matter. A similar system, teacher training in the county normal schools of Wisconsin, was authorized in 1899 and is still in operation.

Rural teacher training in state normal schools was initiated at Kalamazoo, Michigan, in 1901 through the far-sighted vision of J. B. Waldo and under the able leadership of Ernest Burnham, father of the movement, who for twenty-six years has faithfully served and glorified the same position. Alfred Bayliss, former state superintendent of Illinois, moved next in establishing a rural department with a rural training school at Macomb in 1906 under the direction of Caroline Grote and Mabel Carney. Then came the influential activities at Kirksville, Missouri, in 1907-1908 under Marie Turney Harvey, Harold W. Foght, and Leslie B. Sipple, all inspired by President John R. Kirk. Following this, other centers developed widely over the country, including especially the work at Cheney, Washington, by N. D. Showalter and Margaret Curran; that at Farmville, Virginia, by Fannie W. Dunn; at Rock Hill, South Carolina, by Hetty S. Browne and W. K. Tate; and at Normal, Illinois, under the presidency of David Felmley in 1911. From this date forward, stimulated by the Roosevelt Commission on Country Life, the movement has developed steadily until it now involves 85 percent of all public normal schools and teachers' colleges in the country.

2. Present Practice in the Specialization of Rural Training in Normal Schools and Teachers' Colleges

a. The Situation in 1926-27. In 1926-27, William McKinley Robinson (16) of Kalamazoo, Michigan, then in the United States Bureau of Education, found 152 normal schools and teachers' colleges, 83 percent of the entire number, offering courses in rural education or otherwise differentiating their work for prospective rural teachers. Of these 152 institutions, 115, or 62 percent of the entire number, employed special rural instructors; 84 provided rural-school practice; 75 offered special rural curricula one, two, or three years in length; and 76 others offered special rural courses, including rural sociology, rural-school management, and rural-school methods, in the order named.

In the same year (1927), R. L. Bunting and Verne McGuffey (7: 716-727) investigated nine specific phases of what normal schools and teachers' colleges were doing for the preparation of rural teachers under the following heads:

1. The classification of a distinct rural group of students.
2. The offering of distinct curricula for rural teachers.
3. Special practice teaching for the rural group of students.
4. Rural life clubs among students preparing for rural work.
5. Extension service to rural teachers and communities.
6. Rural teacher-placement.
7. Special equipment for the rural-service department.
8. Budgets for rural teacher training and other rural work.
9. The number of instructors devoting time to rural interests.

Replies from 149 institutions showed that 85 percent were participating in one or more of these nine phases. Twenty-nine institutions, chiefly in the Mid-West, were sharing in all nine aspects and rendering relatively six times as much service to rural schools as similar institutions not committed to the theory of rural specialization; 60 had a distinct group of students preparing to teach in rural schools; 113 offered differentiated rural curricula from one year to four years in length; 54 were maintaining 350 one- and two-teacher rural practice schools, and 41 institutions reported the use of 80 consolidated or village schools for practice purposes; 45 rural clubs were reported with a total membership of 3,885 students; 91 of the 149 institutions were engaged in one or more rural extension activities; 50 reported placement activity for rural graduates; 44 provided separate offices for their rural staffs; 28 furnished departmental rural budgets; and

103 institutions employed 424 rural-education specialists, an average of 4 such instructors per school.

b. The Situation in 1929-30. During the year 1929-30, the writer undertook to classify all state normal schools and teachers' colleges in the United States on a basis of rural service. This effort was based on a study of catalogs, questionnaire inquiries, personal correspondence, and visiting. From this analysis a descriptive classification of eight groupings resulted, and the numerical distribution of institutions indicated in the following list was made:

CLASSIFICATION OF STATE NORMAL SCHOOLS AND
TEACHERS' COLLEGES ON A BASIS OF RURAL SERVICE

For the Academic Year 1930-31 (Exclusive of Summer Sessions)
Made from a Study of Catalogs, Questionnaire Inquiries, and
Personal Correspondence and Visiting
(174 Institutions included; no private, Negro, and urban types)

I. *Institutions which offer special courses in the rural field, provide some special practice in typical rural schools, employ one or more designated rural instructors, and enroll a group of students preparing specifically for rural school teaching in one-teacher, two-teacher, or consolidated schools.*

Sixty-seven institutions are included in this list. These, together with the five described later under Group II, constitute the 72 public normal schools and teachers colleges doing most for rural education in the United States.[3]

II. *Institutions which make all the provisions just listed, but in which all the students enrolled, rather than a special rural group, take the rural instruction offered.*

Five schools constitute this unique group; namely, those of Connecticut at Danbury, New Britain, New Haven, and Willimantic, and the normal school at Salisbury, Maryland. Practically all graduates of these institutions do their first teaching in rural schools.

III. *Institutions which make all the provisions previously listed under I except those for special rural practice.*

Eleven schools are included in this group, which, with the 72 just listed under I and II, make a total of 83 institutions employing special rural instructors.

IV. *Institutions which offer one or more special rural courses but employ no designated rural instructor; that is, institutions in which the rural*

---

[3] The names of the institutions grouped under each of these headings must unfortunately be omitted for lack of space, but a complete list, including a directory of the names and addresses of all special rural instructors employed, may be obtained upon request by addressing the writer of the chapter at Teachers College, Columbia University, New York City.

courses are taught by staff members whose major interest is in some other field. This group may be further divided into two subgroups: (a) *Those which provide special rural practice in typical rural schools* and (b) *Those which do not provide special rural practice.*

This group as a whole includes 28 institutions, 5 of which have rural training schools.

V. *Institutions offering no special rural courses of any kind but maintaining one or more rural practice schools.*

Seven are included here.

VI. *Institutions maintaining neither courses nor practice schools specialized for rural-school needs but conducting some occasional rural activities, as holding rural-school conferences, fostering Rural Life Clubs, and so forth.*

Four institutions answer this description.

VII. *Institutions making no definite provision whatever for rural education in any specialized sense.*

This group includes 48 schools some of which are highly urbanized, but the majority of which have large rural constituencies.

VIII. *Institutions which make no specialized rural provision in either courses or practice teaching but which declare their environment to be so rural that all their instruction has to be, and is, adapted to rural-school needs.*

Four institutions made this report; namely, Arcata, California; Hattiesburg, Mississippi; Billings, Montana; and Castleton, Vermont.

c. Outstanding Institutions. The three foremost institutions of the United States in rural-teacher training are those at Kalamazoo and Ypsilanti, Michigan, and at Cedar Falls, Iowa. These lead not only in number of rural students and instructors but also in length of service, curricula offered, number of rural training schools, and other respects. Normal, Illinois; Winona, Minnesota; Aberdeen, South Dakota; Kutztown and Shippensburg, Pennsylvania; and Farmville, Virginia, rank well also; while Salisbury, Maryland, seems to be conducting the best and most plentiful rural-school practice in the United States. Connecticut, Illinois, Kentucky, Michigan, Minnesota, Missouri, Nebraska, North Dakota, Oklahoma, Pennsylvania, and Wisconsin provide specialized rural training in all, or practically all, of their teachers' colleges; and New York and California after long indifference have recently established new and vigorous departments in several of their normal schools.

3. Current Demand and New Trends

The current need for trained teachers is in rural schools. As previously shown, 35 states report a surplus of teachers but *not of fully trained teachers and not in rural schools.* In Alabama (1), for example, 1,158 rural teachers were needed last year but only 207 city teachers. Notwithstanding this situation, many training institutions persist in preparing an oversupply of grade teachers, and take little thought of rural needs. Earl N. Rhodes, to cite a single instance, found in a study of graduates covering data for five years that Bloomsburg, Pennsylvania, had been training twice as many primary teachers, three times as many intermediate teachers, and four times as many junior-high-school teachers as were needed, but only one-fourth as many teachers for rural schools as could have been used.

Because of this shortage of grade openings, graduates of teachers' colleges are going increasingly into rural schools for their initial experience. Placement records are inadequately kept by most institutions, but in New York State (12), rural and semi-rural districts used 64 percent of all new teachers in 1926-27. In Connecticut, the State Department reports 40 percent of all normal-school graduates going first into strictly rural schools in 1929, while a similar tendency can be detected even in the less-urbanized Mid-West. This drift toward rural-school placement is in turn causing a trend in some sections for having all graduates partially prepared for rural schools. These new developments, together with the desirability of giving all American teachers a more adequate understanding of our complete national life, urban and rural, agricultural and industrial, constitute strong argument against too much differentiation in the preparation of teachers for rural schools.

III. PROBLEMS AND MAJOR ISSUES INVOLVED

No activity in the whole realm of teacher training raises so many controversial issues as the question of preparing teachers for one- and two-teacher rural schools. Chief among these questions are the following:

(1) Is specialized training needed for rural teaching?

(2) If so, what amount and type of differentiation is desirable during pre-service preparation in (a) courses, (b) practice teaching, and (c) social and educational leadership?

(3) What follow-up and extension activities are desirable on the part of state teacher-training institutions for the benefit of their rural graduates?

(4) What type of organization (departmental or non-departmentalized) best promotes the adequate pre-service and in-service preparation of rural teachers, and what special staff is required for this purpose?

(5) Do candidates specifically prepared for rural schools actually locate in them and, if so, how long do they remain?

(6) Is the practice of limited certification for one-teacher and semi-graded rural schools a wise state policy even when on the same level as certification for urban elementary schools?

(7) Why do normal schools and teachers' colleges fail to make adequate provision for the preparation of rural teachers?

(8) Why are trained teachers; that is, two-year normal-school graduates, not attracted to rural schools, and how may their interest be enlisted?

(9) What is the function and program of the state in this whole matter of procuring effective and well-prepared teachers for the children of farm areas?

Realizing that the answers to these questions are mostly matters of opinion, the writer submitted them to total or sampling groups of (a) presidents of normal schools and teachers' colleges, (b) directors of rural education in state teacher-training institutions, and (c) county superintendents. Jury judgments of this type were received from 76 presidents representing thirty-eight states, from 66 directors representing twenty-nine states, and from 100 county superintendents representing twenty-two states. These replies will be quoted from time to time throughout the following discussion, particularly when more objective data are lacking.

1. Need of Specialized Training for Rural Teaching

Present practice on the part of teacher-training institutions has been shown to indicate rather universal belief in specialized preparation for rural teachers. So, too, do the jury judgments received. All the rural directors, all but five of the normal-school presidents, and all but two of the county superintendents affirm this belief, further evidence of which is to be found in the recommendations of the various recent state surveys, particularly in those of Virginia (13:273) and Texas (20:247). Again in 1927, Robinson (17:485) interrogated 29 leading American educators on this point and found 21 of them to favor partial differentiation.

The chief reasons for partial differentiation in rural teacher-training, according to the jury judgments collected for this chapter, are to be found:

a. In the physical, social, and economic differences of country and city life.

b. In the different experiences of rural and urban children.

c. In the different organization, handicaps and opportunities of rural schools involving greater responsibility and demands upon the rural teacher (11 : 58 ff.).

d. In the general retardation and neglect of rural schools.

The vote upon these points was practically unanimous among all three groups, with some negative attitude toward the validity of Item *d* as a reason.

In support of the specialization just indicated, it is generally maintained by students of the subject that differentiation in teacher training should vary inversely in proportion to the difficulties and differences of the prospective field of location, and also in proportion to the general education, experience, and maturity of those being trained, as well as to length of the period of preparation and shortages in social background. From this it follows that there is *more reason for partial differentiation in the preparation of rural teachers than in special provision for any other group.*

2. Amount and Type of Differentiation Desirable in the Preparation of Rural Teachers

The amount of differentiated rural instruction, as proposed in the questionnaire submitted, will vary somewhat in different situations, but should include at least:

a. One course in nature study and agriculture, or elementary science, to explain the physical environment of country life. The agriculture presented here is to stress the appreciation aspects of farming, not the vocational.

b. A course in rural sociology and economics (or rural-life problems) to explain the social and economic aspects of rural living. The chief purposes of this course will be to develop appreciation and to define the function and relationships of the teacher and the school in rural society.

c. A third course in rural education (various titles are used) to consider the necessary adaptations of the educative process to rural-school conditions and the farm child's experience. This course should begin with an introductory survey of the significance, conditions, and needs of rural schools throughout both the nation and the local state; then include a study of desirable adaptations in curriculum, technique and method, organization and management, community relations, and some phases of rural-school administration and supervision.

d. Some special practice teaching in typical rural schools under good supervision.

 e. Membership in a Rural Life Club during the period of training. This experience will afford training in social and educational leadership but should not mean exclusion from other student organizations.

 The vote on these proposals was again highly affirmative from all three groups, with almost complete approval (five votes lacking) of the course in rural sociology. All the rural instructors and 97 percent of the county superintendents favor a special course in rural education, but 5 of 66 presidents see no necessity for such an offering. Nature study and agriculture are questioned by only 15 votes in a total of 212, and then chiefly because of the term, *nature study* (*elementary science* is preferred). All the answers but 2 from presidents and 6 from county superintendents advocate practice teaching in rural schools; and all but 2 rural instructors, 10 presidents, and 9 county superintendents out of 64, 54, and 79 voting, respectively, endorse membership in a Rural Life Club as a means of leadership training.

 This general attitude on the part of those replying is again in harmony with the practice of normal schools and teachers' colleges offering specialized rural courses in this field. It has also been further and widely supported by discussions and addresses from national leaders in education for the last twenty-five years (3:16).

3. Follow-Up and Extension Activities for Rural Graduates

 Rural-school teachers, representing the lowest standards of the profession, have always been closely associated with the idea of in-service training. It is therefore not surprising to find all rural instructors, 64 presidents, and 92 county superintendents endorsing the statement on extension service. The 8 presidents and 3 county superintendents replying negatively seem to think supervision of every type the legitimate function of the state and county office of education.

 The type of extension work approved is indicated by the purposes stated in the question; namely, to evaluate and assist graduates in the field, to inform the rural staff, and to stimulate the general development of rural-school and country-life improvement throughout the territory of the teachers' college in coöperation with the division of extension teaching (5).

4. Type of Organization Most Effective in Promoting Specialized Training for Rural Teachers

This question as to the best internal organization within the teachers' college for the specialized preparation of rural teachers is the most debated issue in the whole field of rural-teacher training to-day. That some specialized treatment of the professional curriculum for the various types of public-school teachers is desirable, is now generally accepted by most the administrators of teachers' colleges and others concerned. The points at which such specialization should occur for rural-school teaching, and the content and character of the courses necessary in its realization are also fairly well agreed upon. There is definite disagreement, however, as to the best organization for providing this specialized treatment, and more particularly as to whether it is possible or desirable to predetermine or attract prospective teachers to the rural field far enough in advance to permit specialization in their preparation. Two opposing camps have thus developed lately, even among those whole-heartedly devoted to the rural school and desirous of giving it the best possible advantage. The first group stoutly maintains that rural teaching with all its handicaps can be and should be made to appeal to young people in our teacher-training institutions, and that under these circumstances the best organization may be realized through a coördinated but distinct department or division of rural education enrolling a partially differentiated group of students who have definitely chosen to prepare for rural-school service. The second group, for reasons presented later, believes such departmentalization and election of rural teaching to be impossible or at least inadequate and unwise under present conditions. Members of this group would have the specialized rural courses that are outlined in this discussion required of all elementary candidates in the teachers' college, both rural and urban.

This difference of opinion regarding departmental organization for rural work is clearly reflected in replies to the following statements set up on this point:

a. A recognized department of rural education within the teachers' college, distinct but properly coördinated with other departments or interests, is the best organization for providing the differentiation desirable in rural-teacher training.

b. The staff of a rural-education department should consist *as a minimum* of at least two specialists giving full time to rural-education courses and activities. One of these is to be known preferably as the Director of Rural Education and the other as the Supervisor of Rural Practice. In addition to these, rural critic teachers will be essential, and other instructors should be added as enrollment grows.

c. The rural department should have headquarters in a special office and be supplied with enough teaching, correspondence, and extension equipment to insure efficiency.

d. It should also have a specified departmental budget or some other arrangement for funds sufficiently large and definite to meet the demands of the various activities for which it is responsible.

e. A departmental organization for the preparation of rural teachers as just outlined is preferable to separate rural normal schools for this purpose.

On the question of departmental organization, 58 rural instructors and 80 county superintendents voted favorably; 6 and 13, respectively, voted unfavorably. It is significant here that those most closely associated with young rural teachers, both in their pre-service training and initial employment, should hold this view regarding the effectiveness of departmental organization. Presidents, on the other hand, reflect greater divergence of thought on this matter, with 36 favoring and 25 opposing departmentalism, while 3 frankly state that they do not know how to vote on the question without further study. Here again the vote is significant in that it reflects the deep currents of industrialism affecting all American life, and suggests necessary modification of former rural practice in terms of this change.[4]

The other statements quoted in this connection regarding rural staff, office, supplies, and budget received overwhelming confirmation from rural instructors and a majority vote on each item from presidents and county superintendents, thereby indicating a disposition to treat the rural department fairly, once the idea of departmental organization is accepted.

The remaining statement regarding the inadvisability of separate rural normal schools was vigorously upheld by all groups voting, indicating the general opposition throughout the profession as a whole toward this lingering suggestion of extreme ruralization.

---

[4] Proposals for such modifications have been made by the writer as explained more fully in Footnote 5.

5. Placement and Tenure of Candidates Specifically Prepared for Rural Schools

This matter was not included in the jury-judged statements quoted in this discussion since it was realized that those interrogated had little current data on the subject. Charles E. Benson (6:20) found in 1920, however, that 6 percent of all graduates of teachers' colleges were entering rural schools. It is known that this percentage has increased strikingly, but present figures are wanting either for all graduates or for graduates of rural curricula; so, too, are figures on the tenure of teachers in rural positions.

The most adequate inquiry thus far conducted in this field is that made in 1926 by W. M. Robinson. This study showed (15:25) that, of 1,596 students completing the one-year rural curriculum in thirty-three institutions, 1,380 (86.4 percent) planned to enter one- and two-teacher rural schools; 80 (5 percent), larger open-country and village schools; 7 (0.4 percent), city schools; and 90 (5.6 percent), schools to continue their education. Of 706 students in the same institutions completing the two-year rural curriculum, 189 (26.8 percent) planned to enter one- and two-teacher schools; 470 (66.6 percent), larger open-country, consolidated, and village schools; 11 (1.5 percent), city schools; and 36 (5.1 percent), schools to continue their education. Data collected the same year from graduates who had completed the two-year rural curriculum during the five-year period ending June, 1926, showed that in a total of 307 teaching years since their graduation 49 percent of the time was spent in one-room rural schools; 7.5 percent in two-room rural schools; 7.5 percent in three-teacher or larger schools of the open country; 13 percent in village schools; and 12 percent in city schools. On the other hand, graduates of non-rural two-year curricula who entered rural schools upon graduation spent but 35 percent of their total teaching time in one and two-teacher schools. Thus, from this one study, at least, it appears that graduates of rural curricula do enter rural schools and that they give a longer period of service in schools of this type than do graduates of non-rural curricula.

6. Limited Certification for Rural Teachers

Next to the question of departmentalized organization no question of rural-training policy has provoked more controversy than that of limited certification, by which is meant awarding to rural-curriculum

graduates certificates good only in rural schools. The Chairmen of
this Yearbook Committee opposes this practice on the ground that it
will cause students to avoid the rural field. In this he has support
from others, including almost exactly half the presidents, half the
rural instructors, and half the county superintendents responding to
this inquiry. On no other question was the vote so evenly divided or
the comments so interesting. However, it is well to call attention to
the view, held by some in the 'limited' camp, that it is not the certificate, limited or otherwise, which deters young people from rural
schools to-day, but rather the basic social, economic, and educational
conditions behind the certificate as indicated under Subdivision 8.
Let the state and the profession set the necessary machinery in motion
to remove these handicaps, and teaching in the rural school would
then become so attractive that limited certification would be positively
necessary to prevent a stampede to its doors.

7. Why Normal Schools and Teachers' Colleges Are not Making Adequate Provision for Training Rural Teachers

The replies to this question in the jury-judged statements are most
revealing, in that each group finds the chief cause of neglect lying
outside its own jurisdiction and control. Forty rural instructors
and 30 county superintendents see the hostile attitude of administrators and other faculty members as a chief cause, for example;
whereas only 12 of the presidents view the situation in this way. The
cause receiving the highest vote from all groups contributing is lack
of real demand for specialized rural training on the part of both students and public. Little is said, however, of the responsibility of
teachers' colleges and other state institutions of higher learning for
creating demand rather than merely following it.

Other reasons, listed in a descending order of mention, were: lack
of funds or funds diverted to other purposes; lack of state leadership
and program; competition from county normals and high-school training classes; low certification requirements permitting untrained candidates to enter the field; the pressure of university standardizing
agencies which emphasize academic courses in the teachers' college
and divert attention from the practical type of course needed for
rural teachers; lack of practice facilities; lack of well-trained rural
instructors; and the advent of consolidation, which, it is believed,

will make special rural training unnecessary. Five institutions believe they are doing all that is possible or necessary now.

8. Why Trained Teachers Are Not Attracted to Rural Schools

"Low salary" heads the long list of ready reasons under this inquiry, and when it is recalled that the median salary (9:36) for rural elementary teachers is $761 a year as contrasted with the urban elementary median of $1,129, the validity of this vote is apparent. Next in order comes social isolation, scoring almost as high as salary; then poor living conditions; lack of professional recognition and encouragement; unfavorable working conditions, including janitor work, old buildings, and lack of teaching equipment; complexity and demands of the rural-teaching task; lack of sympathetic supervision during the initial stages of teaching; failure of rural instructors and others to present the attractive side of rural teaching; short and uncertain tenure; lack of specialized preparation; and contact with urban-minded faculty.

Notwithstanding the deterring effects of these various factors, the great majority of those replying—all but 5 of the rural instructors, three-fourths of the presidents, and 75 out of 85 county superintendents—believe that good students can be attracted into rural training courses even now, if only superior rural instructors are employed and the president and faculty lend their support.

These convictions are supported by the study by Robinson (15:21) previously mentioned, in which 75 percent of the experienced rural graduates in reply to the question, "Would you choose the rural curriculum again if you were entering the normal school?" replied in the affirmative.

9. Function of the State in Procuring Well-Prepared Teachers for Rural Schools

The theses submitted for consideration under this head were these three:

a. We shall ultimately solve the whole rural-school problem, baffling as it has proved, and have a well-prepared teacher in every American classroom, rural as well as urban.

b. In realizing this goal for farm children, it will first be necessary to institute broadly conceived state programs (a) for the reorganization of rural schools; that is, consolidation and larger unit; (b) for teacher training; and (c) for the general improvement of country life, especially in its economic aspects.

    c. The present surplus of teachers affords an unprecedented opportunity for correcting this whole situation and should be widely used by states and training institutions to this end.

The expressions of faith brought forth by the first of these statements were heartening indeed. Only two of 59 presidents, seven of 61 rural instructors, and eight of 82 county superintendents had any doubt as to the ultimate solution of the rural-school problem. On Item *b* the vote was entirely unanimous, indicative of the almost complete unanimity with which teacher training is now regarded as a state function. On Item *c* an overwhelming percentage of all three groups voted in the affirmative.

IV. SUMMARY

1. The need for trained teachers to-day is in rural schools. Elsewhere there is a surplus of teachers.

2. Because of this surplus and the demand of cities for professional experience before employment, graduates of teachers' colleges are going increasingly into one-teacher, two-teacher, and consolidated schools.

3. This development, together with the accepted practice of differentiating professional curricula and preparing candidates for specific fields of teaching, has resulted in an increased interest in rural preparation among the executives of teachers' colleges and has fostered a conviction on the part of some that all candidates in training should have at least partial preparation for rural work.

4. The attitude expressed here is noticeably prevalent in industrialized areas, particularly in some of the New England and Middle Atlantic states, where urban influence predominates. But in the agricultural regions, more particularly in the Mid-West, where rural life is less affected by city influence, rural teaching ranks with other phases of the profession on a basis of free choice. Here, and in general throughout the South also, it is still the practice to differentiate training for those intending to enter rural schools and to organize separate departments of rural education similar to other major groupings in the teachers' college.

5. In all parts of the country, both agricultural and industrial, to judge from the replies received in this inquiry, there is a growing

conviction that the American rural heritage, as best exemplified to-day in typical farm life, contains elements of essential educational value which should be rightly understood, appreciated, and transferred to succeeding generations. To insure this understanding, some policy-makers in teacher training advocate an orientation course in *Modern American Civilization* which will explain the recent industrialization of American society and its effects upon both farm and city life, and would have this course pursued by all students in the teachers' colleges.

6. The majority of teacher-training institutions in the United States (83 percent) differentiate some of the instruction provided for prospective rural teachers, basing their special offerings upon the distinctive conditions and problems of rural living and learning. Special courses are usually given in rural sociology and economics, nature study and agriculture, and various phases of rural education. Special rural practice in one-teacher, two-teacher, and consolidated schools is also provided, and rural students' clubs are commonly fostered as a means of leadership training.

7. At least two specialists in the rural-school field, one known generally as the Director of Rural Education and the other as the Supervisor of Rural Practice, are usually employed to have charge of rural-education activities in the normal school or teachers' college.

8. The preparation of public-school teachers is now commonly re-garded as a state function and the educational forces of most states are attempting to unite in working out a comprehensive program for teacher training with due emphasis upon the needs of rural schools. In this, the larger economic and social needs of country life are also being simultaneously attacked, in so far as possible, because of their controlling influence upon all phases of rural education and social work.[5]

9. From the data collected for this study, it is evident that, not-withstanding much progress in recent years, the preparation of rural teachers is still the most neglected, extensive, and challenging prob-lem in the whole field of teacher training; a problem, furthermore,

---

[5] An additional chapter, presenting constructive proposals and techniques for the training of rural teachers in terms of the conditions presented in this chapter and with the present industrialization of rural life especially in mind, has had to be omitted from this Yearbook for lack of space. Individuals interested in this phase of the subject may procure a copy of this section by addressing the writer at Teachers College, Columbia University, New York City.

that involves not only the basic welfare of rural life but much that has thus far been deemed important and essential in our whole national character and stability.

BIBLIOGRAPHY

1. Alabama. *Annual Report, 1929.* Montgomery, 1929. Pp. 136-137.
2. ANDERSON, C. J. "Wisconsin's greatest educational challenge." *Wisconsin Jour. of Educ.,* 60: 1927, 162-163.
3. BAGLEY, W. C. "Nature and extent of curriculum differentiation in the training of rural-school teachers." *Professional Preparation of Teachers for Rural Schools.* Washington, 1928. Pp. 16-21. (U. S. Bureau of Education Bulletin, No. 6).
4. BAGLEY, WILLIAM C., and others. *Rural School Survey of New York State; The Teaching Personnel.* Ithaca, 1923. Vol. IV. Pp. 96-97.
5. BATHURST, EFFIE G. *A Teachers College Follow-Up Service—Its Factors and Development in an Uusupervised Area.* New York, 1929. (In preparation for 'Teachers College, Columbia University, Contributions to Education.')
6. BENSON, CHARLES E. *The Output of Professional Schools for Teachers.* Baltimore, 1922. P. 20.
7. BUNTING, R. L., and McGUFFEY, VERNE. "Preparation of rural teachers." *Teachers College Record,* 29: 1928, 716-727.
8. California State Department of Education. *Biennial Report, 1928.* Sacramento, 1928.
9. Gaumnitz, W. H. *Salaries and Salary Trends of Teachers in Rural Schools.* Washington, 1929. Pp. 36, 41. (U. S. Bureau of Education, No. 6).
10. LEE, JOHN S. *A Study of Teacher Training Offered in Secondary Schools of the United States.* 1930. (Unpublished Doctor's dissertation on file in the Library of Teachers College, Columbia University).
11. McGUFFEY, VERNE. *Differences in the Activities of Teachers in Rural One-Teacher Schools and of Grade Teachers in Cities.* New York, 1929. Pp. 58 ff. (Teachers College, Columbia University, Contributions to Education, No. 346).
12. New York State Department of Education. Educational Measurements Bureau. *Teacher Demand in New York State.* (Mimeographed report. Albany, 1929).
13. O'SHEA, M. V. *Public Education in Virginia.* Richmond, 1928. 273 pp.
14. PEIK, W. E. *The Training of Teachers in North Dakota.* Bismark, 1930. (Unpublished study prepared for the State Board of Administration.)
15. ROBINSON, WILLIAM M. *The Professional Preparation of Teachers For Rural Schools.* Washington, 1928. Pp. 21-25. (U. S. Bureau of Education Bulletin, No. 6).

16. ROBINSON, WILLIAM M. Washington, 1927. (U. S. Bureau of Education, Rural School Circulars Nos. 21 and 25).

17. ROBINSON, WILLIAM M. "The Problem of Differentiating Rural Teacher Preparation." *National Education Association Proceedings*. Washington: 1928, p. 485.

18. STRAYER, GEORGE D., Director. *Report of Florida Educational Survey Commission*. Tallahassee, 1929.

19. U. S. Bureau of Education. *The Public School System of Arkansas*. Washington, 1923. P. 28. (U. S. Bureau of Education Bulletin, No. 10).

20. WORKS, GEORGE A., and others. *Texas Educational Survey Report; General Report*. Austin, 1925. Pp. 151 ff., 247-249.

CHAPTER VII
THE SUPERVISION OF RURAL SCHOOLS

NORMAN FROST, M. S. PITTMAN, and HELEN HAY HEYL

The contributors to this chapter present their material in three sections: I, The Development of Rural-School Supervision; II, The Supervisory Personnel in Rural Schools; and III, An Evaluation of Rural-School Supervision.

SECTION I
THE DEVELOPMENT OF RURAL-SCHOOL SUPERVISION

NORMAN FROST
Professor of Rural Education
George Peabody College for Teachers, Nashville, Tennessee

Supervision, as a distinct function, is almost entirely a development of this century; thus, before 1900 the 'supervisor' and 'superintendent' were used as synonymous terms (1).[1] The attempt to provide supervisory assistance for country teachers has taken two distinct lines, with many compromises and confusions between them. First, there has been an attempt to reduce the work of the administrative officer, so that he may have more time for aiding teachers. The variety of schemes tried have included reducing the size of the administrative unit, providing office and clerical help, employing assistant superintendents, and increasing the supervisory work of the school principal with a corresponding reduction of his teaching load.

All these schemes are being tried in rural schools. The administrative unit of limited size is the predominant feature in New England, New York, and to some extent in West Virginia. The superintendency of the independent district having a population of less than twenty-five hundred accomplishes much the same result. Permissive legislation for the employment of office and clerical assistance has been passed in most states. Assistant superintendents are employed in Louisiana, Ohio, Pennsylvania, and Illinois. The prin-

[1] Numbers in parentheses refer by number and page to the bibliography at the end of this chapter.

cipalship in rural areas has grown in importance with the spread of the consolidated school. The 'affiliated' system of Minnesota is an interesting variant of this trend, and at Rock Hill, South Carolina, a consolidated high school has employed a supervising principal who has general and supervisory duties in all the elementary schools that send pupils to the high school.

The combination of administrative and supervisory duties involved in this plan has the obvious advantage of making local educational leadership available to small areas. Its weakness seems to lie in the broad demands made upon these officials, and the insistent and time-consuming nature of their routine administrative duties (9: 90f.).

2. The second form of supervisory assistance provided for rural teachers is the employment of supervisors somewhat protected from administrative demands. This attempt takes several different forms: the state supervisors of rural schools; district supervisors working in coöperation with state departments of education and teachers' colleges, as in Missouri and Oklahoma; helping teachers; and special or general county supervisors.

Supervision of this sort has the advantage of rendering a specialized service to teachers. Its chief difficulties seem to lie in the necessity of readjusting local school units wherever the county unit is not already established, and in the fact that, since the supervisory positions are new to the school system, they are likely to be discontinued whenever financial difficulties arise.

These two lines of supervisory effort have resulted in two types of supervisory aid: first, staff members of state departments of education assigned to rural schools; and second, regional supervisors working in areas larger than the county but smaller than the state. In 1916, there were 46 state officials assigned to supervise rural schools; in 1922, there were 118; in 1928, the number had grown to 172. The number of states employing these officials for the same dates was 26, 33, and 38. Mrs. Cook (3) states that the "tendency is to emphasize the 'professional' leadership and instructional supervisory phases of the work of state rural school officers." Regional supervisors are sometimes employed by teacher-training institutions, with or without help from state departments of education in paying their salaries. No study of the extent of such work has been found.

3. The third form of rural supervision is secured by the appointment of a county superintendent of schools. The work of these officials

is largely administrative, but many of them do render extremely effective supervisory service to their teachers. These officers and their duties will be discussed in greater detail in the section dealing with administration.

4. The fourth type is characterized by the county supervisor of schools. Cole (2) prepared a table showing the number of rural supervisors of instruction employed in the various states. This begins with four supervisors employed in Connecticut in 1903, and goes through the school year 1928-29, when 817 such supervisors were employed in 29 states.

5. The district superintendent or supervisor represents the fifth attempt at supervision. Within this classification are included the superintendents of townships or groups of townships in New England, the supervisors of schools in judicial districts in West Virginia, and the superintendents of the 'independent' districts so prevalent in most of the states. The superintendents of the independent districts of less than twenty-five hundred population probably constitute a large and important element in the supervision of country schools. No report has been found giving comprehensive data concerning them.

6. The sixth type of supervision is exercised by the principals of country schools. Gaumnitz (4) gives the number of principals and supervisors in the rural schools in 1926 as 14,347. This includes only those devoting half or more of their time to such work. The number of supervisors employed in rural schools that year is given by Cole (2) as 280. Subtraction gives 13,067 as that number of rural principals devoting half or more of their time to their duties as principals—this includes the high-school principals. Data have not been found to show whether or not this number is increasing; in view of the continued consolidation of small rural schools, it seems likely that it is. At any rate, this group of principals performs a large share of rural-school supervision.

Some comparison of the supervisory situation in town and country schools may not be amiss. According to figures given by Gaumnitz (4), for each supervisor or principal in country schools there are 33.1 teachers, 16.1 schools, and 907 pupils. For each city-school supervisor or principal, there are 16.1 teachers, 1.2 schools, and 558 pupils. Great as the progress in providing supervision for country teachers has been, the situation is still far less satisfactory than in urban schools.

SECTION II

THE SUPERVISORY PERSONNEL IN RURAL SCHOOLS

M. S. PITTMAN
Director of Training, Michigan State Normal College
Ypsilanti, Michigan

A questionnaire which was devised for the purpose of obtaining information regarding the professional equipment of the rural supervisory personnel was sent to all the states, and replies of some sort were received from all. The data, however, were so incomplete from 25 states that they have been omitted. From the information gathered from the twenty-three remaining Table I has been compiled. Analysis reveals that there were 1,731 county superintendents, including the 5 district superintendents of the state of Nevada, the 208 district superintendents in the state of New York, and the 36 district superintendents of Vermont. Of this number, definite information was given as to the qualifications of 1,487: 112 hold master's degrees, 438 hold bachelor's degrees, and 937 have less academic preparation than that indicated by these academic degrees.

The reports indicate that 16 of the 23 states have supervisors of rural schools, and the best available data on the qualifications of the supervisors were reported. There were 592 supervisors employed, including the 26 supervisors in the state of Connecticut where the unit of supervision is not absolutely comparable to that in the other states. Of these 592, 90 hold master's degrees, 169 hold bachelor's degrees, and 311 have less than the bachelor's degree; data were not secured for 22.

Data were received from 15 of the 23 states indicating the qualifications of the supervisory officials (superintendent or principal) of rural consolidated schools. In these 15 states there were 3,199 such officials. Of the 3,199, data were secured for 1,893. Of these, 182 hold master's degrees, 1,530 hold bachelor's degrees, and 181 have less formal education than an academic degree represents.

A comparison between the qualifications of these supervisory officials in the three leading non-county unit states with the four leading county-unit states reveals interesting implications with reference to the effect of the character of the unit of school control.

California, Wisconsin, and Pennsylvania, with a total of 342 supervisors, were compared with Maryland, North Carolina, Alabama, and

TABLE I.—THE NUMBER AND THE QUALIFICATIONS OF THE SUPERVISORY OFFICIALS OF VARIOUS TYPES OF RURAL SCHOOLS IN TWENTY-THREE OF THE FORTY-EIGHT STATES

	COUNTY SUPERINTENDENT				RURAL SUPERVISORS				SUPERVISING OFFICIAL OF CONSOLIDATED SCHOOL			
	Total	M.A.	A.B.	Less	Total	M.A.	A.B.	Less	Total	M.A.	A.M.	Less
Alabama	67	10	29	28	53	12	32	9	....	....	....	....
California	58	....	....	....	130	7	20	103	....	....	....	....
Connecticut(a)	....	....	....	....	26	13	9	4	172	(b)	(b)	(b)
Delaware	7	5	2	....	(b)	(b)	(b)	(b)	47	21	14	12
Florida	67	3	16	48	10	2	6	2	70	1	32	37
Georgia	161	5	63	93	(b)	(b)	(b)	(b)	(b)	(b)	(b)	(b)
Idaho	44	....	2	42	4	3	1	....	60	24	20	16
Iowa	99	(b)	(b)	(b)	....	....	....	....	386	25	351	10
Louisiana	63	4	43	16	17	5	10	2	289	19	220	41
Maryland	23	18	3	2	52	14	20	18	(b)	(b)	(b)	(b)
Michigan	83	....	13	70	10	1	3	6	72	13	41	18
Minnesota	87	(b)	(b)	(b)	22	(b)	(b)	(b)	400	(b)	(b)	(b)
Missouri	114	2	29	83	9	6	3	....	398	(b)	398	(b)
Nevada(a)	5	1	4	....	(c)	(c)	(c)	(c)	(b)	(b)	(b)	(b)
New Mexico	31	....	1	30	1	....	....	1	(b)	(b)	(b)	(b)
New York(a)	208	14	57	137	(a)	(a)	(a)	(a)	77	(d)	(d)	(d)
North Carolina	100	23	51	26	32	14	13	5	502	77	398	27
North Dakota	53	....	19	34	2	....	....	2	657	(b)	(b)	(b)
Pennsylvania	66	18	40	8	102	13	39	50	(b)	(b)	(b)	(b)
Texas	264	3	20	241	12	....	3	9	(b)	(b)	(b)	(b)
Vermont(a)	36	2	24	10	(b)	(b)	(b)	(b)	(b)	(b)	(b)	(b)
Wisconsin	72	2	15	55	110	....	10	100	28	2	26	(b)
Wyoming	23	2	7	14	....	....	....	....	50	....	30	20
Total	1,731	112	438	937	592	90	169	311	3,199	182	1,530	181

(a) Not quite comparable to other states.   (b) Not reported.   (c) None.   (d) Not available.

Louisiana, with a total of 154 supervisors. Of the 342 supervisors in California, Wisconsin, and Pennsylvania, 20, or 5.8 percent, hold master's degrees; 69, or 20.2 percent, hold bachelor's degrees; while 253, or 74 percent, have less schooling than an academic degree represents. Of the 154 supervisors in Maryland, North Carolina, Alabama, and Louisiana, 45, or 22.7 percent, hold master's degrees; 75, or 48.6 percent, hold bachelor's degrees; while only 34, or 28.7 percent, have less training than is indicated by an academic degree.

SECTION III
AN EVALUATION OF RURAL-SCHOOL SUPERVISION

HELEN HAY HEYL
Rural Education Bureau
State Education Department, Albany, N. Y.

In the past few years, about a dozen studies have attempted directly to evaluate rural-school supervision. Several other studies on elementary supervision in general have included groups of rural-school children and their teachers. All save one study, that made by Morgan (8) in Kansas, have shown that rural supervision results in valuable gains to children in the mastery of knowledge and skills over the amounts gained by children whose teachers are unsupervised. These gains vary from 6.9 percent of superiority of the supervised group in one and two-teacher schools over the control group in the same type of school, as found by Sherwood (12: 8) in Indiana (with 14.3 percent gain for all types of schools measured during the first year of this experiment, and 30 percent gained during the second year) to the 94 percent of superiority found in Pittman's earlier study (11: 78ff.) and the 126 percent greater progress of the supervised group in consolidated schools of North Carolina over the unsupervised group as reported by Southall (13: 31).

1. The Effect of Experts

It should be noted that with the exception of Misner's study in Washington (7), Morgan's in Kansas (8), and a few others, these studies have been carried on as special experiments by expert supervisors usually working with experts in state or college departments of education. Frequently, too, such experiments have been inaugurated with the avowed hope of demonstrating the value of supervision, and have been carried on under very favorable conditions, especially in matters of finance, supervisory load, supplies, clerical assistance, office equipment for the supervisors, and the like. It is well that this should be so from the point of view of setting standards, but it may be questioned whether or not equal results may be expected of the average supervisor working under ordinary handicaps.

2. What Does the Average Supervisor Accomplish?

Morgan (8) attempted to answer this question in his study of supervision in Johnson County, Kansas, in 1926. His problem was: What is the effect of supervision in rural schools when it is carried on as an everyday job of supervisors such as are commonly employed in cities?

The study involved 4 elementary schools in the Shawnee Rural High School territory, which included 14 elementary schools and about 50 teachers. Four other elementary schools were studied as a control group, one inside the high-school territory and three outside.

In studying the two groups of schools the equivalent groups method was used. Factors equated were enrollment; mental ability of pupils; their social and economic status; the training, experience, and success of their teachers as rated by the county superintendent. About 275 pupils were studied in each group. The plan followed was to study the effectiveness of supervision by the progress which pupils made in mastering the tool subjects: reading, arithmetic, and spelling. As a check, both groups were tested, also, in history and literature to see if the same differences existed in the content subjects as in the tool subjects. Mr. Morgan was the supervisor in charge.

The total gains made by the experimental group over the control group was 14.8 percent; but Morgan found that the actual difference in achievement was very slight, if any. This is shown in Table II, where

TABLE II.—DIFFERENCES IN ACHIEVEMENT OF THE EXPERIMENTAL AND CONTROL GROUPS (From Morgan)

	Experimental Group	Control Group
Reading..	107.8	107.9
Arithmetic computation........................	96.6	81.1*
Arithmetic reasoning...........................	97.5	96.4
Spelling.......................................	84.8	66.7
History and literature.........................	37.9	38.9

*In arithmetic computation the control group was above standard in all grades save one at the beginning of the study. The chance for gain was therefore small.

it will also be seen readily that the only important difference in gain is in spelling. An interesting factor here is that the improvement of spelling received special emphasis in the supervisory program.

Throughout his study, Morgan attributes the small gains to the fact that the grade was well above standard norms in the initial test. This raises the question, whether or not a measurement of gain in a tool subject is a sound measure of the efficiency of supervision. Would a comparison between the intelligence of pupils and their actual achievement be a sounder basis for comparison of the effects of supervision?[2] In any event, Morgan's conclusions are significant. He says:

1. Supervision increased the achievement of pupils in the tool subjects only to a slight degree.
2. Focusing on a single problem brings a high return, as in the case of spelling where scores were doubled in several grades.
3. New plans introduced by the supervisor upset the old and caused some confusion which may have invalidated the results to an extent during the first year of the study.
4. The teaching ability may have varied more greatly than could be determined.
5. Supervisory methods may need modification or enrichment.
6. It is the opinion of the investigator that he placed too much stress on testing and not enough on how to teach.
7. He believes that the problem of reclassification may lead to better results later.
8. For more exact measures, the study should be continued for several years.

A similar study was reported by Misner (7) in 1927, from Stevens County, Washington. Misner found the average rate of progress in the experimental group in the tool subjects to be 1.38, while the control group progressed at the average rate of 1.29. The superiority of the experimental group was thus .09, a rather negligible difference.

Misner's problem dealt with the Union High School, of which he was supervising principal, and four district schools, feeders to the high school. Seven rural schools acted as the control group. Opposition to supervision caused the plan to be modified, but in general the following principles were carried out.

1. Supervision was not limited to any subject to the neglect of all others.
2. The teacher, rather than the supervisor, chose the problem to be taken up first.
3. The work with teachers and pupils was individualized.

---

[2] Suggested by Warren W. Coxe and tested in the South Glens Falls School System, New York State.

4. Regular visits were made to each school, but the supervisor was also subject to call.

5. The high-school needs were always met before the rural-school needs were met.

Visits were made on an average of one to each teacher every two or three weeks. They varied from forty-five minutes to an entire morning in length. The Otis Classification and the Stanford Achievement tests were given on the first and last visits. These were corrected by the supervisor and studied with the teacher on the second visit to ascertain: school weaknesses, pupil weaknesses, and needed kinds of remedial work. Pupils shared in solving each problem undertaken. Three were studied in detail. These were: (1) how to study, which included an investigation of general factors that were demonstrated through geography and history study; (2) how to gain proficiency in silent reading; and (3) how to gain proficiency in arithmetic operations.

Misner used the equivalent-groups method, pairing 53 pupils in each group. The schools were equated in community environment, experience of teachers, and type of school. The total number of pupils tested was 222, from which the 53 pairs were selected. After 134 to 144 days of supervision, the two groups were again measured and the gain for each pupil determined.

Although the average gain in rate of progress reported by Misner was only .09, as pointed out, it should be added that in amount of progress the experimental group averaged 6.976 percent, which is equal to 12 days based on a school year of 172 days, and is comparable with what Sherwood (12:10) reported for the one and two-teacher schools in Indiana during the first year of the Indiana experiment. This is a fair amount of gain in these subjects and may be sufficient to justify supervision; nevertheless, there are implications in these studies which may well cause us to ask, whether, in attempting to demonstrate the value of supervision, we are not placing undue emphasis upon gains to be expected in tool subjects to the neglect of more valuable phases of education.

3. Are the Results of Supervision, as Measured, of Lasting Value?

Another interesting problem arises in connection with the permanence of gains to be expected from supervision. Miss Marshall (6) attempted to discover this in 1928 by studying the possible carry-over influence of the Indiana experiment. This careful piece of work reveals some discouraging facts. Marshall attempted to answer two questions:

Was there any carry-over effect from two years of supervision? First, as shown by a comparison of the Johnson County pupils who were under supervision with the Whitney County pupils who were not under supervision? (Whitney County was a control county during the experiment.) Second, as shown by a comparison of the Johnson County pupils who were not under supervision with the Johnson County pupils who were. (Forty-five children had moved into Johnson County since the experiment closed.)

The conclusions reached were: (1) The carry-over effect of the two years of supervision was not significant in comparison with the progress made in Johnson County during two years of supervision. (2) There seemed to be less progress in Johnson than in Whitney the same two years. (3) Supervised children in Johnson, however, had a significant advantage over the unsupervised children in Johnson County except in spelling.

Whatever criticisms may be made of these smaller studies, there are implications in them which should not be ignored, and students of rural education may well begin to ask what factors other than pupil progress in the fundamental subjects, should be considered in evaluating the effects of supervision.

4. How Can the Experts Be More Expert?

There are at least six clearly recognized major aims of elementary education (10:13), namely, to help every child:

1. To understand and practice desirable social relationships
2. To discover and develop his own desirable individual aptitudes
3. To cultivate the habit of critical thinking
4. To appreciate and desire worth-while activities.
5. To gain command of the common integrating knowledge and skills
6. To develop a sound body and normal mental attitudes

With six such challenging aims, we make a weak case for supervision when we base claims for its efficacy upon its contributions to but a single aim, and this is the narrow field of the fundamentals. Terrebonne, of Louisiana, was clearly conscious of this when he attempted (14) to introduce new items into his program of measurement and checked physical plant, teaching equipment, administrative needs, objectives of supervision, and incidental results of the supervisory program. Whatever criticisms may be made of his study, this widening of scope is commendable.

5. What Other Factors Should Be Included in Studying Supervision?

In a broad study of the values of supervision many items might be included in addition to a scientific survey of achievement. We should begin to look more to these unmeasurable factors for some of the larger values to be expected from a supervisory service that is truly helpful. Child-development programs, character-education projects, personality studies, and emphasis upon mental hygiene are major topics which begin to appear frequently in progressive supervisory programs. These cannot be easily measured, yet no one doubts their value as experiments, even though educators are still uncertain about many features in such programs. We need studies which will clear up these uncertainties as well as studies which measure achievement in subject matter. Educational accounting through objective measurement should not be neglected in rural education: on the contrary, it should be encouraged until a testing program becomes an integral part of every supervisor's program; but this part of the program should occupy only its fair share of the supervisor's time, as was pointed out by Kibbe (5) in her Wisconsin study, and it should be remembered that such accounting measures only a small part of the educational product.

If we turn to the average rural supervisor and ask him how he checks the results of his work, we shall perhaps begin to find some of the unmeasurable items that ought to be considered in evaluating the whole program. Cole, in his excellent study (2) on the status of rural supervisors of instruction in the United States, devotes Chapter VIII to this important problem. In reply to the question, "By what means do you measure the value of supervision?" Cole tabulated the replies of 400 rural supervisors as follows:

	Percent
Partially in terms of increased interest of the teachers	60.0
By increased interest of the pupils	59.7
By increased professional ability of teachers	56.5
By increased community interest in education	47.0
By means of initial testing at the beginning of the school year followed by testing at the end of the school year and comparison of the initial scores with the final scores	45.2
By means of educational testing and comparison with age and grade norms	36.7

Other methods of measurement, recorded in smaller percentages are: the attitude of teachers toward professional growth, the use of objectives as checks on progress, purposeful pupil activity, increases in pupil attendance, the growth of pupils to fit into community life, exhibits of work done in schools, better living conditions within community, further work of pupils after leaving local school, the attitude of teachers towards supervision, and the like.

In concluding the summary of this topic Cole points out that

> under present working conditions, it is doubtful if rural supervisors should be criticized for not using more objective measurements in determining the value of their supervision. To be scientifically accurate, objective testing of supervisory results requires much comparison, controlling, testing, tabulating and interpretation of results. These processes take a great deal of time. After the procedure is all completed, we have measured only a small part of the educational product. . . . Objective measurement should not be discouraged. . . At the same time, subjective measurement is defensible and valuable. Some results of supervision perhaps shall never be measured; they must be judged. The obvious difficulty of such subjective measurement lies in the danger of overevaluating and the supervisor accepting all the credit for the improvement in education within a school or community.

This statement is followed by an interesting example of what Cole conceives to be a good subjective estimate of supervision and he then concludes:

> It would seem that such subjective evaluations should have a place along with the more objective measurements in supervision. A broad view of the results of supervision is to be commended along with a detailed analysis of the results.

We need to have many such evaluations made by skilled experts as well as by average supervisors on the job.

6. In Conclusion

We have come a long way in supervision since the supervisor's duty was defined as the obligation "to cast a genial atmosphere over the classroom;" but we are still a long way from an achieved science of supervision. While the scientific movement in education is itself young, rural supervision is still younger. We shall do well, therefore, to face frankly the present meager factual basis for our work, and to give thoughtful criticism and generous support to all scientific beginnings which are so rapidly growing in number, such as efforts to make more objective the evaluation of teachers and teaching, surveys of supervisory organizations, reports of remedial programs of supervision based upon surveys of instruction, factual studies of supervisory activities. Meanwhile, we shall do well to give due recognition to the continued need for subjective evaluations of other unmeasurable, but vastly important, services of supervision.

BIBLIOGRAPHY

1. COLE, W. E. *The Development of Supervision of Instruction.* 1928. (Master's thesis on file in the Library of Cornell University)
2. COLE, W. E. *The Status of Rural Supervisors of Instruction in the United States.* 1930. (Doctor's thesis on file in the Library of Cornell University)
3. COOK, KATHERINE M. (U. S. Bureau of Education, Rural School Circular, No. 29.) Washington, 1928.
4. GAUMNITZ, W. H. *Some Comparative Statistics of Public School Education in Urban and Rural Communities.* Washington, 1928. (U. S. Bureau of Education, Rural School Circular No. 27)
5. KIBBE, DELIA. "An analysis of the activities of rural supervisors." *Elem. Sch. Jour.,* 28: 1928, 346-352.
6. MARSHALL, JUSTINE E. *A Study of Achievement of the Pupils in Johnson and Whitney Counties.* (Master's thesis on file in the Library of Indiana University)
7. MISNER, FRANK. *A Study of the Comparative Achievements of Pupils in Supervised and Unsupervised Rural Schools."* 1927. (Master's thesis on file in the Library of the State College of Washington)
8. MORGAN, DAVID ANSEL. *The Effects of Supervision in Certain Rural Schools of Johnson County, Kansas.* 1926. (Master's thesis on file in the Library of the University of Chicago)
9. National Education Association. "The principal studies his job." *Research Bull. of the Nat. Educ. Assoc.,* 6: 1928, 90-91.
10. New York Council of Superintendents. *Cardinal Objectives in Elementary Education.* Albany, 1929. P. 13.
11. PITTMAN, M. S. *The Value of School Supervision.* Baltimore, 1921. Pp. 78ff.
12. SHERWOOD, HENRY N. *Value of Rural School Supervision: Results of Two-Years Demonstration in Indiana.* Indianapolis, 1925. P. 8. (Indiana State Department of Public Instruction, Educational Bulletin, No. 84)
13. SOUTHALL, MAYCIE. *A Study of the Value of Supervision in Consolidated Schools.* Raleigh, 1925. P. 31. (Educational Publication, No. 106)
14. TERREBONNE, LUCIUS P. *An Experiment in Parish-wide Supervision.* 1929. (Master's thesis on file in the Library of Louisiana State University and Agricultural and Mechanical College)

CHAPTER VIII

PROBLEMS IN THE ORGANIZATION AND ADMINISTRATION OF RURAL SCHOOLS

THOMAS L. BAYNE, JR., JULIAN E. BUTTERWORTH,
M. G. NELSON, AND R. E. JAGGERS

From the multitude of problems in this field four have been selected for consideration. The first two articles deal with the much-discussed question of the relative efficiency of small and large schools; the third raises certain fundamental questions regarding types of local school units; the fourth presents a critical summary of studies in the analysis of the rural-school administrator's work; while the fifth shows the status of the organization of state departments for rural-school service. Lack of space has, in most cases, made it impossible to mention more than representative studies touching these problems.

SECTION I

MEASURING THE COMPARATIVE EFFICIENCY OF SMALL AND LARGE SCHOOLS

THOMAS L. BAYNE, JR.
Cornell University, Ithaca, New York

I. COMPLEXITY OF THE PROBLEM

Thoughtful students of education realize that many of the generalizations which have been made upon the basis of massed data are of questionable value because the complexity of the problem in question is often obscured. This is illustrated in the comparisons which have been made between the average scores of pupils in small schools (ungraded) and the average scores of pupils in large schools (graded). Writing on larger school units, Haggerty (18: 210)[1] said:

---

[1] Numbers in parentheses conjoined with citations refer by number and page to the references listed at the end of this chapter.

The consolidated school has been widely recommended as an effective means for improving rural education, and in New York State as well as elsewhere considerable consolidation has taken place. The test results in the survey apparently justify such larger school units.

Perhaps Dean Haggerty would qualify this statement at the present time, but it still appears to represent the position of many educators. Before we can say that this position is sound, we must answer at least three questions: First, are the achievements of pupils in all small, ungraded rural schools inferior to the achievements of pupils in the average graded school of larger size? Second, what are some of the factors which effect the validity of comparisons between small schools and large schools? Third, what are some of the administrative considerations which must be taken into account along with the scores made on standardized tests by pupils in the two types of schools? The first two questions will be considered by the present writer; the third question will be treated by Dr. Butterworth. No doubt there are many other problems involved in this complex issue.

II. ARE ALL LARGE SCHOOLS SUPERIOR TO ALL SMALL SCHOOLS?

A recent bulletin by Covert summarizes many of the studies which have been made of the educational achievements of one-teacher and of larger rural schools. Studies made in Kansas, Kentucky, New York, Texas, and Virginia showed (11:19) that the pupils in the larger schools did better on the average than pupils in the small schools. It does not follow that the pupils in *all* the small schools in each of these states did less well than the pupils in the average large school.

In this bulletin we discover that in Tulare County, California, the small schools did as well as the larger ones in reading, that in Arizona there was little difference between educational achievements in some small schools and some large ones (11:6), that in Oklahoma similar results were obtained (11:7). A study of rural-school instruction and supervision in Colorado by Shriber and Hopkins (30) showed for the schools included in the investigation that the two-room schools did better than the larger schools in the towns.

III. ABILITIES OF THE PUPILS IN SMALL AND IN LARGE SCHOOLS

What are some of the factors which effect the validity of comparisons between small schools and large schools? The quality of the pupil material conditions the achievements of the pupils in schools of a given type. In a number of studies the overageness and underageness of the pupils for each grade are used as an indication of the brightness of pupils. Most of these studies show that the pupils in the smaller schools are more retarded than the pupils in the larger schools. It should not be overlooked that data on the retardation of pupils are complicated by the differences in standards of promotion and in age of entrance.

Another method of determining the quality of the pupil material in the different types of schools has been to use the results of intelligence tests, mostly of the group form. On this part Haggerty (18:152) says:

> The fundamental item in defining standard levels of advancement is an objective statement of the requisite capacity for pursuing the educational program of a particular grade, and intelligence tests offer probably the most satisfactory means for giving such an objective statement.

In New York State, the pupils in the one-teacher schools scored lower on the Haggerty Intelligence Examination, Delta 2, than did the pupils in the four-teacher schools. If it is true that this test measures the "requisite capacity for pursuing the educational program," then the quality of the pupil material in the small schools is not so good as in the larger schools, and the lesser achievements of the pupils in the small schools in reading, spelling, and arithmetic would be due in part to this factor. But it is well to be cautious here since a comparison of the content of a group intelligence test with the content of standardized tests in silent reading, word meaning, and arithmetic will convince the reader that the group intelligence tests contain much material akin to that found in the achievement tests.[2]

Kruse (20) compared small schools and large schools and used group intelligence test scores as rough measures of the quality of the pupil material. The pupils in the smaller schools scored lower on the intelligence tests as well as on the tests of achievement. Kruse says (20:120): "It would appear from our data that the conclusions commonly reached regarding the effectiveness of the small school as compared with the larger school are not warranted." He also pre-

---

[2] On page 167 of his report, Haggerty discusses intelligence-test scores as measures of native endowment. Doubtless he might qualify his statements at the present time.

sents some data (pp. 121-127) on the tendency for the small rural schools to lose their more capable pupils, especially in the upper grades, to the larger rural and urban schools. He raises the question (p. 124) : "How do those pupils in the larger rural schools, who are resident outside of the district in which they are attending school, compare with all the pupils in these schools on the one hand, and with the pupils of the small rural schools on the other hand?" His answer is (p. 126) : "The intelligence quotients, which represent the ratio of mental age to chronological age, show very close agreement of the 'outside of district' pupils and pupils of large schools, and marked superiority of the former to the pupils of the small schools." Kruse cautions the reader that environmental factors may be at work here, and also points out (p. 119) that one of the achievement tests, the reading test, probably measures very much the same traits as the intelligence test used.

M. J. Van Wagenen, in his comprehensive study of *Comparative Pupil Achievement in Rural, Town and City Schools* (35) used an intelligence test, as well as a number of achievement tests, in Grades VII and VIII, testing approximately twenty-five hundred pupils in rural schools having an eight-month term, fifteen hundred in rural schools with a nine-month term, and two thousand each in four groups of town and small city high schools. The boys and girls in each grade were compared separately. Mid-scores (rough average scores) were computed within each grade for each group for quarter-year mental-age groups. In other words, the intelligence-test scores were taken into account in making the comparisons for the achievement-test scores. The pupils in the graded schools excelled the pupils in the ungraded schools.

In a study by Wilson and Ashbaugh (36) the boys and girls were compared separately. Pupils in the different types of schools were paired for the comparison on the basis of intelligence-test scores. The pupils in the consolidated schools surpassed the pupils in the rural schools, in general, by small but consistent differences in the achievement tests.

In the West Virginia survey reported by Cavins (7), in the Laurens County, South Carolina, survey reported by Frost (15), and in the Utah survey (34) somewhat similar methods were used and results similar to the foregoing were obtained.

IV. Length of the School Term as a Disturbing Factor

The length of the school term has been a factor which has been taken into account in the more recent studies of the educational achievements of the small rural schools and the larger schools. Kruse (20:59f.) says:

1. The fifth and seventh grades of schools of six-, seven-, eight- and nine-month school years make very near the same achievement in reading.

2. In addition, division, and spelling the increased achievement in schools of longer term is appreciable in amount and fairly regular with increased length of time.

3. It appears, from the facts just given, that the schools have in these grades little influenced the reading ability of the pupils; but do have marked influence on the achievement of pupils in arithmetic and spelling.

4. There is evidence that the pupils in the schools of longer terms are more able than the pupils in the schools of short terms. This holds for both grades V and VII, but the variation in mental ability is more regular in relation to length of year in the seventh grade than in the fifth.

Van Wagenen (35) found that the pupils in the schools having a nine-month term made somewhat higher scores on the achievement tests than pupils in the schools having an eight-month term. F. P. O'Brien (27) found only slight differences between one-teacher schools having an eight-month term and similar schools having a seven-month term.

The superiority of the achievements of the pupils in schools having an eight-month or a nine-month term over the achievements of pupils in schools having a shorter term may not be due altogether to the extra training received. Kruse has suggested that there may be a difference in the quality of the pupils between the two groups of schools. Van Wagenen attempted to take this into account by making his comparisons for the achievement tests in terms of mental age. There is a further possibility, namely, that the communities which have longer terms are the communities in which there is a greater interest in the schools. Where there is greater interest in the schools, there is apt to be greater pressure to do good work brought to bear on pupils by their parents.

C. E. Myers (24) used a measure of instructional efficiency which included a number of factors. Using his particular formula, he arrived at indices which showed the smaller schools to be superior to the larger schools. However, he makes one assumption which has considerable influence upon the indices he uses, namely, the assumption that the achievement of pupils should be in direct proportion to the length of the school term. This assumption is not necessarily correct, and his indices are in error to the extent that this assumption and others he makes are in error. As a matter of fact, when we take Myers' data and compare the small schools with the large schools, using the mean score for a given age group, say eleven years, no months to eleven years, eleven months, within a given grade, say the sixth grade, we find that the larger schools do about as well as the smaller schools.

V. How Significant Are the Differences in Achievements?

Suppose that we accepted the differences between the achievements of the pupils in the small schools and of the pupils in the larger schools at their face value. How significant are these differences as to magnitude? Who knows? It is a common practice to state the differences in terms of what is called 'a school year of progress' in the particular subject, say reading. For example, in Table 5 of the Texas Educational Survey Report (20:70) we find that the median score for the fifth-grade pupils in all schools, excluding cities, was 43.0. The median score for those of the sixth grade was 45.7; the difference between these two medians is 2.7 and may be thought of as constituting a year's progress in reading. That this difference and similar differences are rather small in terms of magnitude of score is not surprising when we keep in mind the extent to which the achievements of the pupils in one grade overlap the achievements of the pupils in an adjacent grade. Such a definition of a year's progress in a subject may be misleading if the reader infers that it is the difference between the scores of the same group of pupils at the beginning of the school year and at the end of the school year. It may also be misleading if he infers that the test measures everything that the pupils have learned in that particular subject. How significant the differences between the achievements of the pupils in the small schools and the pupils in the larger schools are it would be difficult to say.

It would seem in the light of the limitations of the studies which have been made of the comparative achievements of small and large schools that sweeping generalizations should not be made, that there should be further attempts to control some of the factors which effect the validity of such comparisons, that specific problems should be attacked, and that consideration should be given to administrative factors involved in the consolidation of schools.

VI. Some Problems for Further Research

There are many problems suggested for further study by what has been done in comparing small and large schools. The limitations of our measuring instruments and the large number of factors to be taken into account present almost insuperable difficulties. Nevertheless, we can undertake such studies and be ready to admit the serious limitations of whatever we do. A few of these problems are: (1) a study of the entering ages and grade progress of pupils in small and in large schools; (2) a study of what becomes of the bright pupils in the small schools, in which the pupils would be given the best available tests when they enter the first grade and traced in their subsequent progress, to get some light on the question of whether or not the large schools tend to attract the abler pupils from the small schools; and (3) a study of educational progress in small and in large schools. The status of the pupils would be measured at the beginning of the school year, throughout the school year, and at the end of the school year. It is doubtful if the tests available at the present time are comprehensive enough for such a study. In all such studies the administrative aspects of the problem must be kept clearly in mind.

SECTION II

ADMINISTRATIVE FACTORS IN PLANNING A POLICY REGARDING SMALL AND LARGE SCHOOLS

Julian E. Butterworth
Cornell University, Ithaca, New York

I. The Influence of Conditioning Factors

The final concern of the educational administrator is, of course, the providing of such experience as will stimulate the development of those abilities considered significant by society. Various agencies, with their many conditioning factors, contribute to the attainment of this end. On the one hand, there is the school; on the other hand, there are the home and the community with all those experiences that influence the child during his out-of-school life.

Within the school there are such factors as these which influence the educational product to greater or less degree: the length of the school term; the scope of the curriculum and its suitability for the particular groups involved; the quality of the instruction as affected by the ability, training, experience, compensation, and working conditions of the teacher; and the adequacy and suitability of the building to house the curriculum and its equipment to provide the aids useful in its presentation. All these and other conditioning factors are in turn influenced by the wealth of the community, the willingness of its citizens to pay taxes, and the educational intelligence of the citizen body in supporting a progressive school program. The recognition of the influence of such conditioning factors on the educational product is the first step in planning a policy regarding small and large schools.

II. Measuring These Conditioning Factors in Small and Large Schools

The next step for the thoughtful administrator is to raise the question with himself as to whether it is the small or the large school that is likely to provide in greater degree the conditioning factors desired. Investigations of this matter have usually provided a convincing answer. Thus, to cite merely one of many studies that have been made, Larson (21 : 54) found from a study of schools in 98 of the towns in Connecticut that the one-room school was inferior to the consolidated school in holding power, in the training and experience of the teacher, in the net salary paid, and in the school opportunities, and the living conditions provided for the teacher.

Three reservations must, however, be kept in mind. First, not all consolidated schools are superior to all one-room schools in all particulars, and such differences as do appear are not uniform in degree. Thus, while the median training of one-room teachers in Indiana, in 1923, represented about 12 weeks beyond the high school and that of elementary teachers in the city schools more than 36 weeks beyond the high school, yet about 8 percent of the one-room teachers had had a longer training than the median of city teachers (16 : 278). Second, most of these conditioning factors are not inherent in a school because of its largeness or smallness. While, under ordinary conditions, as varied a curriculum cannot be offered in one-room as in larger schools, the former may have teachers as well trained, as experienced, and as well paid as the latter, and may have a building as well adapted to its needs. Third, the educational result depends not only upon the facilities available but also upon the energy and the intelligence with which they are utilized.

III. SUGGESTED RESEARCHES

A sound policy regarding small and large schools will not, then, be developed merely by falling back upon the results of such investigations as Dr. Bayne has analyzed. Conditioning factors—many of which are of an administrative nature—must be taken into account. Progress on this whole question would, therefore, seem to involve such investigations and researches as the following:

1. In a particular territory where the policy is being considered, what are the conditioning factors that now operate and what would they probably be if the policy were changed? This calls for a survey type of investigation showing details regarding teachers, curricula, length of term, buildings, equipment, and the like as they are now, and as they may reasonably be expected to be under the proposed policy (10).

2. The possibility of improving the conditioning factors without changing the policy regarding small or large schools should be surveyed. This will call for an investigation regarding such matters as the ability and willingness of the small schools to provide needed funds, the effect of the present system of state aid on the equalization of opportunities regardless of the size or the wealth of the community, the feasibility of transporting the pupils, and the availability of high schools.

3. Experiments should be conducted similar to the one now going on under the direction of Dr. Fannie Dunn of Teachers College, Columbia University, to see what changes may be made in these conditioning factors in small schools and with what results.

4. Educational results in small and large schools should be measured. Here the investigator should employ improvements in the techniques of collecting and interpreting data such as Dr. Bayne has suggested.

5. The most significant, as well as the most difficult, type of research in connection with this problem is probably that which seeks to measure the influence of the more important conditioning factors upon the desired type of pupil development. While our efforts in this direction seem thus far to have been of value chiefly in showing the complexity of the problem and the inadequacy of our techniques, we shall probably see considerable progress during the next decade.

SECTION III

TYPES OF LOCAL SCHOOL UNITS

Julian E. Butterworth
Cornell University, Ithaca, New York

Our American conception of government demands a large delegation of responsibilities to those administrative units that are close to the people. What are these units controlling education in the rural areas and how should they be evaluated?

I. Existing Types of Local Units in the Rural Areas

The existing types of local school districts in rural communities may be described thus: (1) 'The common school district' is a small area, limited in wealth and population, maintaining usually a school of one teacher and offering usually not more than eight grades of work. (2) 'The consolidated district' is a combination of smaller districts (in which the schools themselves are usually, though not always, brought together at one point) to make possible better educational offerings. (3) 'The community district' is similar to the consolidated district, though in this type emphasis is given to the inclusion of those areas that form a natural community. (4) 'The union high-school district,' formed under various names in several states, is a type of organization under which a number of elementary schools, without giving up their organization for elementary education, combine for secondary-school purposes. (5) 'The township' (or, in New England and New York, 'the town') places under the control of one board all public schools within the boundaries of that political area. (6) 'The county organization' is a local unit in which there is provided one board of education with practicaly full control of all schools within the county except those in the cities and larger villages.

(7) The 'city-county organization' places under one control all schools within the county whether they be in the urban or in the non-urban sections of the county.

II. THE STATUS OF THESE DISTRICTS

The common-school district is found in each state in which the town, township, or county is not the local unit for school administration. The number of such districts varies from state to state.

The latest estimates of the Office of Education, those for 1927-28, give the total number of consolidated schools as 17,004. Since the difference between the consolidated district and the community district is the degree to which community factors are emphasized, and since these are largely qualitative, there is, at present, no way of dividing the figures given between these two types of districts. The union high-school district is found not infrequently in states where the common-school district prevails. California and Illinois appear to have more than most states. The township is the unit of administration for rural schools in Indiana, New Jersey, Ohio, Pennsylvania, West Virginia, and in some cases in Michigan, Iowa, North Dakota, and South Dakota. The town is the local unit in the New England States.

It is more difficult to classify the county-unit states because of varying conceptions as to what constitutes a 'county unit.' Monahan (23: 17), in 1914, listed eighteen states as having this form of organization, recognizing, however, that only six had given 'practically the entire management and control' of the schools to the county boards. Cook (9: 6), in 1922, classified ten states as having the county as the unit of administration. Burris (4: 36-48), in 1924, designated sixteen items of control that a 'satisfactory county system' should possess and graded each of eleven states according to these standards. The present writer (6: 357-361) classified the states using the county as an educational unit into four groups.

Through these various studies of county organization we have had impressed upon us that there is not one type of county control but several. Scarcely any two states have exactly the same type and degree of control, so that more exact definition is the first step in the evaluation of the county unit.

The city-county district is the logical development in the county-unit states where the cities, as well as the villages, are included in the school organization of the county. It is found, also, in other than the so-called 'county-unit states.' Information received from the various state departments of education indicate that there are about 125 such organizations that include a city of 2,500 population or larger.

III. How Should These Units Be Evaluated?

A certain school of administrative thought appears to have accepted the county or the city-county as the most desirable unit for the administration of rural education. Without going into detail, their arguments emphasize ease of administration; the centralization of responsibility, both lay and professional; the equalization of educational burdens; and the stimulation of educational opportunities which such a larger unit makes possible.

One of the outstanding students in the field of rural education emphasizes another criterion; namely, the development of social solidarity (37:560). The present writer (5) has emphasized also certain social and psychological factors and has suggested two criteria for the local unit, namely, that it should be of such size as will provide the facilities required to make a modern school, and that it should be composed of such constituent groups that citizens will find it possible, and will be encouraged, to work together on their educational problems.

These social and psychological factors should be carefully evaluated. The suggestion of their importance comes from the conception that education cannot in the long run make greater progress than the ideals of the citizen body permit and that the sociological make-up of the school district is a real factor in the development of these ideals.

IV. Is There a Best Type of Local Unit?

In much of our writing there is the implication that, in meeting the deficiencies in prevailing local units, one type is to be preferred. How sound is this implication? In answering this question, whatever criteria may finally be accepted as most significant in the determination of the type of local unit, numerous specific factors must be taken into account. Four of these may be cited:

1. The ability of the local district to support the desired educational program. This is determined partly by the wealth of the community, partly by the prevailing standard of educational costs, partly by the sums available through the state for purposes of equalizing opportunities among the various subdivisions of the state.

2. The number of pupils enrolled must be sufficient to provide adequate curricula at reasonable cost. Ashbaugh's recent study of small high schools in Ohio (1) indicates that 73.7 percent of all the high schools in that state had, in 1927-28, an enrollment of one hundred or fewer in the four upper grades. This means that unless the community is unusually wealthy a varied curriculum for various types of students is out of the question.

3. The stage of the development in coöperation for social ends is also likely to be an important consideration in determining the type of local unit. The group that is to coöperate effectively for the development of a progressive educational program should be large enough to provide the resources needed and varied enough in its composition to be stimulating. It should be sufficiently small and homogeneous, however, so that genuine coöperation may be developed if it does not already exist.

4. The quality of leadership available in developing an interest in educational affairs will be an important factor. Under leadership of the highest type unfavorable conditions may be overcome. Unless there is a fair chance that the available leadership is adequate to compass this, it is a question how far the local unit should go beyond existing bounds until that leadership may be changed.

One study of this problem, that of Smart (31:49ff.), suggests that a union school district is the most feasible solution for some conditions, while an Ohio study (28:43ff.) suggests that a county unit or a city-county organization is to be desired for that state.

V. Needed Researches

If the preceding analysis is sound, studies dealing with such questions as the following are needed.

1. What type of local unit is desirable in a particular situation?

The answer to this will call for the setting of tentative standards regarding the number of grades to be desired, the breadth of the curriculum, the quality of the instruction, the amount and nature of adult instruction, if any, the extension instruction of pupils just beyond school age, if any, and the like. It will then be necessary to secure data, for the particular time and place, regarding the wealth needed to provide these facilities, the number of pupils necessary to justify that type of school and to provide classes of economical size. It will call for such objective data as may be secured on the social and psychological factors suggested.

2. The last sentence suggests these important problems: How significant are these social and psychological factors; how may they

be measured; and if they are significant, how far and under what conditions may they be developed?

Such specific questions as the following are involved: How easy is it to get actual physical contacts in the territory tentatively proposed as the local unit? Are there racial, national, religious, occupational, or business groups that would be likely to affect coöperation for educational purposes? Is there so much homogeneity because of similarity of occupation, educational experience, age groups, and the like that there is a lack of stimulus within the group? Questions such as these suggest the need for our securing the specialized service of the rural sociologist and the social psychologist.

3. As such studies as the preceding are made under all sorts of conditions, we may then begin to generalize on such questions as these: When each state has developed that type of local unit most suited to its needs, will there be one or several types of local units? Within any state will there be one or several types? Will effective thinking on this whole question be promoted by deciding upon certain types of units or by setting up ends that it is desired to attain through the local school unit?

4. Particular attention should be given to an evaluation of the city-county organization.

Existing units of this type should be studied intensively with particular reference to such matters as these: a comparison of school facilities offered in the rural and the non-rural sections of the district; the voice that each section of the county has in the control of school policies; the extent to which the curriculum is adapted to the needs of each group; the understanding of the problems of rural life and education evidenced by the professional officers of the district.[3]

While all of the foregoing problems have aspects making the use of objective data feasible, there are many intangible factors involved. This is likely to be more true here than in some other types of researches, because of the importance of the philosophy of government and of education involved. All will doubtless agree, however, that these intangible matters should be teased out, scrutinized, and evaluated as best they may.

---

[3] One such study (33) that presents data on a few of these points shows lower salaries for teachers, a much lower percentage attending high schools, and fewer special promotions of pupils in certain grades in the rural than in the urban sections of the county.

SECTION IV
ANALYZING THE WORK OF THE RURAL-SCHOOL ADMINISTRATOR

M. G. NELSON
Professor of Education
New York State College for Teachers, Albany, New York

I. STATEMENT OF PURPOSE

The administrators of a modern business balance accounts and take inventories at regular intervals in order to determine the amount of profit or loss. Those responsible for the conduct of an efficient business incessantly analyze its activities because continued success depends upon efficient conduct of the various processes.

School administrators are not stimulated to do this because their board of directors (board of education) demands neither inventory nor balance sheet. Being left to themselves, they are apt to do what intrudes upon attention at the moment. The result is a trial-and-error type of administration which is dependent upon a superintendent who engages in those procedures he likes and avoids those he dislikes. A similar lack of detailed analysis and planning would place any business concern in the hands of a receiver.

To meet this condition definite attempts to measure administrative activity have been made in recent years. In city situations much has been accomplished by means of the survey, but surveys are less frequent in rural units. However, a number of studies have been made of the work of the rural superintendent and principal. These studies have considered two aspects: (1) the work of the high-school principal, as he is called in the East, or superintendent of the village school, as he is called in the West, and (2) the work of the county or district superintendent.

These studies are of sufficient interest and value to warrant the presentation here of their significant features.

II. SUMMARIES OF SELECTED STUDIES

1. Studies Analyzing the Activities of School Principals or Village Superintendents

Bell's study (3) classified school systems on the basis of pupil enrollment. Prepared forms were sent to 1000 superintendents who were selected from a total of 1469. Each superintendent was requested to keep a diary for seven consecutive days. An analysis of the 211 usable replies yielded 38 different activities which were then classified under these nine major headings: (1) relations with community, (2) relations with workers, (3) curriculum, (4) students (including teaching), (5) physical maintenance, (6) finance, (7) clerical, (8) professional study, and (9) recreation.

Belknap (2) studied 150 superintendents of graded schools which had a school census population of not more than 500 pupils and employed 6 or more teachers.

The median superintendent spent four daily periods in teaching, two in administration, two in supervision, and two in clerical work. Two periods per day were given to athletics during particular seasons, two periods to orchestra and dramatics, and two periods to other activities.

In Feelhaver's study (12) the high schools accredited by the University of Nebraska were classified on the basis of pupil enrollment and the data for 144 of them were derived by using work sheets covering seven consecutive days, a blank for seasonal duties, and a blank for personal information. The major activities considered were instructional load, administrative load, instructional supervision, professional load (institutes, committee work, professional reading), supervision of study hall, lunch rooms, corridors, and library, clerical load, extra-curricular load, community activities, and recreation and outside work.

Ferriss, in his study of the rural high school in New York (13: 23-29), derived his data mainly from the following sources: statistics and reports of the State Department of Education, the replies of 405 principals to a questionnaire, and visitation of over 75 rural high schools. The major activities considered were teaching-load, supervision, total, supervision, secondary, supervision, elementary, office work, pupil activities, and non-pupil outside activities.

The requirements set up by Harrold (19) limited his study to 167 schools and only 58 principals furnished usable answers to his questionnaire. Each principal was requested to indicate by a system of check marks those activities which he considered 'most important,' 'most difficult,' 'least important,' and 'least difficult.' The frequency of performance was measured by requesting the principals to check the frequency with which each activity was performed as 'not at all,' 'yearly,' 'monthly,' 'weekly,' and 'daily.'

Again by means of the questionnaire McGee (22) sought to ascertain: the actual time distribution of superintendents and the theoretical time distribution for superintendents as reported by university professors. Data were sought from all towns between one thousand and two thousand population in the states of Iowa, Nebraska, and Colorado; replies were received from 110 of 245 superintendents. The major activities considered were teaching, clerical duties, administration, supervision, professional growth and study, and community leadership.

Usable replies to a questionnaire were received by Nanney (25) from 110 of 250 superintendents and the data were checked by 11 personal interviews. Her questionnaire was in the form of a check list which contained the following items: check if (1) performed, (2) best learned on the job, (3) best learned in school, (4) duty is easy, (5) duty is hard, (6) performed daily, (7) performed weekly, (8) performed monthly, and (9) performed occasionally. The duties checked were classified under the following major headings: administration and organization, supervision, clerical and routine, professional growth and study, community leadership, teaching, and recreation.

2. Studies Analyzing the Activities of County Superintendents or Comparable Administrators

The purpose of a study by French (14) was to discover what records should be kept. Each of 36 basic activities were analyzed for the purpose of determining what record items were needed in order to carry on that activity most efficiently. This list was then checked by comparison with actual records being kept by district superintendents and afterward criticised by seven specialists in educational administration.

Gunn (17)[4] utilized daily records furnished by 50 county superintendents and covering periods ranging from six to twenty-four days each. Estimates were made by them of the amount of time given to the same activities for one year. In addition, the opinions of 58 experts in the field of administration and supervision were secured.

---

[4] An outline of this study was furnished by the librarian of the college. The original study could not be secured owing to the fact that George Peabody College does not loan thesis studies to other institutions.

The major activities included were: office activities, supervisory activities, general professional activities, civic activities, boys' and girls' clubs, civic clubs and fraternal organizations, travel, and observation of class work. The length of the county superintendent's day was found to be 8.64 hours.

Nelson (26) sought to ascertain the relative importance and difficulty of thirty-six basic activities, to determine how the district superintendent distributed his time, and to list those influences that determined his distribution. The total number of superintendents was 208; relative difficulty and importance was reported upon by 108; and information regarding the distribution of time was supplied by 116. The data were secured from the state department of education and from a questionnaire. The major activities considered were: teachers, pupils, and classrooms; communities, parents, and school officials; state departments, reports, and clerical-office routine; and personal professional improvement.

The data presented by Soper and Baer (32) were secured by questionnaire and by examination of actual records of clerical work performed during the weeks of February 17 to 23, and November 10 to 16, 1929. Eighty of the 208 district superintendents of schools in New York State furnished information for this study. A wide range was reported for time spent on clerical work.

III. Comments on the Procedures Used and Suggestions for Future Analyses

1. The Type of Analysis

Nine studies analyzed the administrative activities from the point of view of time distribution. One study had the activities checked for daily, weekly, monthly, and occasional occurrence. Five studies reported the activities on the basis of the percentage of time used. One employed minutes, another employed periods, and still another used both minutes and periods. Five of the studies required the keeping of some form of record, such as a diary. Seven studies used the questionnaire, and four studies used the check list.

If the investigators had selected similar procedures, the results would be more readily comparable and more easily utilized by superintendents or principals generally. The desire to improve upon previous studies is quite laudable and should be encouraged; however, the introduction of new methods should not be made unless substantially improved results are probable.

2. The Number of Cases Used

Perhaps the most severe criticism that may be made of these studies is the relatively small number of cases sometimes used as a basis for conclusions. Seldom did the number of cases treated prove to be in excess of fifty percent of the total number possible. This criticism is rather of the administrators themselves than of the investigators. Coöperation of administrators is necessary if improved practices are to be developed.

3. Statistical Treatment

The statistical methods were not commonly adequate. Probable errors were seldom computed, and only a few authors seemed to think that the problem of adequate sampling needed consideration. If the data were too few or unreliable to justify such statistical treatment, it would seem that they were not sufficiently reliable to be used as a basis for any conclusions.

4. The Fineness of Measures Used

There seems to be a tendency for educational investigators generally to attempt to measure with too fine a scale, something like measuring land with a millimeter rule. For example, a certain duty may be performed daily and can be so reported, but a request to report the time spent on the activity in minutes might yield figures so erroneous as to permit no conclusions of value.

5. The Number of Duties Listed in the Analysis

The various studies have not dealt with the same classification of duties. In general, a classification more naturally used for urban studies has been applied. By urban classification is meant dividing duties into the major divisions: administration, supervision, clerical, teaching, and professional improvement. Difficulty arises from the fact that the work of a rural administrator does not naturally divide into such units. There is administration in supervision and also in clerical routine. Until rural investigators adopt a uniform and directly useful terminology their investigations will be handicapped. The rural department of the National Education Association might well appoint a committee to suggest a standard classification of major administrative activities.

6. The Number of Phases Considered

The studies by French and by Soper and Baer are outstanding because their authors have not tried to compass everything. They have limited their work to one phase, the clerical, and they have studied that phase exhaustively. The general, 'panoramic' study is valuable for envisaging larger items, but when it tries to include all the smaller ones, the picture is obscured and confused.[5] The general survey should be made first, then followed by many detailed, analytical studies, each dealing with some limited phase of administrative work.

Probably the greatest service that may be rendered in the field of analyzing the work of the rural-school administrator is to establish standards which may be accepted as reasonable and just by both investigators and the men in the field. When that has been done, perhaps the busy principal or superintendent will realize the necessity of furnishing assistance to those persons who desire to help him take his 'inventory' and strike his 'trial balance.' When this time arrives, no more will the school principal write across a report blank: "My status suits me; with 300 pupils and 14 teachers I've no time to answer this inquiry."

SECTION V

SERVICES RENDERED RURAL SCHOOLS BY STATE DEPARTMENTS OF EDUCATION

R. E. JAGGERS
Supervisor of Rural Elementary Schools
Frankfort, Kentucky

What services are rendered rural schools by the state departments of education? In order to answer this question the available literature was examined and a questionnaire study was made of the present status of this service with respect to the organization for rendering service, the agencies through which the service is rendered, and the specific services rendered.

---

[5] In illustration: one general survey reported upon 127 different items and made the statement that 121 additional items were suggested—248 specific items in all. Another study reported on only five major items. Comparisons between two such studies are manifestly impossible.

I. General Staff of State Departments of Education

Inspection of the published reports shows that the development of public education in the different states has been accompanied by a corresponding increase in the number of persons employed by the states to carry out their respective educational programs. A study made by Schrammel (29:49) in 1926 shows that in 1890 there were only 129 persons employed in the state departments of education in all the states; in 1905 there were 219; in 1925 there were 1890. Persons engaged in this service were carrying out those educational functions for which the lesser units were not held responsible. The median number of persons employed in each state department of education during this period was two in 1890, four in 1905, nineteen in 1915, and twenty-three in 1925. Schrammel suggests (29:56) that one measure of the degree to which a state is able to render service is the ratio between the total number of elementary and secondary pupils and the number of employes in the state departments of education. In 1890 there was one person employed in state departments for every 98,625 pupils, in 1925 one for every 12,296 pupils.

II. Emphasis Placed on Rural Education by State Departments of Education

If the number of persons employed is a measure of the relative value of a particular type of service rendered by state departments of education to the public schools, rural education occupies a high rank. Schrammel (29:71) ranked the states according to the number of persons employed in each of 25 types of services rendered by state departments and found that the rural-school supervisor ranked second in the group; when these 25 types were ranked according to the number of states providing each service, rural-school supervision ranked 6.5.

A review of rural supervision in 1928 by Mrs. Cook (8) indicates that, in 1916, 26 states employed 46 persons as supervisors, inspectors, or agents for rural schools; 33 states, in 1922, had 118 staff members assigned to services in rural schools; and 38 states, in 1928, assigned 172 members of their staffs to the rural-school service. Her study shows that persons assigned to rural-school services are as well trained and receive as much compensation as other members of the staff of the departments of education. Schrammel (29:86) found that in 1925 the median salary of rural supervisors was slightly more than the median salary of the entire staff. The rapid growth in the number of persons assigned to rural service and the relatively high standards in training and salary provided indicate that the field of rural service takes rank equal in dignity and importance with that of other activities of state departments of education.

III. ORGANIZATION OF STATE DEPARTMENTS FOR RENDERING SERVICE TO RURAL SCHOOLS

There are two general types of organizations in state departments of education which render services to rural schools: first, there is the clearly defined rural division of professional service in the department of education with rural-school workers closely associated; and second, there is the department in which the workers are so organized that specialized services are given to all schools by the staff members without regard to whether the schools are rural or urban.

The information from 42 states given in answer to an inquiry shows that in 25 states professional service to rural schools is rendered through a clearly defined division of rural education, while in 17 states the workers in the state departments of education are so organized that specialized services are rendered to all schools without regard to whether they are rural or urban.

According to the questionnaire reports in 25 states in which there is a division of rural education there are 319 persons employed for rendering services to rural schools. Of these, 224 devote all their time to general or specialized services to rural schools, while 95 devote only part-time to such services. Of the 17 states which report no division of rural education, only 4 employ full-time general supervisors; 5 states provide full-time special supervisors; 12 states provide persons for general part-time services; and 5 states provide special part-time services. These 17 states assign 184 staff members to full-time or part-time services to rural schools.

Generally, where persons are assigned for full-time to the services of rural schools, there is a rather distinct division of rural schools in state departments of education, while in departments where only part-time services are rendered, there is no such division. In the 25 states which report divisions of rural education, there is at least one person devoting full-time to rural-school service, while in 17 states reporting no such division only 8 report full-time service.

New York, Michigan, and California have provided well-organized divisions of rural education with a group of closely associated specialists in charge. New York has seven members on the rural education staff; Michigan, 9; and California, 7.

Other states extend service to rural schools under different types of organization. New Jersey provides the helping teacher; in Delaware the state provides local supervisors, while in Nevada five deputies render service as supervisors in five supervisory districts. In fact, all the states extend some kind of service to rural schools. Each state has problems peculiarly its own, and for this reason each must build its organization to meet the conditions to be faced.

IV. AGENCIES THROUGH WHICH SERVICES ARE RENDERED RURAL SCHOOLS BY STATE DEPARTMENTS OF EDUCATION

An examination of the available studies shows that state departments of education are rendering service to rural schools through professional leadership as shown by administrative reforms, higher qualifications of professional personnel, increased appropriations, scientific methods of distributing revenues, and through provisions for better state aid. In addition to this, the professional character of rural schools is being raised; modern methods of administration, supervision, and teaching are being put into operation; problems of administration and teaching are being approached through the survey and other scientific agencies; and the general morale has been raised through a high type of trained leaders provided by state departments of education.

Our own study showed that the following agencies were used *often* and in the order of mention by more than half of the states reporting: (1) circular letters, (2) personal visits to local supervisory and administrative officers, (3) group conferences with local supervisory and administrative officers, and (4) mimeographed outlines. More than half of the states use the following agencies *occasionally*: state-wide conventions of local administrative and supervisory officers, district and regional conferences of local administrative and supervisory officers, county teachers' conferences and institutes, and curriculum committees. At some time during the year all the states reporting use the following agencies: personal visits to local officers, group conferences with them, state-wide and district conventions, circular letters, and mimeographed outlines.

States organized with a division of rural education reported circular letters, personal visits to local officers, group conferences and mimeographed outlines as most frequently used, while those with no rural division reported in order of importance: personal visits, curriculum committees, school and community surveys, teachers' conferences, and institutes.

V. Types of Local Problems with Which State Rural Professional Workers Deal

State departments of education were asked to check a list of thirty local problems in which aid was frequently given to local administrative and supervisory officers. Thirty-seven states checked the problems. These problems are given here in order of frequency of checking: school equipment, classroom visits, planning buildings, in service training, professional growth of teachers, consolidation, health education, scoring plants, water supply, board-member problems, transportation, developing leadership, special education, adult education, community difficulties, length of term, attendance, methods of teaching, rating teachers, trustee relations, colored schools, standard tests, young teachers, office administration, salary schedule, extra-class activities, office assistance, school accounting, making budgets, and selecting teachers.

VI. Summary

This survey of services rendered by state departments of education indicates, then, (1) that the rural service ranks as high as other services rendered by state departments of education; (2) that in state departments of education organized with a division of rural education a greater number of persons devote time to rural-school service than in states which are not so organized; (3) that state departments of education, in making contact with rural schools, use most frequently conferences and visits with local supervisors and administrative officers, and circular letters and mimeographed outlines; (4) that state departments render services most frequently by helping local school officials with local problems.

VII. Further Study Needed Regarding Services Rendered Rural Schools by State Departments of Education

This brief study of the services rendered rural schools by state departments of education raises the major question of what factors operate in determining the efficiency of the organization of state departments of education. The following four problems grow out of this major question.

1. *The Selection and Assignment of the Personnel of State Departments of Education.* What factors should determine the number and training of persons assigned to the different divisions of the department? What should be the relationship between different divisions? What should be the ratio of the number of persons employed in each type of service to the number of persons affected by that service?

2. *The Place of Rural-Education Service in State Departments of Education.* Should there be a clearly defined division of rural education with rural-school specialists closely associated? Should the department of education so be organized that specialized service may be rendered to all schools regardless of whether they are urban or rural?

3. *Relative Efficiency of Agencies or Methods through Which Services Are Rendered to Rural Schools by State Departments of Education.* What are the relative merits of personal visits to local administrative officers, mimeographed outlines and instructions, printed bulletins, and other devices, as agencies through which services may be rendered?

4. *Factors That Should Determine the Problems around Which the State Builds Its Program for Rendering Service to Rural Schools.* Should the state department build its own program for rendering service to rural schools? What factors should determine the types of services included in the state's program? Should the state department hold itself in readiness merely to assist local school officers in developing a program locally conceived? What part of the program of rural education should originate in the division of rural education? What part should originate in the local communities?

BIBLIOGRAPHY

1. ASHBAUGH, E. J. "High school in every school district means too many small schools." *School Life,* 14: 1929, 133 ff.

2. BELKNAP, BURTON H. "The Training and Function of the Rural School Superintendent of Michigan." 1928. (Unpublished master's thesis on file in the Library of Cornell University).

218 THE STATUS OF RURAL EDUCATION

3. BELL, REQUA W. "A Job Analysis of Superintending the Public Schools in the North Central Association." 1926. (Unpublished master's thesis on file in the Library of the University of Oklahoma).

4. BURRIS, BENJ. J. *The County School System: How Organized and Administered.* Indianapolis, 1924. Pp. 36-48. (Education Bulletin No. 73).

5. BUTTERWORTH, JULIAN E. "Defining the local rural school unit in terms of its objectives." *Educ. Admin. and Superv.*, 11 : 1925, 145-156.

6. BUTTERWORTH, JULIAN E. *Principles of Rural School Administration.* New York, 1926. Pp. 357-361.

7. CAVINS, L. V., director. *Survey of Education in West Virginia; Educational Achievement.* Charleston, 1928. Vol. II.

8. COOK, KATHERINE M. Rural School Circular, No. 29. Washington, 1928. U. S. Bur. Educ.

9. COOK, KATHERINE M. *Supervision of Rural Schools.* Washington, 1922. (U. S. Bur. Educ. Bull., No. 10) p. 6.

10. COOK, KATHERINE M. and DEFFENBAUGH, W. S. *The Feasibility of Consolidating the Schools of Mount Joy Township, Adams County.* Washington, 1920. (U.S. Bur. Educ. Bull., No. 9).

11. COVERT, TIMON. *Educational Achievements of the One-Teacher and of Larger Rural Schools.* Washington, 1928. (U.S. Bur. Educ. Bull., No. 15).

12. FEELHAVER, CARL T. "The duties of high school principals in the state of Nebraska." *Sch. Rev.*, 35 : 1927, 190 ff.

13. FERRISS, E. N. *The Rural School Survey of New York State; the Rural High School*, Ithaca, 1922, Vol. VII, pp. 23-39.

14. FRENCH, HAROLD P. "Records of a District Superintendent of Schools in New York State." 1930. (Unpublished master's thesis on file in the Library of Cornell University).

15. FROST, NORMAN, Director. *Survey of Lawrens County. South Carolina Public Schools*, 1928.

16. General Education Board. *Public Education in Indiana.* New York, 1923. P. 278.

17. GUNN, W. W. "Study of the County Superintendent's Time Distribution in Mississippi." 1928. (Unpublished master's thesis on file in the Library of George Peabody College for Teachers).

18. HAGGERTY, M. E. *Rural School Survey of New York State, Educational Achievement.* Ithaca, 1922. Vol. VI.

19. HARROLD, JOHN W. "The Small Union School Principalship in New York State," 1930. (Unpublished study on file in the Library of the New York State College for Teachers).

20. KRUSE, PAUL. *Texas Educational Survey Report; Educational Achievement.* Austin, 1925. Vol. IV.

21. LARSON, EMIL L. *One-Room and Consolidated Schools of Connecticut.* New York, 1925. (Teachers College, Columbia Univ., Contr. to Educ., No. 182).

22. McGEE, RALPH K. "The Distribution of the Town Superintendent's Time." 1927. (Unpublished master's thesis on file in the Library of the University of Colorado).

23. MONAHAN, A. C. *County Unit Organization for the Administration of Rural Schools.* Washington, 1914. (U.S. Bur. Educ. Bull. No. 44).

24. MYERS, C. E. *Measuring Educational Efficiency.* Harrisburg, 1928. (Pennsylvania State Educ. Assoc. Research Bull. No. 3).

25. NANNEY, VIRGIE L. "Analysis of the Duties of Superintendents of Small School Systems." 1925. (Unpublished master's thesis on file in the Library of the Colorado State Teachers College).

26. NELSON, M. G. *A Study of District Superintendent's Activities.* Albany, 1927. 35 pp. (Univ. of the State of New York Bull. No. 890).

27. OBRIEN, F. P. *Conditional Value of a Longer School Year in One-Teacher Schools.* Lawrence, 1926. P. 8 (Bull. Univ. of Kansas, Vol. 27, No. 9).

28. Ohio Institute. "The Problem of Rural and Village School District Organization in Ohio." Columbus, 1930.

29. SCHRAMMEL, HENRY E. *The Organization of State Departments of Education.* Columbus, 1926. (Bur. Edu. Research Monog. No. 6).

30. SHRIBER, J. H., and HOPKINS, L. T. *Improving Rural School Instruction and Supervision in Colorado.* Boulder, 1925. (Univ. of Colorado Bull. No. 214).

31. SMART, THOMAS J. *A Proposed Larger School Unit for an Area in Northeastern Kansas.* Lawrence, 1927. Pp. 49 ff. (Kansas Studies in Educ., Vol. I, No. 8).

32. SOPER, WAYNE, and BAER, JOSEPH A. *A Study of the Clerical Duties of District Superintendents in New York State.* (To be published as bulletin of State Department of Education, Albany).

33. STRAYER, GEO. D., and others. *Report of the Survey of the Schools of Duval County, Florida.* New York, 1927.

34. United States Dept. of the Interior. *Survey of Education in Utah.* Washington, 1926. (U.S. Bur. Educ. Bull. No. 18).

35. VAN WAGENEN, M. J. *Comparative Pupil Achievement in Rural, Town, and City Schools.* Minneapolis, 1929.

36. WILSON, W. K. and ASHBAUGH, E. J. "Achievement in rural and consolidated schools." *Educ. Research Bull.*, 8: 1929, 358-363.

37. WORKS, G. A. "The community unit." *Rural School Survey of New York State; Administration and Supervision.* Vol. II. Ithaca, 1922.

CHAPTER IX

FINANCING THE RURAL SCHOOL

HENRY C. MORRISON
Professor of Education
University of Chicago, Chicago, Illinois

As we travel about the country, we see so many examples of wretched country schools that we wonder if we have really more than scratched the surface with our improvements. We forget that we could find the same kind of educational decrepitude in many ornate and architecturally commendable buildings in the cities. Nevertheless, there are so many positive instances in which superlatively good country schools have been set up that we not unnaturally conclude that what some school districts have done all school districts could do if they would. The question thus raised is the occasion of this paper. Is the rural-school problem at bottom a soluble one through our present fiscal and governmental methods? I assert that it is not.

The stubbornness and persistence of this problem looks rather fateful; but it is not. We have been collecting school facts for many years,[1] and, so far as the broad issue within each of the several states is concerned, we have facts enough. We can see what the facts are and why they are what they are. Meantime, taxationists, rural economists, and students in the field of general economics, have been producing illuminating material which we cannot ignore. The task now before us is to find out the practical bearing of all these facts, and then we shall probably have to make up our minds to submit to a sort of governmental and fiscal surgical operation.

I. CITY AND COUNTRY IN THE SAME BOAT

As a nation, we have carried free and universal education to a point at which we are challenged by the question, Is it possible to support any such system as we have set up, either in city or country?

---

[1] Recall particularly the works of Swift, Russell, Works, Updegraff, F. W. Morrison, Mort, Cavins, and many others; the studies of the Educational Finance Inquiry; many reports of state education offices and state survey commissions; and numerous unpublished university investigations.

The evidence shows that only those communities which are fortunate in economic type can support adequate schools. Further, since the district system sometimes commits management of the schools to local trustees who in the aggregate outnumber the teachers three to one, we can scarcely look for competent management of the school money when the taxes have been collected.

On the other hand, if we turn to the economic structure of the nation as a whole or to that of most of the states, and raise the original question, without preconceptions as to methods of taxation or forms of school government or courses of study, then the clear answer is: It is possible to carry an enrollment under free education up to perhaps age eighteen, and eventually to age twenty-one, for all children and young people, and furthermore the existing enrollment has been one of the critical factors in our recent prosperity.[2] The problem of financing rural schools is in that case only a feature of the problem of financing all schools, of utilizing our singularly adequate economic structure for the support of the school system which is an essential part of that structure. The rural problem is before us simply because a rickety machine breaks down at its weakest point. The farmer is peculiarly the victim of our present system of taxation, and the rural-school district is inherently the weakest point in our district system of school government.

II. OBSOLETE TAXATION

As a young superintendent of schools in an eastern city, I received a salary of $2,000. I paid a poll tax of $2.33 and that was all. In a neighboring farming town lived a young farmer who had taken over a farm which was still under good cultivation and which still possessed a good set of buildings. The farmer had a net cash income of perhaps $600 to $800, disregarding the value of his own labor and interest on his invested capital. His tax bill would be about $100, for local taxes were light in that town. This comparison is an epitome of much of the recent fiscal history of the United States, and it is likewise the heart of one of the two critical factors in the problem of supporting rural schools.

The injustice as between the farmer and myself arose out of the principle that the tax laws of that state measured ability to pay taxes

---

[2] I have elaborated this thesis in my recent study, *School Revenue,* University of Chicago Press, 1930.

by the assessed value of property; the farmer held land, which was thought to disclose tax-paying ability, and the school master did not. The reader will perhaps remind me that I only thought I was escaping and that I really paid taxes in the rent which I paid to my landlord and in the prices with which I liquidated my modest household expenses.

Rent was fixed by supply and demand. In the rare and seldom event of a boom in a New England seaport, rent would have gone up regardless of taxes until new building had steadied the market. In a prolonged period of depression, competitors for tenements would have moved away, and rents would have gone down regardless of taxes, until the point was reached at which some owners would have allowed the city 'to take the property for taxes.' During the boom period, the effect of taxes would have been somewhat to slow up new building and thereby somewhat to affect price levels. But after all, I did pay rent and the landlord paid his taxes out of the rent. So he shifted his taxes to my shoulders? Not so. I paid his taxes in no other sense than I paid his provision bill or his life-insurance premiums; and in no other sense than the school district paid my poll tax.

And then there were the grocer to pay, the tailor and the drygoods merchant, the electric light company, and more others than it is pleasant to recall. All of these paid taxes on the real estate used in business and, at least theoretically, on their equipment and stock in trade. They fixed prices at enough to cover these taxes and likewise their store rent, clerk hire, raw material, labor, fuel, and so on. Otherwise they could not have stayed in business.

But the price levels themselves were fixed by supply and demand. Every now and then some trader would have to give up, and thus competitions would be lessened. Local prices would either go up a little or else cease to fall. Taxes had little or nothing to do with the matter.

But nearly all these traders had profits, the compensation of the enterpriser, and these profits paid no taxes whatever, any more than my salary paid taxes, unless the traders owned residences, and then they paid taxes which were small in proportion to their ability to pay.

My farmer operated in a local market, but the bulk of the farmers who grow the great staple crops, or produce dairy and vegetable crops for the uncertain metropolitan markets, receive prices which are fixed beyond their capacity to control. They cannot throw off taxes as do the merchants and manufacturers. To quote Seligman's trenchant statement:[3]

> The Western farmer, the price of whose wheat is fixed in Liverpool by the conditions of production in countries thousands of miles distant, will not get a whit more for his products if his taxes are doubled. He and he alone must bear the burden of the tax.

---

[3] *Shifting and Incidence of Taxation*, (5th ed. revised, 1927), p. 266.

What was true of my income held equally for incomes from dividends, royalties, interest on moneys loaned that could be hidden or removed from the assessors' knowledge. Thus the great problem of the taxation of intangibles. Tyros commonly says: "If they would only make these tax dodgers (meaning holders of the kind of property mentioned above) pay up, we should have money enough." Be that as it may, here as elsewhere the farmer gets the bad end of the situation and rural-school revenue suffers. In the first place, farming communities ordinarily have very little income from securities with which to help pay taxes which are levied against their land and buildings. In the second place, the farmer's personal property is tangible and is discovered. You may conceal property in a municipal bond, but you cannot very well hide a cow or a mowing machine.

Excessive and vicious taxation has gone far to destroy the tax base. When we studied the rich and ample land of the Illinois and Iowa prairies, we found[4] that in numerous instances local taxation was appropriating more than 100 percent of the farmer's net cash income and a great deal more than 100 percent of his true net income. Still later, the North Carolina Tax Commission[5] disclosed the same phenomenon. Ely has said:[6]

Taxes on lands are steadily and rapidly approximating the annual value of farm lands; and in a period varying from state to state, but in most of the states in a relatively short period—a period so short that some of us may live to see it, if the movement continues unchecked—the taxes will absorb farm values, the farmer's land will be confiscated by the state and our farmers will become virtually tenants of the state.

The patent injustice of the system bears as truly but much less heavily on the city-property owner. The injustice to the farmer is exacerbated by the outrageous selfishness and complacency of the city dweller who not only refuses to do justice but is continuous in his contemptuous reference to the farmer's chronic desire for government aid.

III. Income Taxation

We pay all our taxes out of income. Our ability to pay may be measured in a variety of ways, some of them good and some of them

---

[4] Educational Finance Inquiry, 1924; *The Financing of Education in Iowa* and *The Financing of Public Schools in Illinois.*

[5] *Report of Tax Commission,* 1929.

[6] Ely, Richard T. *The Tri-State Development Congress Proceedings.* Duluth, 1924.

very bad, but however ability is measured, the bill is paid out of income. Hence, in the last analysis, income itself is fundamentally the basis of valid measurement.

If taking perhaps 12 percent of the net cash income of the farmer who has served us in our illustration was a reasonable exaction, then the schoolmaster should have paid at least $240 instead of nothing at all, and so in proportion with other salary earners, wage-earners and city earners in general. If all had really paid, even in simple proportion to ability as measured in income, then the burden on the farmer and teacher alike would have been much less than the figures cited.

Time was when the value of property, that is, what it would sell for, was a pretty good measure of ability, since nearly all incomes were derived from property and mostly from land. The value of property was closely related to the income which could be derived from it. But the industrial revolution changed all that. A new kind of society came into existence in which income was far more in the form of wages, salaries, interest, dividends, royalties, and profits than in the form of income from property. In recent years the difference has been enormously accentuated. Nevertheless, property continues to be the fundamental measure, long after it has ceased to be any valid measure at all.

Taxationists are almost unanimously agreed that the use of individual and corporate income as the fundamental measure of ability is altogether the most scientific basis of taxation and further that which can be made to comport most accurately with justice and expediency.

Taxation, however, is not only a matter of economics but a matter of government as well. No system could honestly and competently be operated by untrained local officials selected on a political basis and dependent for reëlection on the good will of the people they tax. Some of the more progressive states, led by Wisconsin in 1911, have set up state income taxation administered by non-political state officers holding their positions by appointment rather than by election.

Nor will sundry schemes for the discovery of new sources of revenue in new forms of taxation ever prove a solution. Almost all such schemes are merely new ways of tapping income. They are not only apt to tax most heavily those who can least afford to pay, but they are a prolific occasion of needless readjustments in business, with all the misery which even normal and necessary readjustments cause.

State income taxation is, then, the first and fundamental step in the solution of the problem of rural-school support, and for three reasons: First, because elementary justice requires it. It is a mere outrage that the American farmer in the aggregate should pay about 30 percent of his income in taxes when a large proportion of his fellow citizens go scot-free, and another large proportion seldom go above 5 percent or 6 percent of income comparably reckoned. Second, because rural schools, quite apart from tax support, require the maximum of prosperity and well-being in the farmhouse. The solution of the problems of rural economic life is difficult enough at best without handicapping the farmer at the outset with an impossible tax load. Third, because in modern society the bulk of the true taxables is in urban communities[7] and income taxation alone can reach most of it.

IV. State Aid

If we were to utilize the most just and scientific system of taxation at present in sight, the local tax revenue in country towns would be, for a long time at least, much less than it is now. Here there appears the second of the two critical factors in our problem, namely, an obsolete form of political and fiscal unit, the school district.

In the eighteenth century, in Massachusetts, as soon as the Indian menace was finally removed, people began to move back from the "center town." Little knots soon formed minor social centers in remote corners of the townships. Partly, no doubt, because of the particularist tendencies of Congregationalists, but chiefly for geographical reasons pure and simple, these centers became self-governing school districts, and they were eventually recognized in a series of statutes. In general, they were each empowered and required to levy taxes for the support of the school, to elect officers to manage it, and in general each district was constituted a corporation with power to sue and be sued. Thus appeared a political organism which was very much in accord with Anglo-Saxon genius. It was admirably adapted to the political limitations of frontier society, and it moved westward with the New England migration.

---

[7] For readers who would like to pursue the study of taxation, the following list of readings is suggested: Comstock, *State Taxation of Personal Income*, 1921; also *Taxation in the Modern State*, 1929; Lutz, *Public Finance*, 1924; Plehn, *Introduction to Public Finance*, (5th. edition), 1926; Seligman, *Essays in Taxation* (10th edition revised), 1928; and also *Shifting and Incidence of Taxation* (5th edition), 1926.

The fateful thing about the frontier district was that it established a pattern of political and fiscal thinking which persisted long after the society which had given rise to the organism had disappeared. The school district is still with us, a sort of political vermiform appendix. Even the great cities are still districts, with all the attributes of the frontier districts. We are interested, however, particularly in the fiscal anomalies which the method of governing a state school system through many hundreds and even thousands of self-governing local agencies of the state presents.

1. The Local School District Not an Economic Unit

The center of these anomalies rests in the principle that the local school district, whether it be the small frontier type, the township district or some of the modifications thereof, is no longer a self-contained economic entity. In the days in which the district system came into being, economic society in the United States was strikingly homogeneous. You might divide up a state according to convenience, and the parts, however small they might be, would be likely to be pretty much the same in kind. Under such conditions it made little difference whether districts were large or small. A large district might have twice as many children, but, if such were the case, it would probably have twice as many taxable resources to apply to their schooling. In short, the school district was a serviceable form of school government in precisely the same kind of society in which the general property tax was an acceptable method of taxation. But that society was disappearing in the East more than a hundred years ago, and it rapidly disappeared everywhere after the Civil War.

The story of its disappearance is familiar to every school child who understands the Industrial Revolution. Local communities of all sorts became differentiated in type. Some of them became all but exclusively agricultural. Others became mill towns or trading centers or railroad towns. Others still became largely residential. And finally there emerged the great metropolitan cities which form a class by themselves. So far as financial resources were concerned, the effect was to produce conditions not unlike those which can be seen in any considerable city. Some parts of the city are occupied largely by factories, but the people who work in the factories, including those who draw large salaries, do not live in that part of the city. Other parts are occupied by wholesale and retail merchandising establishments, banks, office buildings, and the like, but hardly anybody at all lives there. The city is approximately an economic unit; it would be entirely such if it included the stretch of farming land which is necessary to support the inhabitants and if there were no politically distinct residential suburbs.

In such a city the bulk of the actual tax-paying ability is in the residential sections, for people and not property pay taxes. It would be ridiculous to have the city divided up into districts for school purposes, although that is exactly what used to be done. The school system of practically every city is coterminous with the city itself; the city has become the district. Political scientists are beginning to see that not even the residential suburbs can be allowed to exist independently of the city.

Now scarcely any modern rural-school district, large or small, is such an economic unit or ever can be. Most of the states, though not all of them, and some counties, are approximate units; that is to say, the activities of the people as a whole cover pretty much the whole economic field, and the returns in popular income from these economic activities are for the most part somewhere within the state.[8]

All the studies which have thus far been made have for their chief exhibit an enormous range among school districts in taxable resources behind each child to be schooled; and the smaller the districts, the greater this range. The facts themselves do not amount to much, but the reason why the facts are what they are amounts to a great deal. The reason as we have seen consists in the fact that economic and social changes have utterly broken up the kind of society in which the school district was founded, and the essence of the change is in differentiation in economic communities.

2. Local School Support Does Not Mean Local Self-Government

The second fallacy to which the school-district method of thinking has given rise is the notion that local support and government of schools is an instance of local self-government. The tax-supported system of public schools is, and always has been, a state system or nothing. The only justification of the use of the taxing power for

---

[8] There is a sharp qualification to make in the cases of the predominantly agricultural, the predominantly industrial, and the predominantly mining states; but that is a long story, and it would lead us far from the problem of rural-school support if we were to follow it out.

the support of universal education is in the principle that schools are intended to produce intelligent citizens and that people are citizens of the state wherein they reside and of the United States. Most of the residents of a given community were schooled elsewhere. The schools are so far state institutions that not even municipal ordinances apply to school buildings. The issue is not between localism and the state, but between a system in which administration is assumed by the legislature and support is left to the ancient school district, and one in which administration is committed to an executive board and support is assumed by the state as a whole.

Local self-government applies only to those matters in the conduct of which the local community alone stands to benefit or lose. Like the general property tax and the school district itself the notion that schools are peculiarly a local concern is a carry-over from an earlier state of society.

Now, the historical evidence is clear that in the period when state school systems were being laid down the founders had in mind a concern for the principle that support should be derived from the state as well as raised locally. Hence, the state school funds of unhappy memory. More recently there has emerged the notion of 'state aid,' a curious inversion in political thinking. Nobody speaks of state-aided courts or national guard, for these are accepted functions of the state. But neither in constitutional foundations nor in closely reasoned principle are they any more functions of the state than are public schools. We use the term 'state aid' because long habituation has accustomed us to a pattern of thinking which is localistic in character.

State-aid acts necessarily attempt to measure the amount of aid which shall be given. Thus arises the principle of equalization. We forget that adequate citizenship training in rural schools, which is the only kind of equalization we ought to be interested in, may involve great inequality in financial support. We are thus led to a study of financial equalization, in order to see what is involved.

V. EQUALIZATION

The problem of equalization reduced to its lowest terms may be stated thus: In a system composed of many districts very greatly differing among themselves in ability to maintain schools of minimum standards, so to distribute state money that the burdens upon the several districts will be made equal. The solution must be in the form of a mathematical formula written into the statute, applied by a ministerial officer, and checked by court interpretation. We thus have two fundamental terms here, *ability* and *burden*, and in order to use them in a valid formula the two must mean the same thing in all districts. Let us see if they do or can.

1. Ability

Ability is expressed by some derivative of the ratio *resources: load*. Resources must be measured in terms of property values and largely in terms of real estate values (as long as the general property tax is the basis of our fiscal system), but a given total assessed valuation, as experience shows, does not and cannot mean even approximately the same thing in any two districts.

Further, even granted that the assessment ratio could be made uniform, a given aggregate local valuation means utterly different things in different types of districts so far as it is related to tax-paying ability:

1. Income from the property taxed may be almost the only income in the district. This is especially true in rural townships.

2.. There may be an immense amount of income in addition to income from the property taxed. This is apt to be the case in residential cities.

3. The income of local taxpayers may nearly all be derived from the property which is taxed, but still may be greatly out of proportion to the value of the property. This is true of many mill towns in which the value of the industrial product depends on the skill of workmen, demand for the product, and other similar factors, rather than on expensive plant and equipment. Sometimes the opposite condition exists, especially in mining towns, and the value of the industrial property is such that it can be determined for taxing purposes only by some arbitrary agreement.

4. In some districts, the school support constitutes nearly all the local tax obligation, while in others it is only a minor fraction.

5. A given aggregate valuation may be the base of taxes which are very largely thrown off by the tax-payers, while another may represent taxes which in their nature cannot be shifted. As we have seen, the condition last named is particularly true of rural townships.

Now all the variables which have been named, and others as well, appear endlessly among school districts. If it could be shown that there is some constant relationship among them, then an involved equalization formula might be worked out, but it has not been shown and probably cannot be.

2. Load

The term 'load' is usually expressed as number of educables or some derivative thereof, such as teacher-quota, number of teachers, and the like. We ought to bear in mind that any such derivative is meaningless apart from the term 'cost,' and cost is meaningless unless it is referred to some constant such as 'standard school' or 'minimum schooling.' Thus the constant employed is brought under scrutiny.

Now we school people, and the great body of citizens as well, are, or ought to be, concerned with the education of citizens and equal opportunity for all children. We are not interested in a nine-months' school or the elementary school or the high school, or even in qualified teachers. These are merely adventitious characteristics of the machinery which we hope will produce good citizens. We are interested in the program of studies of the citizenship school, the more accurate and scientific in its definitions the better. And then we are interested in achievement tests or some other educational measures related to such a program. Hence, as soon as we attempt to arrive at the essential meaning of our constant, the term 'load' comes to be expanded into the expression, "Cost of standard schooling for m educables." In this expression, m is a variable, but it is a well-conducted and amenable variable, since it means the same thing everywhere. "Cost of standard schooling" is, however, a wayward and perverse variable; that is to say, it refuses to bear any constant relation whatever to m.

1. What accountants call *overhead* varies greatly from district to district for the same number of pupils. The outstanding example is overhead in the one-room school, in which the cost of standard schooling is much the same for six pupils or thirty. There are, however, many other examples, a notable one being disproportionate capital costs in the cities.

2. Teachers' salary cost for equivalent schooling varies in two opposite directions even in districts of much the same type. (a) The actual personal service cost is related to local cost of living, the local purchasing power of the dollar. Hence, the unscientific character of the state-wide minimum salary acts. (b) A differential must in the long run be paid to teachers who work in remote or otherwise unattractive communities.

3. Staff work actually needed for equivalent schooling varies tremendously. In general it is greatest in metropolitan cities, mill towns, and decadent rural townships. It is least in residential cities, trading centers, and the better type of rural townships. Under our existing localism and

particularism, districts which need staff work and exceptionally qualified teachers least commonly spend most on both items.

From all the foregoing, it follows that the factor 'ability,' dependent as it is on 'load,' cannot be measured apart from an elaborate, continuous, and very expensive state survey. It is not likely that this will be done or that any statute can be drafted which will distribute state money even approximately in proportion to need.

3. Burden

When we think in terms of a valid constant, even though the constant must necessarily be a virtual and not an actually determined quantity, 'burden' is expressed by the ratio *Cost of standard schooling* : *Resources*. Similarly, 'ability' as *Resources* : *Load* becomes *Resources* : *Cost of standard schooling*.

Thus 'ability' and 'burden' are reciprocal terms and our analysis of ability applies to burden as well.

4. The State Equalization Fund

State aid through an equalization act implies a state fund of some sort (either the income from permanent invested funds or from the rental of school lands) or an annual appropriation set up by the legislature.

The first of the two sources has become almost negligible, at least for large-scale rural aid. The second involves taxation, and however taxation may be applied, the effect is to introduce another type of variable into a situation which is already hopelessly complicated.

I. If the state tax is a general property tax apportioned to the different minor civil divisions to be levied and collected, then it may easily happen that the aided district contributes as much or even more to the equalization fund as it receives in aid. At all events a state-aid act is not even approximately either an equalizing or an aiding act if it fails to include the burden of the state tax as a factor in the formula of distribution.

2. If the fund is secured through state-wide income taxation, while the local districts make no use of income taxation, then it is probable that the richer districts which receive little or nothing of state aid will contribute most heavily to the fund in state-tax money; for, as we have repeatedly seen, incomes which are at present untaxed tend to concentrate in the richer districts. Nevertheless, the result is wholly indeterminate and under such acts we can at best hazard the guess that on the whole the act is in the direction of equalization.

3. If the equalization fund rests on a state corporation tax, then the state money is a sheer addition to the aggregate of amounts raised locally to the extent that the stock of domestic corporations is held by out-of-the-state investors. To the extent that it is held within the state, the effect is the same as that of the state income tax.

Finally, the use of taxation for the purpose of creating an annual distributive fund is prone to run counter to the principles of the state constitution. Without wearying the reader with a further discussion of the political principles underlying the school district as an agency of the state, suffice it to suggest that the district principle itself is inherently incompatible with the principles of equalization funds. The friends of education in general and of rural schools in particular may from time to time succeed in circumventing the objections of supreme courts or even in securing constitutional amendments *ad hoc,* but in so doing we only contribute to the needless complexity and puzzledom of our civil structure itself.

5. Effort

Effort is an administrative term which implies a measure of local volition in raising money. If it were possible to find a valid measure of ability, then 'effort' would be expressed by the ratio *Money raised locally : Ability.* Equalization acts ordinarily include 'effort.' To that extent, such an act ceases to be equalization and becomes a grant-in-aid. On the other hand, if effort is not in the act, then the local districts will tend to relax. The paradox is a beautiful illustration of the logical absurdity of the whole system. Nevertheless, the term has a very important bearing on our study of rural schools.

Effort is commonly taken to mean tax rate for school purposes. Now the tax rate in country towns is often less, sometimes much less, than in cities. Further, the assessment ratio is often less. Hence officials, legislators, and too often students think that these tax rates are objective guides which show that in fact ''the farmers are not trying to help themselves.'' In reality, such facts are almost always superficial and misleading. Our brief glance at some of the essentials of taxation and our study of the term 'resources' must, as it seems to me, convince the reader that a given tax rate in a country town may easily be a minor fraction of the city tax rate in the same year and still represent greater effort. The farmer commonly has only the income from the farm which is taxed with which to pay taxes.

The city man commonly has very much more income with which to pay taxes than the income which is derived from the property which is taxed.

6. Equalization Acts Rest on a False Basis

We have an abundance of factual material which shows enormous *prima facie* inequalities as between the districts of the several states, but nobody has ever measured the actual inequalities. In all probability, they are much greater than the superficial disclosures make manifest.

The equalization acts as a permanent remedy rest upon a fundamentally false method of thinking in that they accept the school district as a valid political unit, whereas, as we have seen, the district belongs to a social order which has long been obsolete. It is a singular misfortune for rural schools and for the rural economic community that we should have been so long preoccupied with this method of solving the problem, for we are thus led to postpone the inevitable radical reform of our system of taxation and of the governmental structure upon which our school system rests.

So long as the support of public schools is looked upon as being primarily a local concern, the richer cities and other local communities will inevitably tend to spend all their available resources on their own schools, or on schools which are falsely believed to be their own. The result will tend to be, as it often is, what are in effect extremely expensive tax-supported private schools in communities in which the great body of mercantile and industrial incomes congregate. Every such local system, inevitably, in the long run, means poor and weak schools somewhere else, chiefly in country towns, but also in many mill towns and in some metropolitan cities.

7. What the State Aid Program Has Accomplished

On the other hand, the equalization and state-aid program has accomplished some definite results in the direction of progress. In the states which have been active, money has been made available for schools in poorer towns, often to the great advantage of public education. While that is, as it seems to me, mere symptomatic treatment, palliatives are sometimes desirable. Much more important, the long agitation out of which the equalization acts have arisen has very evidently been helpful in getting the public into the habit of thinking as citizens of the several states and not merely as community in-dwellers.

VI. THE WAY OUT

For at least three-quarters of a century, the original school district has been evolving under fiscal and administrative stress and in a few of the states the process has gone far. We have not the space to study in detail the emergence of the township, consolidated and city districts, the county district in some of the southern states, the advanced type of planned district in Utah, and finally the state unit in Delaware. Everywhere the expanding district is a sort of evolutionary response to local pressure in which the tendency is to find a political unit which more nearly corresponds to an economic unit.

The establishment of township districts and of consolidated districts is a case in point. A more striking instance is that of the city district in which all the resources of the city were made available for the support of all the schools in the city, regardless of the resources of the several wards. A proposal to go back to the old and forgotten system and to write an equalization clause into the city charter would be looked upon as the act of a madman—and so it would be.

The recent county-unit movement, especially in some of the southern states, is clearly a movement in the direction of natural evolution, at least in those county units in which the local district is abolished altogether, and a county board of education lays taxes upon the county as a whole and furnishes schools, as and where they are needed regardless of local resources. The Utah modification of the county unit is an interesting instance of a planned development in the line which we have recognized as having natural validity. Here the state is divided into forty districts, each of them, as far as possible in a state which is still sparsely settled, economically comparable with each of the others.

The end of the road is found in Delaware, in which, outside of the city of Wilmington, the state itself is the fiscal unit, and the schools are supported by a state income tax. Much may doubtless be required for rural schools there, but, so far as fiscal support is concerned, Delaware has nearly solved her problem, in that she has placed the economic resources of the state behind every school in the state, regardless of local resources. When Wilmington shall have come into the state system, the fiscal problem will have been fully solved.

Our conclusion is, then, that *the ultimate solution of the fiscal aspect of the rural-school problem everywhere is clearly to be found in consolidation of the varied economic resources of each of the several states and in the use of a scientific system of taxation to reach those resources and to apply them as needed to the maintenance of a state system of citizenship schooling. The solution of the rural-school problem is part and parcel of that of all the schools.*

VII. FEDERAL AID

In a study of this sort, the question of the participation of the federal government will not down. Aid for rural schools is no doubt one of the most appealing of the many demands which are constantly being made upon the national treasury, but the appeal is nearly always based upon the need which is felt and perhaps on the desire to gratify a large section of voters rather than upon a competent analysis of the situation.

There is much reason to think that we as a people will eventually have to utilize the federal resources in the support of all schools and not merely rural schools alone.

In the first place, we are as much concerned with producing intelligent citizens of the United States as we are concerned with citizenship in any of the several states. If we are going to submit questions of even foreign policy to popular vote, then the responsibilities of popular education are materially increased. If the more backward states are unable or unwilling to maintain efficient schools, then the more enlightened states suffer in all their federal relations and indeed in national relations as well.

In the second place, our economy is national in scope, not state or local. Commerce between the states is untrammeled; our banking and credit system is national in scope. Title to property is not confined within state lines. Industrial income which is an enormous resource in the payment of taxes refuses to settle and be taxed in the state in which the industrial property is located.

In the third place, and probably by reason of the foregoing, the federal government is a much better tax-collecting agency than the state governments and immeasurably better than the local governments.

Nevertheless, the problem of school support is a state problem before it is a federal problem. The Constitution leaves education to the states, but the state constitutions do not leave it to the local communities. The states are sovereign, and the school districts are agencies of the state.

So far as federal aid is a possibility, it would have to be apportioned much as the states have attempted to apportion equalization funds, and we do not know enough about interstate economics to write any such apportionment. The effect of any federal act at present in sight would without much doubt be to allot funds where they are least needed or at least not in accordance with needs.

We are accustomed to compare property valuations behind each census child in different states, and we naturally find somewhat the same inequalities, although much less in range, which we find among the districts in any one state. Still better, we compare popular incomes and find much the same order of differences. It does not follow, however, that the respective states differ in ability to support schools in anything like the range shown by such comparative statistics. Whenever we get an economic area which is large enough, the aggregate of popular income becomes approximately the aggregate of consumption as the people deal with each other. The question then becomes, not how much money is there, but rather how does the local school support tie into the general economic structure. For this reason, when we compare property valuations behind each child to be educated in the districts of the several states, the actual range in ability to support schools is apt to be greater than the figures show, whereas when we compare states either in respect to property or popular income the school range tends to be less than the statistical indications. A favorite comparison is that of California with Mississippi. Superficial comparison shows much more available wealth in the former state than in the latter, and doubtless there is more. Nevertheless, the very fact that popular income per school child is greater in California is in itself evidence that the purchasing power of a given salary is materially less. People in Mississippi tend to trade with each other at a lower price level.

Further, wherever a state is extensively urbanized, the principle of increasing cost of government per thousand of population served very greatly complicates the comparison which seems so simple when property valuation or popular incomes are compared. New York and South Dakota are very different types of states; most persons would probably rate the former as wealthy and the latter as relatively impecunious. Nevertheless, when factors are taken into consideration which ought to be counted, the disproportion in ability to support schools is a different kind of disproportion than that which appears on the surface. These and many other critical factors run through the comparisons in a bewildering tangle which ought to give us pause before we embark on an extensive program of federal aid.

CHAPTER X

COÖPERATIVE EXTENSION WORK IN AGRICULTURE AND HOME ECONOMICS[1]

T. H. EATON
Professor of Rural Education
Cornell University, Ithaca, New York

I. A GENERAL PICTURE

The United States Department of Agriculture maintains a division known as the Extension Service. Of this 'service' the principal subdivision is the Office of Coöperative Extension Work. In every one of the forty-eight states, and the Territory of Hawaii, the land-grant college of agriculture maintains likewise an extension service. The federal and state services together perform a function known as 'coöperative extension work in agriculture and home economics.' This function involves the employment of more than six thousand paid workers and approximately two hundred fifty thousand workers active without pay. It affects demonstrably the lives of several million rural people; directly or indirectly it has touched, according to careful estimate, three in four families among the rural population of the United States. To its support went in the past year a sum in excess of twenty-three million dollars, 94.5 percent of which was supplied from public tax monies. Of the total, 39 percent came from federal appropriations, 28 percent from state appropriations, and the remaining 33 percent from county and local appropriations and the gifts of

---

[1] At the request of the Committee Professor Eaton prepared for this Yearbook an extensive chapter upon coöperative extension work which set forth in detail the present status and the trends of this work as determined by some three months of careful investigation of sources and painstaking compilation of data. When an unexpected demand for condensation of some material and omission of other material was made of all contributors, Professor Eaton, at my request, and at the 'eleventh hour,' withdrew his original chapter and wrote a new one less than half the length of the original. It is due Professor Eaton to acknowledge this excellent spirit of coöperation and also to inform the reader that what the author feels now to be a "cursory account" is not a mere statement of impressions but presentation reasonably well supported by factual data here omitted.—*Editor.*

organizations and individuals within the counties. Over a period of fifteen years the coöperative extension work in agriculture and home economics shows a consistent growth in size of staff and in financial support. Increase of support from federal sources is large, but that of support from the states is larger still, and the percentage supplied from private sources decreases. The service, then, represents a public undertaking of a very considerable and a growing importance.

On the legal side the work finds its sanction in the federal enactment of 1914 (the Smith-Lever Act) and subsequent legislation, notably the Capper-Ketcham Act of 1928; in the states such sanction appears in acceptance of the provisions of the federal enactments and in supplementary legislation.

II. General Scope of Extension Work

The scope of coöperative extension work in agriculture and home economics as to educational objectives, instructional content, and persons to be served, is not closely defined in federal legislation, in rulings of administrators, or, so far as I can discover, anywhere else. Suggestion of scope, however, appears in the federal legislation as follows: [The Smith-Lever Act was passed] "in order to aid in diffusing among the people of the United States useful and practical information on subjects relating to agriculture and home economics, and to encourage the application of the same." That the work is intended to serve most directly the rural people of the United States appears in the provision that federal grants to the states "shall be allotted annually in the proportion which the rural population of each state bears to the total rural population of all the states." The official conception of function is suggested by a statement of the Federal Director of the Extension Service: "The aim of all extension work should be toward better, happier, and more comfortable homes. Whether this is brought about by improvement and stabilization of the farmer's economic position, by bringing new information and new viewpoints to the farmer's wife, or by the training of his boys and girls in the 4-H clubs, this aim should always be kept in mind. Improvement of rural life is the real object of the Smith-Lever Act, and in our interpretation of it we should always have that object in view." Again he says: "The aim of coöperative extension service is to aid farm people to increase their net incomes and to improve their living conditions." This latter emphasis is reflected in the customary official measurement of success for coöperative extension work in terms of the number and distribution of 'improved practices' adopted on farms and in homes.

III. DIVERGENT CONCEPTIONS OF AIMS

Emphasis upon material results leads easily to confusion of activities of direct service with those of education. In recognition of this difficulty the Secretary of Agriculture ruled in 1922 as follows: "It is clear...that the work of the coöperative extension employees...is educational. These extension workers are public teachers...charged with giving instruction and practical demonstrations...Their work covers the entire rural field, which includes economic production, economic marketing, and the development of better home, community, and social conditions...[It] is not a part of the official duties of extension agents to perform for the individual...or for organizations the actual operations of production, marketing, or the various activities necessary to the proper conduct of business or social organizations." This ruling has had a marked and wholesome effect to sanction efforts 'to help rural people to help themselves,' as against the practice of 'doing things for rural people.' Nevertheless, extension workers still very often act to recruit and 'sign up' members for economic and other associations, not infrequently to organize such associations, sometimes to manage them, occasionally to buy and sell commodities, and here and there to repair farm and home equipment, and otherwise to do for rural people what they should learn to do for themselves.

It is safe to say, without fault-finding, that the aim of economic efficiency and material improvement is still dominant in the work of the coöperative extension service, nearly, if not quite, everywhere. But there is an increasing number of extension workers, particularly among those 'on the firing line' in the counties, who hold that ends of understanding and appreciation, not necessarily measurable in 'changed practices' of the material sort, are both legitimate and desirable objects of educative service; who hold, too, that the worth of the rural population, in the larger sense, is by no means to be measured by their contribution to the consuming needs of the urban population.

Thus it comes about that the phrase, "subjects related to agriculture and home economics," receives a varied interpretation; and the trend, on the whole, is toward a liberal interpretation. So the conception of agriculture tends to grow from mere productive husbandry among the rural population to include the mode of life of the rural family and the rural aspect of our civilization. Much the same story is told for home economics. The conception of it enlarges gradually to include, beyond the responsibilities of the housewife in matters of food, shelter, and clothing for the family, the organization of family life in all its extended implications.

IV. DIVERGENT DEVELOPMENT OF PRACTICE

These differences in conception of aim for extension work tend to be reflected in practice. Thus, at one extreme, under the philosophy that finds its ends in 'changed practices' and 'improved conditions,' one is likely to discover: (1) a program restricted closely to 'practical needs'—namely, such as can be met by readjustments in material environment; (2) definiteness in 'goals of accomplishment'— for example, so many farmers keeping purebred bulls, so many housewives using a household budget, so many boys and girls drinking a quart of milk every day; (3) a ready-made content of simplified prescriptions worked out by experts for dealing with difficulties; (4) methods of 'selling the idea and giving directions for its application.' At the other extreme, under that philosophy which finds the educational objectives of coöperative extension work in 'enriched experience' and 'fuller social life,' one is likely to find: (1) a program of rather vague aspirations; (2) 'goals of accomplishment' in terms of 'meetings held' and 'contacts made'; (3) a content largely of 'stimulating get-togethers'; (4) methods hortatory and entertaining. Between the extremes are all degrees in combination of breadth with definiteness.

There is no question that coöperative extension work has gone far toward helping rural people to help themselves. There is little doubt, either, that it can move further in this direction by enlarging the scope of its program, by increasing both the range and the definiteness of its educational objectives, by liberalizing the content of its teaching to include both the foreground of practicality and the background of meaning, without divorcing the one from the other, and by combining with the objectivity of its characteristic method, the demonstration, developmental teaching that leads beyond factual information to initiative and resourcefulness in the discovery and solution of significant problems by the rural people themselves.

V. Bases of Organization of the Work

The organization of coöperative extension work is based upon two lines of cleavage: (1) a division according to 'subject-fields'—namely, agricultural extension in "subjects relating to agriculture," and home economics extension in "subjects relating to home economics"; (2) division according to 'persons reached'—namely, work with men (farmers), work with women, and work with rural boys and girls. The results of this double classification in differing administrative systems among the states are a bit confusing to the uninitiated. Two examples of this seeming confusion may be presented. First, in most counties of most states, and in some states altogether, only two classes of county agents may be found, the county agricultural agent and the county home-demonstration (home-economics) agent. These two are responsible for work with boys and girls. In other states a third type of agent, the county '4-H club' agent, is found, who is responsible only for work with boys and girls, but in both agriculture and home economics. Second, in several states poultry and garden work, because farm women in the main engage in such, is in charge of the home-demonstration agent. Nevertheless, workers in the field seem well agreed that the double classification presents no serious difficulties. The most pregnant criticism seems to be that it permits easy evasion on the one hand or duplication of effort on the other, in respect to the needs which men and women share. There is no little evidence that joint undertakings of men and women in extension are comparatively rare, despite the marked overlapping of agriculture and home economics under a liberal interpretation. Moreover, the home-demonstration agent seldom works with men, and except where he is the sole agent, the county agricultural agent seldom works with women, unless it be in connection with the 4-H clubs for boys and girls.

VI. Organization Compared with That of the School

In organization of program there is a rough similarity between that of coöperative extension work and that of a large school. In a state, or county, or 'local community,' the 'extension program,' like the 'program of studies' in a school, means commonly the sum of all educative undertakings of the service. A 'line of work,' or 'major project,' corresponds roughly to a 'course of study.' A 'minor project,' or subproject, corresponds to a 'subject-course.' For example, consider a major project in live-stock improvement for farmers or a major project in nutrition for farm and village women: the first is likely to include subprojects in swine breeding, upgrading the dairy herd, flock improvement with sheep, etc.; the second to include subprojects in food selection, food preparation, child feeding, control of constipation, diet for overweight, etc. The parallel between such an organization and the course of study in science in a high school is not far to seek—general science, biology, physics, chemistry, etc. The word *project* in extension is not, in the main, used as the schoolman is likely to use it—for example, in 'project method'—but to indicate an undertaking projected and carried through by the extension service.

In the case of agriculture for adults, at least, the project system of organization in the program is extremely flexible. On the whole the farmer is able to "take what he wants and leave the rest." In home economics there is commonly a greater formalization. Very often to receive the benefits of the service a woman must join a 'project group' (like a class in school) that meets at more or less regular intervals with 'a project leader,' and carries through to 'completion' certain required activities of study and practice. Sometimes the project leader is a specialist from the college, sometimes the county home-demonstration agent, but most often, a 'local leader,' unpaid, working with the occasional assistance of the county home-demonstration agent or the specialist or both. Sometimes the prescription of uniform requirements in home-economics projects reaches a level of standardized rigidity sufficient to warm the heart of a college registrar; such, for example, that to 'get what she wants' a woman must first complete a series of prerequisite undertakings in which she has no interest whatever. But, of course, such prescription is rare. With boys and girls, again, some formalization exists, but seldom in most states to the extent of involving prerequisites to a desired project.

In the work with boys and girls, called generically the '4-H club work,' the term *project* is used also much as the schoolman is accustomed to use it; for example, the boy at home carries on a 'home project' in growing an acre of potatoes from certified seed or the girl carries on a 'canning project' involving the conservation of thirty quarts of tomatoes, ten quarts of sweet corn, and ten quarts of string beans. But in many states the award of the club insignia for 'completion' means more than a satisfactory production job and the handing in of records and 'story'; it means that the youngster has to his or her credit other 'achievements,' such as making bird-houses, identifying flowers and trees and insects, taking part in community beautification, making exhibits at fairs, attending club meetings regularly, and the like. Membership in a corn club signifies, for instance, usually, much more than an experience in growing corn according to directions furnished in a bulletin.

It is generally agreed among extension workers that the formalization of instruction among women, and sometimes among boys and girls is due to the comparative ease of assembling groups for successive and regular meetings—a procedure that is rarely possible with farmers. With the boys and girls, too, it appears that the incentives of extraneous reward and of competition serve to enable prescription quite impossible with farmers. Some workers in the junior field are of opinion that close association with the public schools makes for increase in uniformity and prescription, as against flexible adjustment of offerings to the needs of individuals and small groups. In some instances this opinion seems supported by the practice of granting 'school credit' for specific achievements in approved forms of club work.

VII. The Scope of the Extension Program

The actual scope of the extension program as revealed in range and variety of project content and other forms of teaching is extremely difficult to discover. It is safe to say that summarization of annual reports from counties to state authorities and from state authorities to the federal government by no means reveals the full scope. The reports are made on standard forms that of necessity compress a wide variety of undertakings into a single category; for example, one can learn that in the state of New York 309 project groups distributed through thirty counties and enrolling 5,256 members followed the project in Home Health and Sanitation, but from the reading one can gain no idea as to how much or how little was included in the study of health and sanitation. But study of the annual reports from the states, of the monthly reports within states, and of planned and approved county programs, together with observation of extension activities, proves that the subjects actually dealt with, even in the 'same project,' vary from state to state, from county to county, and from worker to worker. Hence the suggestion of uniformity among the states to be gathered from a casual reading of the project totals for the nation is quite misleading. In range of projects some programs are generous, some restricted; in range of content within a project some are generous, some restricted. In one state, for example, 1,089 different topics were dealt with by speakers and demonstrators from the college at extension meetings. Nevertheless, the following generalizations can be well supported: (1) The economic problems of rural life are overwhelmingly preponderant in effect upon the extension program. (2) Recognition in the program of the needs of women, though it has gained a bit in fifteen years, still lags far behind the work with farmers. (3) The social aspects of rural life in which men and women and children have similar, if not always common needs, hold still a very minor place in the extension program.

VIII. The Staff of Extension Employees

1. In the States and Counties

The staff of extension employees in every state divides roughly into two classes: the state or college staff, for the most part resident at the college and working out from it; and the county staff, resident in the counties and working there. The college staff divides again into two classes: the administrative and supervisory group, often called 'the central office workers'; and the 'specialists,' or 'subject-matter workers.' County employees fall into three classes: county agricultural agents and assistants; county home-demonstration agents and assistants; county 4-H club agents and assistants.

A typical central-office staff includes a director, a state leader of county agricultural agents and his assistants, a state leader of home-demonstration agents and her assistants, and a state leader for boys' and girls' club work and his assistants. A typical staff of 'subject-matter specialists' includes at least one person designated to each of the following fields: agronomy, horticulture, forestry, animal husbandry, darirying, poultry husbandry, agricultural engineering, agricultural economics, foods and nutrition, clothing and textiles, home management.

A county fully organized as to the skeletal minimum of staff includes the following: for the southern states, a county agricultural agent and his assistant for 4-H club work with boys, a county home-demonstration agent and her assistant for 4-H club work with girls; and for most of the other states, a county agricultural agent, a county home-demonstration agent, and a county 4-H club agent. A few counties in some states have a considerably larger staff, created by addition of assistant agents in each of the three lines; but very few states have reached the skeletal minimum in all counties served by extension work. Indeed, the most representative county staff for the country as a whole consists of one county agricultural agent without colleagues or assistants, charged with conduct of all three lines of work.

By states the total number of employees in coöperative extension work ranges from 377 (Texas) to 16 (Rhode Island), with a median of 114 (Florida). The ratio of extension employees to rural counties in the state averages 1.57 for the country, and ranges from 7.12 (Connecticut) to 0.87 (Nebraska). The central-office staff ranges in size from 25 (Texas) to 3 (Delaware), with a median of 11 (Kansas). The specialists range in number from 76 (New York) to 4 (New Mexico), with a median of 18 (North Dakota). The percentage ratio of specialists to total extension staff ranges from 38.6 (Connecticut) to 4.2 (Texas), with an average for the country of 18.9—one in five of extension employees is a specialist. The number of county agricultural agents ranges from 201 (Texas) to 3 (Rhode Island), with a median of 54 (Florida). The total number of such agents is 2,700. The home-demonstration agents range in number from 135 (Texas) to 3 (Rhode Island), with a median of 15 (Missouri). The total of home-demonstration agents is 1,316.

Here is enough to suggest that the larger rural states are most scantily staffed for coöperative extension work; that the policy with respect to employment of specialists varies widely; and that provision for extension service to women lags far behind the agricultural extension work for farmers. Since work with boys and girls may be performed by an agricultural agent, a home-demonstration agent, an assistant to either, or a special club agent, examination of staff organization gives no certain clue to emphasis upon such work.

It may be worth noting that, by fields of subject matter, the specialists in colleges distribute as follows: agriculture 72.6 percent, home economics 21.4 percent, all other specialists 6.0 percent. It is quite true that the diversity of specialized subjects of the technical order is greater in agriculture than in home economics, but the preponderance of agricultural specialists tends to confirm the conclusion that the extension program as a whole bears heavily upon the side of agricultural industry, as compared with the problems of the home. The 'miscellaneous specialists' include one in three known as 'rural sociologists.' Some of the others belong to the fields of technology in production. This fact suggests again the preponderant influence of the economic factors in determining a program for improvement of rural life. A study of expenditures for the major 'lines of work' during fifteen years points to just as marked an emphasis upon agriculture as against home economics and to a relative neglect of the non-economic still greater than that suggested by the distribution of specialists and other workers in the several fields.

2. In the Office of Coöperative Extension Work

The Office of Coöperative Extension Work at Washington employs some fifty workers. Approximately half of them serve a central-office function; the other half a specialist function. The duties of the office involve for the administrative staff chiefly inspecting, accounting, and advising with respect to the conduct of extension work in the states. The specialists are loaned to the states for special undertakings and advice as to project development. The office supplies 'illustrative material' for extension workers in the states and conducts studies on the order of 'self-survey,' as to methods and results in extension work. It recommends to the federal director of extension approval or disapproval of such projects in the states as involve the use of federal funds, and thus exercises a considerable measure of control over the extension program in states that provide funds little in excess of the federal 'offset' requirements. On the whole its recommendations in respect to program approval favor the promotion of 'changed practices' of the economic order, so that the poorer states are limited in development of a program looking to rural needs not economic. But the power of the federal director working through this office is rather of veto than of direction.

IX. The Function and Influence of State Directors of Extension

The state director of extension exercises a very considerable authority in most states. The scope of the program depends very largely upon him. The differences in program among states are, perhaps, as often a reflection of his philosophy in extension work as a reflection of differences in need and resources for the improvement of rural life. The astonishing lack of extension work for women in certain rich states is, for example, directly attributable to administrative policy. Over the extension system the power and influence of the director in most states is far greater than that of the state superintendent of public instruction over the schools. He deals, however, with a system of education involving no element of compulsion on the part of learners. Extension undertakings for the man, the woman, and the boy or girl, are purely elective. Hence, on the economic side, at least, the extension program rarely underemphasizes the major needs of farm and home. Despite his large authority the state extension director cannot, if he would, impose a program autocratically upon the state, as might a school superintendent with equal powers. Though complaints are heard here and there concerning autocracy at Washington or in the state office, there is little evidence of any large influence of the sort.

X. The Functions of County Agents

The county agricultural agent is responsible immediately or through a state leader to the director at the college; so, too, usually are the county home-demonstration agent, and the county 4-H club agent. In some instances the county agricultural agent is the administrative head of the county extension office, and the other county agents, when such are employed, are responsible directly to him. Administrative organization within the counties varies widely from state to state and sometimes from county to county within the state. For the most part the county organization includes a quasi-official body (or bodies)—corresponding roughly to the school board in the county system of public schools—to whom the county agents are responsible, for example, the executive committee of the county farm bureau or a similar organization of county people. Often the agricultural agent works with one committee, the home-demonstration agent with a second, and the 4-H club agent with a third; and the director or his representatives may work with such committees very much as the state superintendent of public instruction works with school boards in the state. Out of such relations arise some of the most difficult problems of the extension service, and variations of policy in respect to the nature and uses of the county extension bodies are among the most significant differences in extension organization. But there is no room here even to suggest the problems.

Within the county, too, are often local extension administration groups in the several 'local communities' of the county—corresponding, as it were, to the school trustees in a district system of public schools. Sometimes one committee serves for all extension work in the community; sometimes there is a committee or committeeman for each of the three lines of work, the agricultural extension with farmers, the home-demonstration work with women, and the boys and girls' club work.

Variety in the system of administration is wider, perhaps, than is the case with administration of the public schools. But there is marked trend to develop through such means a local participation and responsibility in the administration of extension work. In very few states is the employed county agent looked upon merely as a functionary of the college working in the county in such fashion as the central authorities shall determine. If not often truly the agent of the people of his county working in coöperation with the college, the county agent is at least an agent of the college working in coöperation with the people of the county.

XI. Four Classes of Programs

In accordance with the outline of organization so hastily sketched we find four classes of programs in coöperative extension work; a national program, a state program, a county program, and a local program. For the most part the national program has no existence as such. It means either the sum of all extension undertakings within the nation or the sum of those undertakings that are common to all the states. Sometimes, however, the Washington influence is sufficient to produce something like a real national program in certain lines of endeavor. During the war the extension program was chiefly of national determination; at present the influence of the Federal

Farm Board has largely determined the inclusion of undertakings everywhere in the states to forward the development of coöperative marketing of farm products. Sometimes the state program is something more than the sum of county programs or even the system of 'state-wide' projects in which all counties share. But in most states it is little more. Nearly everywhere the county is the unit, both for the construction and the execution of an extension program. The local community program represents an adaptation of the county program to the particular needs and resources of the community. Some tendency appears, however, here and there, to regard the local community as the basis upon which to build and to carry out programs of extension. In that view the county program is the sum of common undertakings among the several communities of the county; it is made up of the 'county-wide' projects. The state program, by the same token, becomes the system of state-wide projects derived from the county programs, which in turn derive from the local.

The last paragraph may seem like an attempt to suggest distinction without difference. But the attempted distinctions rest upon fundamental differences in conception of extension work. At one extreme is the view that central authority shall plan a program for the people, take it to the people, and carry it out for the people. At the other is the view that extension shall take its programs from the people, and work them out with the people from whom they derive. Space is lacking, unfortunately, to discuss the implications of these two viewpoints upon the whole organization and functioning of the extension service.

That all programs of extension should accord with the significant needs of rural people, is accepted as a postulate by all thoughtful extension workers. On the whole, programs probably do so, else the extension service would by this time be 'on the rocks,' instead of receiving steadily increasing public support. But just how well any program fits the needs of a state, a county, or a local community, one can hardly say with assurance in any present instance. A substantial body of findings, economic and social, is accumulating in many states. But so far as I can discover, except in the case of a few particular projects, little has been done to use such findings as the bases of extension programs for localities studied, and little done, outside of 'conferences,' in the way of searching out facts for the purpose of discovering the needs and resources upon which to build an extension program, county, local, or state. The larger outlines are unquestionably, in most cases, built upon known facts of need; but careful study of needs in this county and in this town, for extension work, is almost as rare as is careful study of the needs of this group of students, for what is offered in this course of study.

Nevertheless, the extension service works under a system of constant check against the needs of the people with whom it deals, as the school in the main does not. On the whole, rural people are getting from the service what they want; first, because they can reject rather promptly what they do not want; and second, because increasingly they come to have a part both in the origination and the execution of the programs of extension. That what they want is not always what we as idealists think they need does not affect the general principle of the pragmatic sanction upon which present programs so largely rest. It is safe to say that present emphasis upon economic needs in rural life is largely a response to the actual demands of country people. They need many things, but they *feel* most distinctly the need for a sound economic basis upon which to build their living.

XII. Methods of Constructing a County Program

In general there are three methods of constructing a county program. The most widely used may be called the 'cafeteria system.' The college, in the light of its examination of needs and within the limits of its extension resources, lays out a series of 'project offerings.' It says, as it were: "Here are things that we can do for you and with you. Which of them seem to you most suitable as undertakings in your county?" The offerings are presented to a more or less representative group of people in the county—often the county farm bureau representatives—and those people make a selection that constitutes the county program for the year or a longer period, determining which projects shall be county-wide and which shall be localized.

A second method, not widely used, but increasingly favored by county workers, if not always by state workers, is that the county and local committees, working with the agents, propose a program to meet the needs as they see them, and submit the proposal to state authority for sanction. If the college has nothing ready prepared to meet this need or that, the question comes, "What have you in the way of resources that can be used to help us in this matter?'' In this case, so to speak, the customer orders his dinner prepared for him.

A third method, not yet discarded in some states, may be called the *table d'hôte* method. In this case central authority prepares a complete program, usually called a state program, and then calls upon the county agent to 'sell' it to the people of his county. This method, at least in states of diversified character, is obsolescent. The tradition of it, however, appears in the often heard assertion that the job of the county agent is to 'put over' the college program in his county.

XIII. Overlapping with Other Agencies

An important factor in sound policy for extension is the determination of the extent to which the service should attempt work for which other agencies are designed or fitted. On the whole, present policy seems to be that of expediency. The extension service steps in to meet a need in what it regards as its field when no other agency is serving that need or when an active agency seems not completely to be meeting the need. So, in many counties, extension workers engage in health work because no health agencies there exist; in many counties extension workers take on work in provision of 'the hot school lunch,' because the school agency is inadequate to meet the need. This policy in the main works well. There are instances of rivalry and duplication of effort and of neglect of clearly appropriate obligations because of diversion of resources, but they are not common.

XIV. Responsibility for Club Work

A particular instance of the bearing of this policy that is of interest to school men appears in the conduct of boys' and girls' club work. The age for club membership is from ten to twenty years in most states. With the development of compulsory education laws, the majority of boys and girls within those age limits are enrolled in the public schools. A study in twelve states shows that boys and girls out of school make up, on the average, less than seven percent of club membership. Since the total enrolment in 4-H clubs, though above 800,000, is probably less than the number out of school in the rural districts, it has been urged that the extension service should confine its junior undertakings to the out-of-school group. The fact remains, however, that the public schools, whatever their responsibility, have not in any large measure attempted to meet the needs of present life of pupils at home and on the farm as club work has done. Moreover, it is quite certain that in the main they are not now staffed to do the work even so well as it is done at present by the agency first in the field. Hence an abandonment by extension workers of the in-school group would immediately result in a loss of certain opportunities for the great majority of those who now enjoy them. If public policy demands that the public schools take over functions that they have neglected, it is probable that they must take over also a considerable part of the junior extension personnel, and something of the organization and method of club work at its best.

There are in boys' and girls' club work four forms of organization:

1. An organization of clubs of boys and girls together, commonly known as 'community clubs,' in which a wide diversity of 'home-project' interests may be represented in the one group.

2. An organization of boys' clubs, or agricultural clubs, including girls, on the one hand, and of girls' clubs, or home-making clubs, on the other.

3. An organization of clubs on the basis of home-project interest, such as pig clubs, corn clubs, sewing clubs, canning clubs.

4. An organization in which club membership is nominal only. The boy or girl works alone at the home project or to meet other requirements and never attends club meetings or takes part in organized group activities, unless it be at the final 'achievement day,' on which the 4-H clans of the county gather. This plan holds where isolated conditions prevail.

There is considerable difference, on the side of theory, as to the educational merits of the several forms; but facts as to the trends in utilization of the several forms are not for the country yet available. In the opinion of the Washington office the 'community club' is gaining relatively upon the others, but the 'project club' is still the most widespread.

XV. The Use of Local Leaders

Club work depends largely upon the use of so-called 'local leaders.' In women's work, too, the use of local leaders is widespread. In work with farmers the local leader is relatively less used and, in the opinion of a majority of state directors, less successful. The local leader is most effective when groups can be brought together, as can be done with women and juniors more readily than with practicing farmers. Despite marked differences of opinion as to the value of local leadership in extension undertakings, particularly those involving efforts at instruction, the number of local leaders in all lines increases. There are now not far from a quarter of a million men and women who thus serve without pay to advance the cause of rural education.

XVI. The Use of Demonstrations

Generalizations upon extension methods cannot be supported by statistical data, except it be as to the frequency of use of demonstrations. The characteristic method of extension work is objective teaching by way of demonstrations. Demonstrations are of two sorts—at least in the classification adopted for report of extension undertakings—'result demonstrations' and 'method demonstrations.'

The result demonstration appears in the exhibit of results from a 'recommended practice.' For example, a farmer produces a result demonstration by spraying all the potatoes in his field except the outside and the middle rows. If the practice of spraying is justified in its effect on the plants, the plants 'tell the story' to the farmer, to his neighbors, or to the group of observers whom the county agent brings to the farm to note the results produced by spraying.

The method demonstration consists in showing people how to do something by doing it. For example, the home demonstration agent shows a group of women how to give an invalid a bath in bed, by bathing a person in bed 'before their face and eyes' instead of merely telling them how it ought to be done; or a local leader demonstrates to a group of club members how to splice a rope by splicing a rope before them and directing them in practice of splicing—not by lecturing about splicing, and drawing pictures of spliced rope on a blackboard. Under pressure of the brief contacts that tend to distinguish his work from that of the school teacher, the extension worker has developed methods objective and direct, of great merit in teaching facts, methods, and standards in a very convincing way. He is given to large use of physically concrete illustrations and examples.

Under the same pressure he has come to lean heavily on words. His voice, his pen, and his mimeograph he keeps busy; and therein, perhaps, is prone at times to do the learner's thinking for him, when his first object is to move the learner to think through his own problem. In that he is like many other teachers, of course.

In educating the people of rural America to objectives in rural life, through media of rural experience, coöperative extension work in agriculture and home economics is characteristically, more than any other agency, an agency of rural education.

CHAPTER XI

GUIDING PRINCIPLES IN RURAL EDUCATION

ORVILLE G. BRIM
Professor of Elementary Education
Ohio State University, Columbus, Ohio

I. INTRODUCTION

Rural education, perhaps even more than non-rural education, is in need of a clarification of its objectives and principles. It has suffered from neglects; it has unthinkingly accepted the criteria and patterns of urban education; it has been buffeted about by conflicting forces within the rural field itself. The demands of the moment for immediately practical procedures have taken attention from the more fundamental issues and a long-term program. In view of this situation and to supplement the impersonal analysis and evaluation of the preceding chapters, it was decided to add a section dealing specifically with the question of guiding principles.[1] While the writer alone is responsible for the following statement of principles, he has used freely the suggestions of criticisms of certain members of the Committee and of many others either engaged in the rural field or familiar with its problems. These theses were prepared primarily to set forth the problem and to stimulate critical reaction rather than to invite or secure agreement.

II. WHAT SHALL BE OUR GUIDING PRINCIPLES IN RURAL EDUCATION?

1. Are the Problems of Education in the Rural Field Sufficiently Distinctive, Significant, and Difficult to Justify Special Classification, Special Emphasis, and Special Study?

---

[1] The plan of the Yearbook Committee was to follow this presentation by Dr. Brim with a series of chapters, by members of the Committee and others, discussing the fundamental principles and policies of rural education from various angles. When the material submitted far exceeded the space allotted, it was decided it would be well to include this one chapter in the present Yarbook even though the discussions logically conjoined with it had to be deferred to a later volume. It is hoped, therefore, that this arrangement will stimulate interchange of ideas among those especially interested in rural education, and thus fructify subsequent contributions by the Society's Committee on Rural Education.—*Editor.*

1. There are few, if any, characteristics of rural life and education that cannot be found *in some small degree* in non-rural life.

2. Most, if not all, differences, however, are differences in degree rather than in kind. One not only adheres to an outworn logic[2] but also sacrifices practical efficiency by denying the existence of a distinctive rural problem just because it possesses characteristics somewhat in common with non-rural life and education.

3. The claim for special classification, emphasis, and study, is based upon the following three features:

(a) The group to be studied and served through rural education is large and basically significant in our social economy.

(b) Social and natural conditions of rural life make progress here more difficult. To these natural handicaps must be added the accumulated results of past neglect and exploitation and the effect of current indifference.

(c) An intensive, rather than a superficial study of the cultural, social, and economic conditions and the professional issues involved reveals distinctive problems in school organization, in curriculum construction, in teacher training and guidance, and in administration and finance. Therefore, it is held that, while the difference is merely a difference in degree, this is great enough to constitute a difference in kind. It would seem a matter of practical wisdom and democratic justice to recognize this problem as one deserving and demanding special attention.

4. This differentiation is not urged with the idea of permanent segregation, for our state and national programs of education must be organic wholes. It is urged rather for the purpose of intensive study in order that the rural situation may be better understood, its problems more effectively met, its contribution to the national program as a whole be realized and in order that it may be reincorporated in the inclusive public-education program in a truer relative proportion to the other major phases of the whole program.

2. What Is the Nature and Scope of the Problem?

1. While it seems evident that the rural exodus has tended to select certain levels and types of intelligence, the major differences between rural and urban people are due to nurture rather than to

---

[2] Bogoslovsky, Boris B. *The Technique of Controversy.*

nature; that is, the distinctive charateristics of rural folk are a result, in the main, of such facts as the limited variety and number of human contacts, the intimate association with living things, the meager contact with many aspects of our complex civilization and social heritage, and the influence of farming as a mode of life upon psychological and social traits.

2. It is difficult, if not impossible, to determine the characteristics and limits of the rural educational problem in any exact degree. It is impossible because whatever trait of rural life one may take, it exists in different degrees in different parts of the country, and it varies gradually until it disappears or is seldom found in urban centers. However, if we center attention upon what might be called *the modes of rural and of urban life,* significant differences appear.

3. It should be the purpose of social and educational research to determine with greater clarity and certainty these distinctive features by which the scope of the problem of rural education shall be more accurately determined.

4. "Rural," for practical purposes, may be assumed to include the open country as a nucleus, plus, to an as yet undetermined extent, certain more concentrated communities which should eventually be classified as rural or urban upon the basis of discovered characteristics. It is a misconception of the problem to seek to limit it to the open country, because the traits that are educationally significant are found in marked degrees in the rural town. The boundary line, however, will never be permanently fixed. For purposes of research, it may well vary with the nature of the specific problem studied.

3. Is the Rural Educator's Problem Inclusive or Supplementary?

1. Should he be responsible for and concerned in all the problems and activities involved in the educational program for people living under rural conditions? An affirmative answer here would seem to imply that any educational program is an integrated whole and the influence of the rural conditions so basic and far reaching in effect that it can be provided for only when the entire educational program is organized in relation to these factors; that is, this point of view would liken any educational program to a chemical compound.

2. Or should he be concerned solely in the peculiar problems that arise in the total educational effort because of the special conditions

under which these people live? This would limit the rural field to the *peculiar rural* aspects of the problem of educating *rural people*. This position seems to imply that the peculiar educational problems that arise because people live under rural conditions are such that they may be considered apart from the general program[3] and the conclusions added to it; that is, it would be in the nature of a physical addition which left the general program unchanged.

3. While the leader in rural education may and perhaps must isolate the peculiar rural features for special consideration and study, in practical life and in practical procedure they are chemically and integrally organized within the total situation. The rural educator must, therefore, in formulating programs and in directing practice consider and be responsible for the entire program.

4. What Are the Objectives of Rural Education?

1. The general objectives of rural education do not differ from objectives of urban education on the same level. Both are concerned in realizing the maximal individual growth and self-expression and in promoting greater social well-being and progress through the on-coming generation. Its responsibilities are to the child and to society as a whole, not to the local group whose children it is educating.

2. The specific objectives, however, the means by which the larger objectives are attained, will, since they are determined by the resources, experiences, and needs of rural children, be peculiar in part to rural life. For example, rural children need stress put upon certain health habits; certain social attitudes fostered by rural life need correcting; interests dormant because of the impoverished or one-sided environment will need specific cultivation.

5. Is Rural Education Responsible for Preserving for the Nation and the World Our Unique Rural Heritage?

1. One function of education is to conserve and transmit to the coming generations the meanings, ideals, and achievements of the race. Living in the open country has apparently tended to foster and strengthen in general certain traits, attitudes, dispositions, such as

---

[3] Attention should be here called to the fact that a genuinely general program does not at present exist. The present program includes any *truly general* features plus special adaptations to the urban mode.

independence, neighborly spirit, a calm disposition, and industriousness, which seem, to those who know them, to have fundamental significance for mankind in general and to be worthy of preservation. In our modern trend toward a more rapid, more crowded, more mechanized social life, these seem in danger of being lost. The far-seeing social philosopher and educator will seek deliberately to determine these significant traits, yet so little known, and to preserve the values for the coming generations. The rural educator who is likely to sense these values most clearly has a special responsibility for bringing them to the attention of the non-rural world.

2. Education should seek, however, to bring to each new generation the best from all cultures wherever these may be found in time or place. It should seek to make each person openminded, critical, and wisely selective rather than a defender of, or missionary for, any particular type of culture. Although it is desirable that these virtues be preserved for coming generations, and duly considered by the rural and non-rural people in forming their own life philosophies, overemphasis here in the education of rural people unnecessarily sacrifices the rural child's larger life to a more balanced life for others.

6. What Responsibility Has the School for Improving Its Community?

1. The major responsibility of a school to its community is to provide it with a group of socially minded, intellectually alert, sanely independent, progressive young people. If this is done, the community is inevitably improved, not only by virtue of the product, better children, but also by the very nature of the educative process; for this educative process, to be effective must relate to the lives the young people are now living and must touch upon the activities, experiences, resources, and needs of the home and community far more closely than it has in the past. Moreover, education means a changed outlook, an improved manner of life. These young people must live out their new visions. They cannot live them out without expressing them in the home, on the farm, in the community where they are. If education does not thus modify these young people and through them their environment, it is not effective.

2. Since education must be lived to be possessed, the school's responsibility to improve the community is increased. In order that

better standards of living, new ideals, and broader outlook taught by the school may be reinforced by the home and actually achieved by the pupils, the school may be compelled at times to undertake more directly the improvement of the cultural level of the home and community. However, all activities fostered by the school should be so selected and directed as to give a maximal return to the child. Whatever value accrues to adults and community (and any education vital and significant to the child will always contribute somewhat to social life) must be secondary to a program which puts child development first. Any program which subordinates the child's welfare to adult or community service is educationally unsound.

7. What Should Be the Nature of the Rural-School Curriculum?

1. The rural-school curriculum should be reorganized in keeping with the principles set forth in Part II of the *Twenty-Sixth Yearbook* of this Society. Paragraphs 24-29 concerning "Changing Conceptions of Learning and of the Subject Matter of the Curriculum" have special significance for the rural school. Its curriculum organization and content have been and are formal and unrelated to the life of the child, community, or society, while the environment abounds with vital material. It is organized upon the subject-matter-to-be-learned basis while the child's life has been teeming with potentially educative activities and experiences. The schools have been unresponsive to the educative possibilities of the environment.

2. The rural school should take on the nature of a laboratory where children should become participators in activities and answer-seekers rather than answer-learners. This school should utilize as an integral part of its program the many varied activities and experiences in the home, on the farm, and in the community. To it children should bring their out-of-school activities and problems for fuller consideration. The work of the school should be so organized as to illuminate, expand, and enrich the meanings of the child's daily experiences and work. The rural school finds in rural life a superior educational laboratory. To neglect it as we have is an educational crime against the rural child.

As rapidly as possible, rural education should in its curriculum meet the standards expressed in the two following paragraphs:[4]

---

[4] *Twenty-Sixth Yearbook* of this Society, 1927. Part II, 18f.

The curriculum should be conceived, therefore, in terms of a suc-cession of experiences and enterprises having a maximum of lifelike-ness for the learner. The materials of instruction should be selected and organized with a view to giving the learner that development most helpful in meeting and controlling life situations. Learning takes place most effectively and economically in the matrix of a situation which grips the learner, which is to him vital—worth while. Traits learned in a natural, or lifelike setting, gives promise of emerging defi-nitely in appropriate conduct. It is the task of the teacher and the cur-riculum-maker, therefore, to select and organize materials which will give the learner that development most helpful in meeting and con-trolling life situations. The method by which the learner works out these experiences, enterprises, exercises, should be such as calls for maximal self-direction, assumption of responsibility, of exercise of choice in terms of life values.

The learner must, in general, as regards any particular problem, conception, or solution of a problem, approximate the best available form of racial organization through his own personal mode of assimila-tion. In helping the learner to reach this approximation, the intelligent teacher will use the methods which have proved by previous educational experience to be most effective. No formulated scheme of assimilation, made in advance, and handed out complete by the curriculum-maker can of itself, be sufficient. To be truly functional for him, the process of assimilation must be the pupil's own. This does not, however, deny the effective part that the good teacher or other expert may have in assisting the pupil. The curriculum maker should arrange activities and materials so as to give the learner carefully planned assistance.

4. In order that a suitable curriculum may be made for rural children, we must determine, in addition to the objectives and guiding principles of education in general: (a) the specific characteristics of the rural natural social environment which determines so largely the attitudes, outlook, and standards of the rural child; (b) the variety of available resources that may be utilized in enriching and expanding a child's experience; (c) the interests, attitudes, and standards of rural children themselves; and (d) practical and fruitful units of work for rural children of different races and age-levels.

5. An application of the principles of the *Twenty-Sixth Yearbook* just quoted would demand special curriculum adaptation, not only for rural children in general, but also for Mexican children within our borders, for Negro children, and for the one-teacher school.

6. Since the special problems of rural-school curricula, as in the case of other curricula, arise out of the peculiar situation of the rural

schools, and must be solved in those situations, this fact should be recognized and faced by the Federal Office of Education, state school systems, and colleges with comprehensive plans for experimental studies in rural education.

7. To promote adequately its broad purposes and responsibilities, the rural secondary school must offer a program of studies sufficiently broad and varied to afford development in all desirable phases of growth and toward ends representing all the major aims of secondary education. It must give recognition to the peculiarities of experience, background, and social and physical environment of rural youth as these have bearing upon effective learning, and an understanding and appreciation of rural institutions and the other aspects of the rural environment. It must also introduce rural youth into the broader aspects of modern life and culture. The rural secondary school should, so far as facilities permit and need justifies, provide boys and girls vocational training in at least the major occupations of the community, where this training is appropriate to secondary-school levels. It is unjust, however, to limit rural boys and girls to vocational secondary schools where training in a rural vocation is a requirement in each curriculum offered. Because of the comparative isolation of rural children and the tendency on the part of certain forces to foredoom them to life on the farm, the rural secondary school faces a crucial issue in vocational guidance. In vocational guidance the school is responsible for making possible, through instruction and guidance, an intelligent choice of vocation, whether this be in country or city.

8. What Should Be the Guiding Principles in the Program for Boys' and Girls' Club Work Fostered by the United States Department of Agriculture?

1. In a democracy the worth of any institution or social agency is measured primarily in terms of its effect upon the health, happiness, and development of those directly involved in it. It is a form of exploitation to use children as a means of promoting the efficiency and well-being of adults (cultural, economic, or occupational) unless this comes as a by-product of a program whose major purpose and value is service to children themselves.

2. On the elementary level and upon the secondary level, so far as these pupils have not chosen their vocations, the entire organization

involved in promoting club work for boys and girls should be concerned primarily with the general development of these boys and girls. Therefore, the entire program of club work should be judged by accepted educational values and standards.

3. The initial purpose in the development and promotion of boys' and girls' club work was primarily to use it as a means of improving agricultural practices and rural life. Its purpose is becoming more educational, yet its organization and many of its techniques are largely characteristic of the earlier purpose. Critical revision of both purpose and practices in the light of educational criteria is needed.

4. Since the interests, activities, and growth of the child are so intimately related to the home, the farm, and the community, he will profit much from a program which seeks the improvement of them. The needs of the child, however, when inclusively considered, are not synonymous with those of the adult. The incidental value which accrues to children from the present club work must not be used to justify or divert our attention from its adult and vocational emphasis.

5. If the function of national, state, county, and local leaders of agricultural club work is to be primarily educational, then adequate professional training in the principles and technique of child guidance should be demanded of them.

6. If agricultural and home-making activities are to be used primarily as a ready and effective means of a generous education for the child, a stepping stone to a larger outlook, then the present expertness in the fields of agriculture and home-making on the part of agents, national, state, and county, and practical efficiency in the same fields on the part of the local leader are not enough. A generous knowledge of our entire social heritage is necessary in order that one may utilize the many leads that arise in these club activities for the maximal educational value for children.

9. Should We Have Two Distinct Agencies, the Public School and the Organization for Boys' and Girls' Club Work, Conducting Educational Programs for Rural Children?

1. Organizations once established tend to become formal, static, and conservative if not definitely opposed to change. New values and practices must frequently be fostered by new organization. While centralizing of authority and leadership makes for immediate economy

and efficiency, it tends to prevent variation and progress. A progressive society will, then, not only permit but encourage the development of new organizations, with new and conflicting points of view, in order that out of these may be achieved a new and better program. There will then be a tendency to integration as each understands and approves the other. Such integration is to be encouraged in order not to multiply beyond the point of usefulness the number of organizations.

2. While recognizing the general value of independent and competing programs and the distinctive contribution of club work, the writer holds that an indefinite continuance of this dual program for children is unsound and unjustified for two reasons: (a) it is inconsistent with the emphasis in education upon the development of an integrated personality and the belief in the principles of integrated learning and an integrated program; and (b) the fostering of the club program has drawn from the rural school many of its dynamic leaders, and has thus weakened and retarded seriously the service and improvement of this major educational agency.

3. As club work becomes truly educational, and as school work loses its formal, bookish, and abstract nature in favor of an experience-activity curriculum, the two programs become alike in purpose, organization, and method. To the extent to which they are kept apart, the club activities suffer for want of enriching and broadening contacts they might have if closely related to the history, geography, civics, and science of the school; the school program likewise suffers because it lacks sufficient contact with the vital problems, interests, and activities of the child's out-of-school life. The best educational results can be realized only when the child's out-of-school experiences and activities and his in-school contacts with the rich resources of our social heritage are integrated into a unified program and made to supplement each other. The life activities and experiences available in his environment are the natural laboratory for a child's education. To rob the school of this is to enforce upon it, in this day of activity education, a barren and ineffective program.

4. Ideally these two educational programs should be merged and the responsibility be placed in the hands of the county superintendent's office. To be worthy of this responsibility, rural educators need a new vision of education. The school has tended to formalize and make rigid everything it touches. It is constrained by stereotypes that seem

to devitalize every experience and activity, every mental adventure that becomes a part of its program. Herein lies the curse of the past and the challenge of progressive education to the rural leader.

5. To safeguard the distinct contribution of club work, there should be provided an assistant county superintendent, responsible for promoting this type of work and aiding the teachers to utilize these out-of-school experiences and problems as a basis for a real integrated experience-activity curriculum. Pending this ultimate solution these two forces (county and state school officers and state and county club agents) should coöperate in such a way as to provide an integrated program with maximal learning for the child.

10. What Special Provision Should Be Made for the Preparation of Rural Teachers?

1. The rural teacher faces problems which in nature and variety differ greatly from those met in the urban school. Some of these, such as multi-graded classes, limited teaching equipment, lack of supervision are more or less temporary. Others, such as limited professional contact, numerous and varied community responsibilities, special problems growing out of rural life conditions, are more permanent. These justify some special preparation for service in rural fields.

2. While special preparation is advocated, prospective urban and rural teachers should be trained in the same institutions and follow in the main a common curriculum.

3. The practice of preparing teachers for rural schools and in high-school training classes, county normal schools, or special rural normal schools was an expedient and should be abandoned. As a permanent national policy it is unwise to predetermine teachers for the rural field either by lower certification or by limited certification. The first is an insult to the rural child, and the second will cause students to avoid the field.

4. Greater emphasis should be given, in the general curriculum just mentioned, upon the consideration of the problems in the field of rural education for these four reasons:

(a) Pre-service preparation should be concerned primarily with the problems a teacher is to meet during her first few years of service. Experience, supervision, and later professional study will aid her to meet later problems.

(b) A large number of the graduates from state teachers' colleges who ultimately teach in the city begin their teaching experience in rural or village schools. Many cities not only have their own local training schools, but also demand from other applicants experience as a prerequisite for teaching in their systems. This, in the main, must be got in small villages and the open country.

(c) Its problems for the teachers in the one-teacher schools are admittedly more difficult.

(d) Supervisory assistance is practically unavailable. The beginning teacher in the city has careful guidance in making necessary adaptations.

5. Each state teachers' college or certain designated state teachers' colleges should provide, in addition, specific preparation for those who wish to teach in rural fields equal *in every respect* to that provided for prospective urban teachers.

6. The preceding statements assume a continuance of the present unintelligent and undemocratic placement of teachers. A fundamental revision is necessary for any permanent solution. Since the rural school presents so many difficulties that have been so little studied and for the solution of which so little help is available, and since rural people are most in need of a cultural educational program, only those teachers who have demonstrated superior ability, initiative, and power of leadership should be permitted to teach in rural communities. The state by additional pay and other forms of recognition should make these positions attractive.

11. What Professional Leadership Shall Be Provided for Rural Schools?

1. Leaders, on the several levels in the rural field, should be as adequately prepared for dealing with their problems as are the leaders for similar levels in the non-rural field.

2. The practice of selecting county superintendents by political methods is an obstacle to securing professional leadership of merit and is to be condemned.

3. Efficiency in administrative and supervisory service demands that the unit of organization be large enough to justify the provision of expert leadership in each field.

4. Since effective supervision of elementary schools requires special fitness for that work, every county or similar unit should wherever

possible provide an expert in elementary-school curriculum and practice.

5. A program of supervision for rural schools should be a coöperative undertaking between the building principal and the county and the state supervisory forces. The distribution of responsibility must be adjusted to special fitness for leadership and time made available for supervisory service. The degree to which the principal is charged with the full responsibility of supervision must be determined by existing conditions, such as the requirement of teaching by the principal, the necessity for combined responsibility for both elementary and secondary levels, and the salaries possible to provide for principals. In very few cases is it to be expected that the principal of a rural consolidated or village school can fully discharge the supervisory duties needed by that school. Smaller schools of one, two, and three teachers have no principal. The supervisor is then, in the rural situation, an agent with relationships and responsibilities differing in many respects from those characterizing urban supervisors, upon whose functions our present theory of supervisory relations and programs have largely been built. The rural-school principal must, however, increasingly bear an important share in the function, and to this end fitness to lead in the study of educational problems on both elementary and secondary levels should be demanded as a prerequisite. The tendency to advance to this position a high-school teacher who knows little about the elementary-school practice or a person trained primarily in administration, with minor attention to modern classroom standards and practice on either level, is unsatisfactory.

6. The readiness of people in rural education to utilize the rural field as a stepping stone to other positions is to be regretted. The indifference of urban leaders to the existing level of educational facilities, standards, and leadership, and the willingness to use this as a training ground for their future teachers, principals, and supervisors is an indication of their lack of thoughtfulness.

12. What Place Has the 'Visiting Teacher' in Rural Education?

1. The movement to provide visiting teachers in rural schools is to be commended in so far as it is recognition of the significance of the home and community environment as a force in the child's education, the complexity of the problem of school attendance, and the

subtle nature of the task of guiding the intellectual, emotional, and social development of the child.

2. The maximal service of this movement will depend upon the extent to which it strengthens the present educational organization by increasing the consciousness and understanding on the part of school people of the social and psychological factors in educational progress and by making available clinical and social service.

3. There is danger that this new movement, as an independent and separate program, will actually operate, through the enthusiasm of its advocates, the appeal of the new, and the emotion-stirring quality of its problems and data, to deplete the financial resources available for school work, detract from its leadership, and further retard its progress. When a visiting teacher program is initiated, it should be a part of the state and county educational organization. Its program, moreover, should be most intimately related to the activities program of the school. Its allegiance should be to the educational organization: its purpose should be the further enrichment of child life.

4. Here, as in club work, is a challenge for rural teachers, principals, and superintendents. If we do not extend our vision and program to meet these problems, another agency more dynamic, more sensitive to life and its needs, will and should take the work over.

13. How Shall the Rural Schools Be Administered?

1. The effectiveness of administrative methods and procedures is to be measured by the degree to which they aid in attaining educational objectives.

2. It is to be expected that as scientific method is employed in the study of administrative problems, the factors influencing the effectiveness of various methods and procedures will enable us to indicate some as generally superior to others. In many phases of administrative work, however, our studies are far from conclusive. For example, we cannot yet be certain which of several types of local districts, for example, consolidated, community, township, and county, is superior. While each of these appear to have definite advantages over such districts as the common-school district and the union high-school district, it would seem that the particular type to be preferred will depend upon the situation in a particular state. Therefore, until all possible types of local districts have been more scientifically evaluated, variation in practice is to be desired. One of the pressing needs to be

cared for in the rural areas is a complete elementary and secondary program of adequate scope and quality available to all. This can come only through some type of larger unit than now prevails in most states.

3. Existing data show that, in general, consolidated schools are superior to small schools, especially to those having one teacher. This superiority, is, however, not inherent in most particulars. The small school may, when proper facilities are provided, give desired growth to pupils in as great degree as does the consolidated or other type of larger school. Consolidation, therefore, should be considered not as an end in educational administration, but as a means for providing those conditions that influence child development—superior teaching, a broad and well-planned curriculum, longer school term, and the like.

4. In a few places, the city-county organization, whereby the city and county are combined into one district, has developed. In view of our limited experience with this type of local unit and the almost complete lack of comparable data, no definite judgment regarding it is at present warranted. Its desirability, from the point of view of the education of rural children, should be determined by such questions as the following: Does it tend to provide a type of curriculum suited to the needs of those children living in the rural areas of the city-country district? Does it encourage the conservation of the desirable elements in rural life as they affect child development? Do the people in the rural areas of the district have a real voice in the determination of educational policies? Does the professional leadership of the district have a sympathetic understanding of rural life and of the educational problems of rural people? Our tentative judgment is that this organization may be desirable under some circumstances and not under others, depending upon the degree to which the points suggested are taken into account.

5. Although progress in the education of rural children depends in great measure upon the educational progress of the parents, and although maximal progress of parents will be secured only by giving them responsibility and by securing their active participation in the problems of community betterment, yet education is so vital to national security and child welfare that responsibility for it should not be left entirely upon the local community. The state must bear an important share in the burden through the establishment of minimal standards and through the exercise of intelligent, aggressive leader-

ship. The best method of organizing the resources of the state to deal with the educational problems of the rural areas remains to be determined.

6. Except where the county or other area comparable to it in size and influence is the local district, an intermediate unit appears to be desirable. Such a unit may: (1) provide a better type of leadership than can ordinarily be secured in the constituent districts, (2) perform certain functions of control not practicable in the local unit that yet need not be referred to the state, (3) assist in equalizing the burdens and opportunities of education when adequate state financing is not in effect, and (4) provide certain special forms of service not possible in the constituent districts. In very few states is any one of these functions now exercised to the degree and in the manner to be desired.

14.   What Provision Should Be Made for Rural Adult Education?

1. A definite and comprehensive program of education for rural adults should be provided not only because the level of culture in the rural community determines so largely the outlook, attitudes, achievement, and intellectual efficiency of the rural child, but also because, limited as the adults are in stimulating social contacts and service agencies, their own achievement and progress is seriously lessened.

2. While a program should be relatively informal and relate specifically to the interests and needs of the group, it should touch all aspects of life, cultural as well as vocational.

3. The present offerings of the Department of Agriculture in its extension program, the offerings of the public school, of universities, and of volunteer agencies should be so organized as to prevent over-lappings and conflicts and to secure maximal service for the rural adults. The present confusion means inefficiency.

4. Since a program for adult education fostered by the Department of Agriculture would not detract from the efficiency of any legally authorized agency for education (as is true on the elementary and secondary level), it seems immaterial whether the major comprehensive program be provided for adults by extending the existing program for vocational education so as to serve all the legitimate educational needs of rural adults or whether such a program be provided by extending the services of the public school. Experience alone can decide which form of service offers greatest promise.